Better Homes and Gardens.

fresh
& easy
MEALS

WILEY

Better Homes and Gardens® Fresh & Easy Meals
Contributing Editor: Cathy Long
Contributing Graphic Designer: Diana Van Winkle
Editorial Assistant: Sheri Cord
Book Production Manager: Mark Weaver
Contributing Photographers: Pete Krumhardt, Blaine Moats
Contributing Proofreader: Candy Meier
Contributing Indexer: Elizabeth Parson
Test Kitchen Director: Lynn Blanchard
Test Kitchen Product Supervisor: Marilyn Cornelius, Jennifer Kalinowski, R.D.
Test Kitchen Culinary Specialists: Marilyn Cornelius, Juliana Hale,
    Maryellyn Krantz, Jill Moberly, Colleen Weeden, Lori Wilson
Test Kitchen Nutrition Specialists: Elizabeth Burt, R.D., L.D.;
    Laura Marzen, R.D., L.D.

Meredith® Books
Editorial Director: John Riha
Deputy Editor: Jennifer Darling
Managing Editor: Kathleen Armentrout
Brand Manager: Gina Rickert
Group Editor: Jan Miller
Art Director: Matt Strelecki
Copy Chief: Doug Kouma
Senior Copy Editors: Kevin Cox, Jennifer Speer Ramundt,
    Elizabeth Keest Sedrel
Assistant Copy Editor: Metta Cederdahl
Proofreader: Joleen Ross

Executive Director, Sales: Ken Zagor
Director, Operations: George A. Susral
Director, Production: Douglas M. Johnston
Business Director: Janice Croat

Vice President and General Manager, SIP: Jeff Myers

***Better Homes and Gardens®* Magazine**
Editor in Chief: Gayle Goodson Butler
Deputy Editor, Food and Entertaining: Nancy Hopkins

Meredith Publishing Group
President: Jack Griffin
Executive Vice President: Doug Olson

Meredith Corporation
Chairman of the Board: William T. Kerr
President and Chief Executive Officer: Stephen M. Lacy

In Memoriam: E. T. Meredith III (1933–2003)

Pictured on front cover: Steak Rémoulade Sandwiches (see recipe, page 133)

All of us at Meredith® Books are dedicated to
providing you with the information and ideas
you need to create delicious foods. We welcome
your comments and suggestions. Write to us at:
Meredith Special Interest Media, 1716 Locust
St., Des Moines, IA 50309-3023.

Our seal assures you that every
recipe in *Fresh & Easy Meals* has
been tested in the Better Homes and
Gardens® Test Kitchen. This means
that each recipe is practical and
reliable and meets our high standards
of taste appeal. We guarantee your
satisfaction with this book for as
long as you own it.

contents

GREAT FOR **KIDS**

Find this symbol on recipes that are sure to be hits with kids and teens.

appetizers
& SIPPERS

Looking for a satisfying snack that's also good for you? How about party foods that fill your guests up but not out? Here you'll find something for every occasion. From snack mixes to dips and chicken fingers to milk shakes, these fun munchies really hit the spot.

(clockwise from top right) **Hot and Spicy Walnuts,** *recipe page 10*
Fruit and Peanut Snack Mix, *recipe page 6*
Oriental Trail Mix, *recipe page 7*

fruit and PEANUT SNACK MIX

For a snack kids will go for, add a 6-ounce package of fish-shape crackers to this three-ingredient mix.

appetizers & sippers

Start to Finish: 10 minutes
Makes: about 12 (½-cup) servings

1　**6-ounce package dried cranberries (1½ cups)**

1　**7-ounce package dried pears, snipped (1⅓ cups)**

1　**cup cocktail peanuts**

1 In a medium bowl stir together all ingredients. Serve immediately.

Nutrition Facts per serving: 212 cal., 8 g total fat (2 g sat. fat), 5 mg chol., 139 mg sodium, 34 g carbo., 3 g fiber, 5 g pro.
Daily Values: 1% vit. A, 2% vit. C, 2% calcium, 6% iron

Nutty Nutrition

The combination of protein from the peanuts and carbohydrate from the fruit makes this an ideal snack. While carbohydrates provide energy, they increase blood sugar levels quickly and are metabolized rapidly, often leaving you feeling hungry again soon. Foods high in protein provide a more lasting feeling of fullness and slow the absorption of the sugars in the carbohydrates. Eating the two together results in an energy-packed snack that stays with you.

oriental TRAIL MIX

Quick to put together, this perfect trail mix features the concentrated nutrition of nuts and dried fruits with crisp rice crackers and the enticing bite of ginger.

Start to Finish: 10 minutes
Makes: 16 (⅓-cup) servings

4 **cups assorted oriental rice crackers**

¾ **cup dried apricots, halved lengthwise**

¾ **cup lightly salted cashews**

¼ **cup chopped crystallized ginger and/or golden raisins**

1 In a medium bowl stir together all ingredients. Serve immediately.

Nutrition Facts per serving: 102 cal., 3 g total fat (1 g sat. fat), 0 mg chol., 78 mg sodium, 17 g carbo., 1 g fiber, 2 g pro.
Daily Values: 9% vit. A, 6% iron

honey-mustard SNACK MIX

Crunchy, spicy, and high in protein, this mix has it all. Take it to the office for a fun midafternoon treat or make it for an at-home movie night instead of plain popcorn.

Prep: 10 minutes
Bake: 20 minutes
Oven: 300°F
Makes: 15 (½-cup) servings

1½ cups crispy corn-and-rice cereal

1 cup bite-size shredded wheat biscuits

¾ cup unblanched whole almonds

½ cup peanuts

2 tablespoons butter

3 tablespoons honey mustard

1 teaspoon Worcestershire sauce

¼ teaspoon garlic powder

⅛ teaspoon cayenne pepper

4 cups plain popped popcorn

1 In a foil-lined 13×9×2-inch baking pan place cereal, wheat biscuits, almonds, and peanuts; set aside. In a small saucepan melt butter. Remove saucepan from heat; stir in mustard, Worcestershire sauce, garlic powder, and cayenne pepper until combined. Drizzle over cereal and nut mixture in pan, tossing gently to coat.

2 Bake mixture, uncovered, in a 300° oven for 20 minutes, gently stirring after 10 minutes. Stir in popcorn. Lift foil to remove baked mixture from pan; cool completely. Serve immediately.

Nutrition Facts per serving: 113 cal., 8 g total fat (2 g sat. fat), 4 mg chol., 87 mg sodium, 9 g carbo., 2 g fiber, 3 g pro.
Daily Values: 2% vit. A, 1% vit. C, 2% calcium, 8% iron

hot and SPICY WALNUTS

Nuts hit the spot as a snack, and this snack is loaded with them. Walnuts have more heart-healthy omega-3 fat than other nuts. Use canola oil in the recipe to boost its omega-3 content even more.

appetizers & sippers

Prep: 10 minutes
Bake: 20 minutes
Cool: 15 minutes
Oven: 300°F
Makes: 8 (¼-cup) servings

1 **teaspoon ground coriander**

1 **teaspoon ground cumin**

½ **teaspoon salt**

¼ **teaspoon freshly ground
   black pepper**

⅛ **teaspoon cayenne pepper**

2 **cups walnut halves**

1 **tablespoon cooking oil**

❶ In a small bowl stir together coriander, cumin, salt, black pepper, and cayenne pepper; set aside. Place nuts in a 13×9×2-inch baking pan. Drizzle with the oil, stirring to coat. Sprinkle with spice mixture; toss lightly.

❷ Bake in a 300° oven for 20 minutes or until nuts are lightly toasted, stirring once or twice. Cool in pan for 15 minutes. Turn out onto paper towels; cool completely. Store, covered, in a cool place.

Nutrition Facts per serving: 214 cal., 21 g total fat (2 g sat. fat), 0 mg chol., 147 mg sodium, 4 g carbo., 2 g fiber, 5 g pro.
Daily Values: 1% vit. C, 3% calcium, 5% iron

spiced chili NUTS AND SEEDS

Pick your favorite nuts and seeds for this snack recipe. Orange juice concentrate spiked with piquant spices gives the mixture a burst of flavor.

Prep: 10 minutes
Bake: 15 minutes
Oven: 300°F
Makes: 16 (¼-cup) servings

- 2 **tablespoons frozen orange juice concentrate, thawed**
- 2 **teaspoons Worcestershire sauce**
- 1 **teaspoon garlic powder**
- 1 **teaspoon ground cumin**
- 1 **teaspoon chili powder**
- ½ **teaspoon cayenne pepper**
- ¼ **teaspoon salt**
- ¼ **teaspoon ground allspice**
- ¼ **teaspoon black pepper**
- ⅛ **teaspoon onion salt**
- 2 **cups unsalted peanuts, hazelnuts, and/or Brazil nuts**
- 1 **cup pecan halves**
- 6 **tablespoons unsalted shelled sunflower seeds**
- 2 **tablespoons sesame seeds**
  Nonstick cooking spray

① In a large bowl combine orange juice concentrate, Worcestershire sauce, garlic powder, cumin, chili powder, cayenne pepper, salt, allspice, black pepper, and onion salt. Stir in nuts and seeds; toss to coat.

② Line a 15×10×1-inch baking pan with foil; lightly coat with nonstick cooking spray. Spread nuts and seeds on foil. Bake in a 300° oven for 15 to 20 minutes or until toasted, stirring once. Cool. Store in an airtight container at room temperature for up to 1 week.

Nutrition Facts per serving: 183 cal., 16 g total fat (2 g sat. fat), 0 mg chol., 59 mg sodium, 7 g carbo., 3 g fiber, 6 g pro.
Daily Values: 2% vit. A, 6% vit. C, 2% calcium, 5% iron

fruit KABOBS

Kabobs are a fun way to serve fruit for parties, and a cool dip adds extra pizzazz. Seasonal substitutes, such as fresh peaches, nectarines, and plums or mangoes, add flavorful variety.

Prep: 20 minutes
Chill: 30 to 60 minutes
Makes: 8 servings

¾ **cup cantaloupe chunks**

¾ **cup honeydew melon chunks**

¾ **cup small strawberries**

¾ **cup pineapple chunks**

2 **small bananas, peeled and cut into 1-inch slices**

1 **cup orange juice**

¼ **cup lime juice**

1 **8-ounce carton vanilla low-fat or fat-free yogurt**

2 **tablespoons frozen orange juice concentrate, thawed**

  Ground nutmeg or ground cinnamon (optional)

❶ On eight 6-inch or four 10-inch skewers alternately thread the cantaloupe, honeydew melon, strawberries, pineapple, and bananas. Place kabobs in a glass baking dish. Combine orange juice and lime juice; pour evenly over kabobs. Cover; chill kabobs for 30 to 60 minutes, turning occasionally.

❷ Meanwhile, for dip, in a small bowl stir together the yogurt and orange juice concentrate. Cover and chill until ready to serve.

❸ To serve, arrange the kabobs on a serving platter; discard juice mixture. If desired, sprinkle nutmeg or cinnamon over dip. Serve dip with kabobs.

Nutrition facts per 1 kabob and 2 tablespoons dip: 91 cal.,1 g total fat (0 g saturated fat), 2 mg chol., 20 mg sodium, 21 g carbo, 1 g fiber, 2 g pro. **Daily values:** 6% vit. A, 78% vit. C, 4% calcium, 2% iron

fruit WITH CREAMY SAUCE

This blend of cottage cheese, applesauce, and honey is good with any fruit combination, so choose whatever piques your interest in the produce department.

Start to Finish: 15 minutes
Makes: 6 servings

½ **cup low-fat cream-style cottage cheese**

½ **cup unsweetened applesauce**

1 **tablespoon honey**

1 **cup sliced nectarines; sliced, peeled peaches; orange sections; or sliced strawberries**

1 **cup sliced apple or pear**

½ **cup seedless grapes**

1 **small banana, sliced**

Ground cinnamon or ground nutmeg

❶ For sauce, in a blender container or food processor bowl combine cottage cheese, applesauce, and honey. Cover and blend or process until smooth.

❷ In a large bowl stir together nectarine slices, apple slices, grapes, and banana slices. Divide fruit among 6 dessert dishes. Spoon some of the sauce over each serving and sprinkle with cinnamon.

Nutrition Facts per serving: 77 cal., 1 g total fat (0 g sat. fat), 1 mg chol., 77 mg sodium, 17 g carbo., 2 g fiber, 3 g pro.
Daily Values: 4% vit. A, 9% vit. C, 2% calcium, 1% iron

tropical FRUIT POPS

You may think you're making this treat for the kids, but as soon as the adults taste them you're going to have to make more. Experiment with gelatin flavors to determine which you like best.

Prep: 15 minutes
Freeze: 6 hours
Makes: 8 large or
12 small pops

½ **cup boiling water**

1 **4-serving-size package sugar-free lemon-, mixed fruit-, or strawberry-flavor gelatin**

1 **15¼-ounce can crushed pineapple (juice pack)**

2 **medium bananas, cut into chunks**

1 In a 1- or 2-cup glass measuring cup stir together the boiling water and the gelatin until gelatin dissolves. Pour into a blender container. Add undrained pineapple and banana chunks. Cover and blend until smooth.

2 Pour a scant ½ cup of the fruit mixture into each of eight 5- to 6-ounce paper or plastic drink cups. (Or pour a scant ⅓ cup into each of twelve 3-ounce cups.) Cover each cup with foil. Using the tip of a knife, make a small hole in the foil over each cup. Insert a wooden stick into the cup through the hole. Freeze about 6 hours or until firm.

3 To serve, quickly dip the cups in warm water to slightly soften fruit mixture. Remove foil and loosen sides of pops from drink cups.

Nutrition Facts per large pop: 65 cal., 0 g total fat (0 g sat. fat), 0 mg chol., 29 mg sodium, 15 g carbo., 1 g fiber, 1 g pro.
Daily Values: 1% vit. A, 13% vit. C, 1% calcium, 1% iron

appetizers & sippers

mango YOGURT POPS

Made with real fruit and fat-free yogurt, these pops are a healthful low-calorie treat. On a hot summer day, the tropical taste of this refreshing snack will hit the spot—for kids and adults alike.

appetizers & sippers

Prep: 15 minutes
Freeze: 4 to 6 hours
Makes: 8 pops

1   teaspoon unflavored gelatin

⅓ cup peach nectar or apricot
    nectar

2   6- or 8-ounce cartons vanilla
    or peach fat-free yogurt
    with sweetener

⅓ of a 26-ounce jar refrigerated
    mango slices, drained, or
    one 8-ounce can peach
    slices, drained

① In a small saucepan combine the unflavored gelatin and peach or apricot nectar. Let stand for 5 minutes. Cook and stir over medium heat until gelatin is dissolved.

② In a blender container combine gelatin mixture, yogurt, and drained mango or peach slices. Cover and blend until smooth. Spoon mixture into eight 3-ounce paper cups. Cover each cup with foil. Cut a small slit in the center of each foil cover and insert a rounded wooden stick into each. Freeze pops for 4 to 6 hours or until firm.

③ To serve, remove the foil and tear paper cups away from pops.

Nutrition facts per pop: 49 cal., 0 g total fat (0 g sat. fat), 1 mg chol.,
28 mg sodium, 10 g carbo., 0 g fiber, 2 g pro.
Daily values: 5% vit. A, 6% vit. C, 6% calcium, 0% iron

Snack Sense

Snacking is important to any balanced diet. It helps your body go with the flow during the day and keeps your energy expenditure on an even keel, with fewer peaks and valleys. When you keep the edge off of your appetite, you tend to eat less during mealtimes. Some of the best snacks to enjoy are those high in protein. Yogurt fits that role very well.

Keep a variety of flavored fat-free yogurts in the fridge. If a savory snack is what you're after, stir some chopped fresh vegetables into plain yogurt (a dash or two of garlic powder or a snippet of fresh herbs are other possible additions). But don't forget: It's important to keep track of snacks and stay within your total calorie allowance for the day.

crispy PARMESAN CHIPS

These homemade chips require no dip or spread since the cheese is baked right in. Look for wonton wrappers in the refrigerated area of the produce section.

Start to Finish: 30 minutes
Makes: 15 servings

30	wonton wrappers
	Nonstick spray coating
2	tablespoons olive oil
1	clove garlic, minced
½	teaspoon dried basil, crushed
¼	cup grated Parmesan or Romano cheese

1 Use a sharp knife to cut wonton wrappers diagonally in half to form 60 triangles. Spray a baking sheet with nonstick coating. Arrange one-third of the triangles in a single layer on prepared baking sheet.

2 In a small bowl stir together the olive oil, garlic, and basil. Brush the wonton triangles lightly with some of the oil mixture; sprinkle with some of the Parmesan or Romano cheese.

3 Bake in a 350° oven about 8 minutes or until golden brown. Cool completely on a wire rack. Repeat with the remaining wonton triangles, oil mixture, and Parmesan or Romano cheese.

Nutrition facts per 4 chips: 70 cal., 3 g total fat (1 g sat. fat), 3 mg chol., 123 mg sodium, 9 g carbo., 0 g fiber, 2 g pro.
Daily values: 0% vit. A, 0% vit. C, 2% calcium, 3% iron

chèvre & TOMATO SPREAD

Goat cheese, with its intense tangy flavor, is a delightful complement to dried tomatoes. Together, they make an ideal spread for entertaining or everyday snacking.

Prep: 20 minutes
Chill: 2 to 4 hours
Makes: 10 (1¼-cups) servings

⅓ **cup dried tomatoes (not oil-packed)**

4 **ounces soft goat cheese (chèvre)**

½ **of an 8-ounce package reduced-fat cream cheese (Neufchâtel), softened**

¼ **cup snipped fresh basil or 2 teaspoons dried basil, crushed**

3 **cloves garlic, minced**

⅛ **teaspoon black pepper**

1 **to 2 tablespoons fat-free milk**

10 **slices party rye bread or 20 assorted reduced-fat crackers**

Assorted garnishes, such as quartered cherry tomatoes, broccoli flowerets, chopped yellow sweet pepper, and/ or small fresh basil leaves (optional)

1 In a small bowl cover dried tomatoes with boiling water. Let stand for 10 minutes. Drain tomatoes, discarding liquid. Finely snip tomatoes.

2 In a bowl stir together the snipped tomatoes, goat cheese, cream cheese, basil, garlic, and black pepper. Stir in enough milk to make the mixture of spreading consistency. Cover and chill for 2 to 4 hours. Serve with rye bread or crackers. If desired, top with assorted garnishes.

Nutrition facts per 2 slices party rye and 2 tablespoons spread:
94 cal., 6 g total fat (3 g sat. fat), 19 mg chol., 202 mg sodium, 6 g carbo., 0 g fiber, 4 g pro.
Daily values: 5% vit. A, 1% vit. C, 2% calcium, 2% iron

creamy SPINACH DIP

Dips typically are loaded with fat, but by combining fat-free cottage cheese and light mayo, you get all the creaminess of a traditional dip without the unwanted extra calories and fat.

Prep: 15 minutes
Chill: 1 to 4 hours
Makes: 8 (about 1¾-cups) servings

1½ **cups fat-free cottage cheese**

⅓ **cup light mayonnaise dressing or salad dressing**

1 **tablespoon lemon juice**

1 **tablespoon fat-free milk**

1 **clove garlic, minced**

½ **teaspoon dried Italian seasoning, crushed**

   Dash pepper

1 **cup finely chopped fresh spinach**

   Assorted vegetable dippers, such as carrot, celery, zucchini, or sweet pepper sticks; cucumber slices; and/ or cauliflower or broccoli flowerets

❶ In a blender container or food processor bowl combine the cottage cheese, mayonnaise dressing or salad dressing, lemon juice, milk, garlic, Italian seasoning, and pepper. Cover and blend or process until smooth. Stir in spinach. Cover and chill for 1 to 4 hours or overnight.

❷ Stir dip before serving. Serve with vegetable dippers.

Nutrition facts per 1 carrot and 3 tablespoons dip: 98 cal., 4 g total fat (1 g sat. fat), 2 mg chol., 281 mg sodium, 11 g carbo., 2 g fiber, 6 g pro. **Daily values:** 207% vit. A, 16% vit. C, 11% calcium, 4% iron

Skinnier Dairy Products

Fat-free milk (previously called skim) and reduced-fat milk (previously called low fat) have been around for years, but now almost every dairy-based product has a low-fat or fat-free version. Great news, since a low-fat diet is essential to controlling weight and minimizing health risks. Fat-free versions of yogurt, cottage cheese, and ice cream are readily available, and the majority of these dairy products have the full flavor we've come to expect. The next time you buy a dairy product, try the reduced-fat version or the fat-free version. You may be pleasantly surprised.

salmon CUCUMBER DIP

Cucumbers provide just the right amount of crunchy texture to this dip, which also can be used as a spread for making dainty tea sandwiches. The salmon makes this snack elegant enough to serve to party guests.

Prep: 20 minutes
Chill: 1 to 4 hours
Makes: 16 (about 2 cups) servings

1　**8-ounce carton fat-free dairy sour cream**

2　**tablespoons catsup or chili sauce**

1　**tablespoon finely chopped onion**

¼　**teaspoon salt**

½　**cup flaked, cooked salmon or canned salmon, drained, flaked, and skin and bones removed**

½　**cup finely chopped, seeded cucumber**

1　**plum tomato, seeded and finely chopped**

1　**tablespoon snipped fresh dill or parsley**

　Whole grain crackers or assorted vegetable dippers

1 In a medium mixing bowl combine sour cream, catsup or chili sauce, onion, and salt. Stir in the salmon, cucumber, tomato, and dill or parsley. Cover and chill for 1 to 4 hours.

2 Serve dip with assorted crackers or vegetable dippers.

Nutrition facts per 4 crackers and 2 tablespoons dip: 86 cal., 3 g total fat (0 g sat. fat), 2 mg chol., 167 mg sodium, 11 g carbo., 3 g fiber, 3 g pro.
Daily values: 2% vit. A, 2% vit. C, 3% calcium, 12% iron

incredible QUESADILLAS

Capture a south-of-the-border attitude with these flavorful snacks. Cooking becomes a fun activity when you show the kids how to use a waffle baker.

Prep: 20 minutes
Cook: 3 minutes each
Makes: 8 servings

½ **cup shredded reduced-fat Mexican-cheese blend**

4 **8-inch fat-free flour tortillas**

4 **low-fat brown-and-serve sausage links, cooked and coarsely chopped**

2 **tablespoons well-drained pineapple salsa or regular salsa**

1 **small red onion, sliced and separated into rings**

2 **tablespoons finely snipped fresh cilantro**

½ **cup pineapple salsa or regular salsa**

Cilantro sprigs (optional)

❶ Heat a waffle baker on a medium-high heat setting. Sprinkle 2 tablespoons of the cheese over half of each tortilla. Top with sausage, the 2 tablespoons salsa, onion, and cilantro. Fold tortillas in half, pressing gently.

❷ Place one quesadilla on preheated waffle baker. Close lid, pressing slightly. Bake for 3 to 6 minutes or until tortilla is lightly browned and cheese is melted. Remove from waffle baker. Cut quesadilla in half. Repeat with remaining quesadillas.

❸ Place the ½ cup salsa in a bowl. If desired, garnish quesadilla pieces with cilantro sprigs. Serve with salsa.

Note: Or cook each quesadilla in a 10-inch nonstick skillet over medium heat for 3 to 4 minutes or until golden brown. Using a spatula, turn quesadilla over. Cook for 2 to 3 minutes more or until golden brown. Remove the quesadilla from the skillet.

Nutrition Facts per serving: 104 cal., 2 g total fat (1 g sat. fat), 8 mg chol., 362 mg sodium, 17 g carbo., 2 g fiber, 5 g pro.
Daily Values: 2% vit. A, 1% vit. C, 4% calcium, 2% iron

artichoke-feta TORTILLAS

Three cheeses, roasted peppers, and artichokes melt and mingle in these tortilla-wrapped treats. They're the perfect appetizer for a casual gathering.

appetizers & sippers

Prep: 15 minutes
Bake: 15 minutes
Oven: 350°F
Makes: 24 servings

Nonstick cooking spray

1 **14-ounce can artichoke hearts, drained and finely chopped**

½ **of an 8-ounce tub reduced-fat cream cheese (about ½ cup)**

3 **green onions, thinly sliced**

⅓ **cup grated Parmesan or Romano cheese**

¼ **cup crumbled feta cheese (1 ounce)**

3 **tablespoons reduced-fat basil pesto**

8 **8-inch spinach, tomato, or regular flour tortillas**

1 **7-ounce jar roasted red sweet peppers, drained and cut into strips**

1 **recipe Yogurt-Chive Sauce**

❶ Lightly coat a 3-quart rectangular baking dish with nonstick cooking spray; set aside. For filling, in a large bowl stir together artichoke hearts, cream cheese, green onions, Parmesan cheese, feta cheese, and pesto.

❷ Place about ¼ cup filling on each tortilla. Top with red pepper strips; roll up. Arrange tortilla rolls in the prepared baking dish. If desired, lightly coat tortilla rolls with additional cooking spray. Bake, uncovered, in a 350° oven about 15 minutes or until heated through.

❸ Cut each tortilla roll into thirds and arrange on a serving platter. Serve with Yogurt-Chive Sauce.

Yogurt-Chive Sauce: In a small bowl stir together one 8-ounce carton plain fat-free yogurt and 1 tablespoon snipped fresh chives.

Nutrition Facts per serving: 75 cal., 4 g total fat (2 g sat. fat), 8 mg chol., 177 mg sodium, 8 g carbo., 1 g fiber, 3 g pro.
Daily Values: 2% vit. A, 26% vit. C, 7% calcium, 4% iron

mini SPINACH POCKETS

A savory spinach and onion mixture fills these miniature stuffed pizzas. The refrigerated pizza dough makes them incredibly easy to prepare.

Prep: 30 minutes
Bake: 8 minutes
Stand: 5 minutes
Oven: 425°F
Makes: 25 pockets

Nonstick cooking spray

½ **of a 10-ounce package frozen chopped spinach, thawed and well drained**

½ **of an 8-ounce package reduced-fat cream cheese (Neufchâtel), softened**

2 **tablespoons finely chopped green onion**

1 **tablespoon grated Parmesan cheese**

Dash black pepper

1 **10-ounce package refrigerated pizza dough**

1 **tablespoon milk**

Bottled light spaghetti sauce, warmed (optional)

1 Line a baking sheet with foil; lightly coat foil with nonstick cooking spray. Set baking sheet aside. For filling, in a medium bowl stir together spinach, cream cheese, green onion, Parmesan cheese, and pepper. Set aside.

2 Unroll pizza dough on a lightly floured surface; roll dough into a 15-inch square. Cut into twenty-five 3-inch squares. Spoon 1 rounded teaspoon filling onto each square. Brush edges of dough with water. Lift a corner of each square and stretch dough over filling to opposite corner, making a triangle. Press edges with fingers or a fork to seal.

3 Arrange pockets on the prepared baking sheet. Prick tops of pockets with a fork. Brush with milk. Bake in a 425° oven for 8 to 10 minutes or until golden brown. Let stand for 5 minutes before serving. If desired, serve with spaghetti sauce.

Nutrition Facts per pocket: 38 cal., 2 g total fat (1 g sat. fat), 4 mg chol., 62 mg sodium, 5 g carbo., 0 g fiber, 1 g pro.
Daily Values: 9% vit. A, 1% vit. C, 1% calcium, 2% iron

Nutritional Powerhouse

Popeye may have eaten spinach to make him strong, but the leafy green veggie does a lot more than that. With only about 25 calories in a half pound, spinach is one of the most nutrient-dense vegetables around. That same half pound also contains a whopping 21 grams of fiber as well as more than three times the recommended daily amount of vitamin A and the phytochemicals lutein and indoles, which can help lower one's risk of cancer and maintain healthy vision.

roasted pepper ROLL-UPS

The spinach and roasted red peppers combine for a bright, colorful filling. The high-fiber and high-protein beans create a very nutritious snack.

Prep: 20 minutes
Chill: 2 to 24 hours
Makes: 6 servings

1 15-ounce can white kidney beans, rinsed and drained

½ of an 8-ounce package reduced-fat cream cheese (Neufchâtel), softened

¼ cup packed fresh basil

1 tablespoon fat-free milk

2 small cloves garlic, quartered

⅛ teaspoon freshly ground black pepper

⅓ cup roasted red sweet peppers, drained and finely chopped

6 6-inch flour tortillas

1 cup packed spinach leaves

1 For the filling, in a blender container or food processor bowl combine the beans, cream cheese, basil, milk, garlic, and black pepper. Cover and blend or process until smooth. Stir in roasted sweet peppers.

2 To assemble, spread about ⅓ cup of the filling evenly over each tortilla to within ½ inch of the edges. Arrange spinach leaves over filling to cover. Carefully roll tortillas up tightly. Cover and chill roll-ups for 2 hours to 24 hours.

3 To serve, use a sharp knife to cut roll-ups crosswise into 1½-inch slices. Serve immediately.

Nutrition facts per serving: 173 cal., 7 g total fat (3 g sat. fat), 15 mg chol., 289 mg sodium, 24 g carbo., 4 g fiber, 8 g pro.
Daily Values: 10% vit. A, 38% vit. C, 5% calcium, 11% iron

appetizers & sippers

nutty CHICKEN FINGERS

A satisfying snack is ready in a jiffy when you make these crunchy coated chicken strips.

appetizers & sippers

Prep: 15 minutes
Bake: 7 minutes
Oven: 400°F
Makes: 3 servings

⅓ **cup crushed cornflakes**

½ **cup finely chopped pecans**

1 **tablespoon dried parsley flakes**

⅛ **teaspoon salt**

⅛ **teaspoon garlic powder**

12 **ounces skinless, boneless chicken breasts, cut into 3×1-inch strips**

2 **tablespoons fat-free milk**

Reduced-calorie ranch-style dressing (optional)

1 In a shallow dish combine crushed cornflakes, pecans, parsley, salt, and garlic powder. Dip chicken in milk, then roll in cornflake mixture. Place in a 15×10×1-inch baking pan.

2 Bake in a 400° oven for 7 to 9 minutes or until chicken is tender and no longer pink. If desired, serve chicken with ranch-style dressing.

Nutrition Facts per serving: 279 cal., 15 g total fat (0 g sat. fat), 66 mg chol., 219 mg sodium, 8 g carbo., 2 g fiber, 29 g pro.
Daily Values: 3% vit. A, 3% vit. C, 4% calcium, 9% iron

wrap and ROLL PINWHEELS

If you can't find colorful spinach or jalapeño tortillas, use plain or whole wheat tortillas to wrap these cheese- and meat-filled finger foods.

Prep: 20 minutes
Chill: 2 to 4 hours
Makes: about 12 (2-slice)
    servings

- 3   7- to 8-inch spinach and/or jalapeño flour tortillas
- 1   5- to 5.2-ounce container semisoft cheese with garlic and herb
- 12   large fresh basil leaves
- ½   of a 7-ounce jar roasted red sweet peppers, cut into ¼-inch strips (about ½ cup)
- 4   ounces thinly sliced cooked roast beef, ham, or turkey
- 1   tablespoon light mayonnaise dressing

❶ Spread each tortilla with one-third of the semisoft cheese. Top cheese with a layer of the large basil leaves. Divide roasted red sweet pepper strips among the tortillas, arranging pepper strips over the basil leaves 1 to 2 inches apart. Top with meat slices. Spread 1 teaspoon mayonnaise dressing over the meat on each tortilla. Tightly roll up tortillas. Wrap each roll in plastic wrap. Chill for 2 to 4 hours.

❷ To serve, remove the plastic wrap from the tortilla rolls; cut each roll into 1-inch diagonal slices.

Nutrition Facts per serving: 103 cal., 7 g total fat (4 g sat. fat), 8 mg chol., 125 mg sodium, 6 g carbo., 0 g fiber, 4 g pro.
Daily Values: 1% vit. A, 29% vit. C, 2% calcium, 4% iron

herbed POTATO WEDGES

You can serve these tasty potato wedges as a snack or a side dish with flavored sour cream, catsup, or both. No matter how you serve them, your kids will eat them up.

Prep: 15 minutes
Bake: 15 minutes
Oven: 425°F
Makes: 8 servings

- 2 teaspoons olive oil
- 2 teaspoons balsamic vinegar
- 1 tablespoon grated Parmesan cheese
- 1 tablespoon fine dry bread crumbs
- ½ teaspoon dried Italian seasoning
- ⅛ teaspoon black pepper
  Nonstick cooking spray
- 2 medium baking potatoes
- ½ cup light dairy sour cream
- 1 tablespoon snipped fresh chives
- ¼ teaspoon garlic powder

1 In a small bowl or custard cup combine olive oil and balsamic vinegar. In another small bowl combine Parmesan cheese, bread crumbs, Italian seasoning, and pepper.

2 Lightly coat a foil-lined baking sheet with nonstick cooking spray; set aside. Cut the potatoes in half lengthwise, then cut each half lengthwise into 4 wedges. Arrange potato wedges skin side down on the prepared baking sheet so they don't touch. Brush with olive oil mixture and coat with Parmesan cheese mixture.

3 Bake in a 425° oven for 15 to 20 minutes or until potatoes are tender and edges are crisp.

4 Meanwhile, in a small bowl combine sour cream, chives, and garlic powder. Serve warm potatoes with flavored sour cream mixture.

Nutrition Facts per serving: 79 cal., 3 g total fat (1 g sat. fat), 5 mg chol., 43 mg sodium, 11 g carbo., 1 g fiber, 3 g pro.
Daily Values: 2% vit. A, 15% vit. C, 5% calcium, 5% iron

chocolate-mint MILK SHAKES

Even adults swoon for a milk shake. This variation takes a childhood favorite and freshens it with a hint of mint flavor. Low-fat and fat-free ingredients keep the fat and calories much lower than a regular milk shake.

appetizers & sippers

Start to Finish: 10 minutes
Makes: 2 (8-ounce) servings

2 cups chocolate low-fat frozen yogurt

½ cup fat-free milk

Few drops peppermint or mint flavoring

1 In a blender container combine frozen yogurt, milk, and flavoring. Cover and blend until smooth. Serve immediately.

Nutrition Facts per serving: 182 cal., 3 g total fat (2 g sat. fat), 21 mg chol., 162 mg sodium, 35 g carbo., 0 g fiber, 8 g pro.
Daily Values: 2% vit. A, 1% vit. C, 24% calcium

Watch What You Drink

Many people typically grab whatever is around when thirst hits. Many perceived healthy beverages, such as juices and sports drinks, are high in calories and sugar. Know that liquids register differently from solid foods in our bodies. After eating 400–500 calories, we feel satisfied. However, after drinking 400–500 calories, we can then go on to eat another 400–500 calories. Keep this in mind the next time you are thirsty.

tropical banana MILK SHAKES

Take a tropical vacation from your day—share this midafternoon treat with your kids.

Prep: 10 minutes
Freeze: 1 hour
Makes: 4 (6-ounce) servings

1 **small banana**

1 **cup orange juice**

1 **cup vanilla low-fat or light**
   ice cream

¼ **teaspoon vanilla**
   Ground nutmeg

1 Peel and cut up the banana. Place in a freezer container or bag; freeze until firm.

2 In a blender container combine frozen banana, orange juice, ice cream, and vanilla. Cover and blend until smooth. Sprinkle each serving with nutmeg.

Nutrition Facts per serving: 97 cal., 1 g total fat (1 g sat. fat), 5 mg chol., 21 mg sodium, 20 g carbo., 1 g fiber, 2 g pro.
Daily Values: 3% vit. A, 55% vit. C, 2% calcium, 1% iron

appetizers & sippers

minty COCOA

Chocolate and mint have always been a great flavor duo. The combination in this beverage is no exception; getting your daily calcium never tasted so good. The Mocha Cooler variation is a must for coffee fans.

Start to Finish: 15 minutes
Makes: 6 (1-cup) servings

½ **cup unsweetened cocoa
   powder**

   **Heat-stable sugar substitute
   equal to ¼ cup sugar, or
   ¼ cup sugar**

10 **striped round peppermint
   candies, finely crushed**

6 **cups fat-free milk**

❶ In a large saucepan stir together the cocoa powder, sugar substitute or sugar, crushed candies, and ¾ cup of the milk. Cook and stir over medium heat until mixture just comes to boiling. Stir in the remaining milk; heat through. Do not boil. Remove from heat. If desired, beat with a rotary beater until frothy.

Nutrition facts per serving: 134 cal., 1 g total fat (0 g sat. fat), 4 mg chol., 128 mg sodium, 21 g carbo., 0 g fiber, 10 g pro.
Daily values: 15% vit. A, 3% vit. C, 31% calcium, 7% iron

If using ¼ cup sugar option: 167 cal. and 28 g carbo.

Mocha Cooler: Prepare as above, except omit the peppermint candies; increase the heat-stable sugar substitute to equal ⅓ cup sugar or increase the sugar to ⅓ cup. Add 2 to 3 teaspoons instant coffee crystals with the ¾ cup milk. Cook and stir over medium heat until mixture just comes to boiling. Remove from heat; stir in the remaining milk. Serve immediately over ice. (Or, cover and chill. Stir before serving over ice.)

Nutrition facts per serving: 117 calories, 1 g total fat (0 g sat. fat), 4 mg chol., 126 mg sodium, 17 g carbo., 0 g fiber, 10 g pro.
Daily values: 15% vit. A, 3% vit. C, 31% calcium, 7% iron

If using ⅓ cup sugar option: 160 cal. and 26 g carbo.

pineapple ginger SPRITZER

You'll find crystallized ginger (candied ginger), the key ingredient in this fruit flavored drink, in the supermarket spice aisle or stocked with the dried fruits. Or, look for it in a specialty food store.

Prep: 10 minutes
Chill: 2 to 24 hours
Makes: 6 (1-cup) servings

4   **cups unsweetened pineapple
    juice**

1   **tablespoon chopped
    crystallized ginger**

    Ice cubes

2   **cups carbonated water,
    chilled**

    Pineapple spears (optional)

1 In a pitcher combine pineapple juice and ginger. Cover and chill for 2 to 24 hours. Strain juice mixture, discarding ginger.

2 For each serving, pour pineapple juice into a tall glass over ice, filling each glass about three-fourths full. Add enough carbonated water to each glass to fill. If desired, garnish with pineapple spears.

Nutrition facts per serving: 101 cal., 0 g total fat (0 g sat. fat), 0 mg chol., 19 mg sodium, 25 g carbo., 0 g fiber, 1 g pro.
Daily values: 0% vit. A, 31% vit. C, 3% calcium, 6% iron

breakfast
& BRUNCH

Greet the day with a delicious breakfast that will keep you going all morning long. When time is short, choose an on-the-go meal, like a Berry-Banana Smoothie or a Breakfast Tortilla Wrap. Or, for more relaxed a.m. fare, try the Spring-Fresh Frittata or Pancakes with Berry Sauce.

Breakfast Bread Pudding, *recipe page 38*

breakfast BREAD PUDDING

If you love bread pudding, here's a great way to start the day. Cubes of cinnamon-swirl bread nestle in a custard made with protein-packed egg product and fat-free milk.

breakfast & brunch

Prep: 25 minutes
Bake: 35 minutes
Stand: 15 minutes
Oven: 325°F
Makes: 6 servings

- 6 slices cinnamon-swirl bread or cinnamon-raisin bread
  Nonstick cooking spray
- 1½ cups fat-free milk
- ¾ cup refrigerated or frozen egg product, thawed
- 3 tablespoons sugar
- 1 teaspoon vanilla
- ¼ teaspoon ground nutmeg
- 1 5½-ounce can apricot or peach nectar (⅔ cup)
- 2 teaspoons cornstarch

1 To dry bread, place slices in a single layer on a baking sheet. Bake in a 325° oven for 10 minutes, turning once. Cool on a wire rack. Cut slices into ½-inch cubes (you should have about 4 cups).

2 Lightly coat six 6-ounce soufflé dishes or custard cups with nonstick cooking spray. Divide bread cubes among the prepared dishes. In a medium bowl combine milk, egg product, sugar, vanilla, and nutmeg. Use a rotary beater or wire whisk to beat until mixed. Pour milk mixture evenly over bread cubes. Press lightly with the back of a spoon to thoroughly moisten bread.

3 Place dishes in a 13×9×2-inch baking pan. Place baking pan on oven rack. Carefully pour the hottest tap water available into the baking pan around dishes to a depth of 1 inch.

4 Bake in the 325° oven for 35 to 40 minutes or until a knife inserted near centers comes out clean. Transfer dishes to a wire rack. Let stand for 15 to 20 minutes.

5 Meanwhile, for sauce, in a small saucepan gradually stir apricot nectar into cornstarch. Cook and stir over medium heat until thickened and bubbly. Reduce heat. Cook and stir for 2 minutes more. Spoon sauce over warm puddings.

Nutrition Facts per serving: 164 cal., 2 g total fat (1 g sat. fat), 1 mg chol., 189 mg sodium, 28 g carbo., 0 g fiber, 8 g pro.
Daily Values: 13% vit. A, 15% vit. C, 9% calcium, 10% iron

blueberry BREAKFAST SCONES

Spread good morning cheer with these orange-glazed scones served warm with a dab of butter.

Prep: 25 minutes
Bake: 15 minutes
Oven: 400°F
Makes: 10 scones

2 **cups all-purpose flour**

¼ **cup sugar**

1 **tablespoon baking powder**

1 **tablespoon finely shredded orange peel**

¼ **teaspoon salt**

¼ **teaspoon baking soda**

¼ **cup butter**

½ **cup buttermilk or sour milk***

¼ **cup refrigerated or frozen egg product, thawed**

1 **teaspoon vanilla**

1 **cup fresh or frozen blueberries**

Nonstick cooking spray

1 **recipe Orange Powdered Sugar Icing**

① In a large bowl stir together flour, sugar, baking powder, orange peel, salt, and baking soda. Using a pastry blender, cut in butter until mixture resembles coarse crumbs. Make a well in the center of the flour mixture. Combine buttermilk, egg product, and vanilla. Add to flour mixture all at once, stirring just until moistened. Gently stir in blueberries. Lightly coat a baking sheet with nonstick cooking spray; set aside.

② Turn dough out onto a lightly floured surface. Quickly knead dough by folding and pressing gently for 12 to 15 strokes or until nearly smooth. Pat dough into a 7-inch circle on the prepared baking sheet. Cut dough into 10 wedges.

③ Bake in a 400° oven for 15 to 20 minutes or until golden brown. Cool slightly on a wire rack. Drizzle Orange Powdered Sugar Icing over tops of scones.

Orange Powdered Sugar Icing: In a small bowl stir together ¾ cup sifted powdered sugar and ¼ teaspoon finely shredded orange peel. Stir in enough orange juice or fat-free milk (3 to 4 teaspoons) to make an icing of drizzling consistency.

***Note:** To make ½ cup sour milk, place 1½ teaspoons lemon juice or vinegar in a glass measuring cup. Add enough fat-free milk to make ½ cup total liquid; stir. Let stand for 5 minutes before using.

Nutrition Facts per scone: 194 cal., 5 g total fat (3 g sat. fat), 13 mg chol., 273 mg sodium, 34 g carbo., 1 g fiber, 4 g pro.
Daily Values: 7% vit. A, 6% vit. C, 10% calcium, 9% iron

breakfast & brunch

Fruit Picking

Fruits are an excellent source of vitamins, minerals, and fiber and contain virtually no fat. That's true whether you're using fresh, frozen, or canned fruit. A couple of things to watch out for: When selecting canned fruit read the label carefully and choose those canned in juice, not syrup; check the ingredient list on frozen fruits for added sugars or sauces and buy those without these additions.

bananas foster OATMEAL

For a breakfast that's quick to make and keeps you going all morning long, add banana slices, toasted pecans, and caramel ice cream topping to a packet of instant oatmeal.

Start to Finish: 10 minutes
Makes: 2 servings

- **2 1-ounce envelopes instant oatmeal (plain)**
- **1 medium banana, sliced**
- **2 tablespoons chopped pecans, toasted**
- **2 to 3 teaspoons caramel ice cream topping**
- **Fat-free milk (optional)**

1 In 2 microwave-safe bowls prepare oatmeal according to package directions. Top with banana and pecans. Drizzle with caramel topping.

2 If desired, microwave on 100 percent power (high) about 30 seconds or until toppings are warm. If desired, serve with fat-free milk.

Nutrition Facts per serving: 230 cal., 7 g total fat (1 g sat. fat), 0 mg chol., 17 mg sodium, 38 g carbo., 5 g fiber, 6 g pro.
Daily Values: 1% vit. A, 9% vit. C, 3% calcium, 9% iron

breakfast & brunch

fruity OATMEAL

Make your morning oatmeal even more satisfying by adding fresh and dried fruits.

breakfast & brunch

Start to Finish: 15 minutes
Makes: 4 servings

- 2 **cups water**
- ¼ **teaspoon salt**
- 1 **cup rolled oats**
- 1 **cup chopped peeled peaches or chopped apple**
- ¼ **cup raisins or snipped pitted whole dates**
- 1 **teaspoon vanilla**
- ¼ **teaspoon ground cinnamon**
  Fat-free milk (optional)

1 In a medium saucepan bring the water and salt to boiling. Stir in oats, peaches, raisins, vanilla, and cinnamon. Reduce heat and simmer, uncovered, for 3 minutes (for quick oats) or 5 minutes (for regular oats), stirring occasionally. Remove from heat. Cover and let stand for 2 minutes.

2 Divide oat mixture among 4 bowls. If desired, serve with fat-free milk.

Nutrition Facts per serving: 143 cal., 2 g total fat (0 g sat. fat), 0 mg chol., 151 mg sodium, 29 g carbo., 4 g fiber, 4 g pro.
Daily Values: 5% vit. A, 5% vit. C, 2% calcium, 7% iron

fruited GRANOLA

This very berry granola starts your day with an appetizing crunch. Bowls of the cinnamon-scented cereal make great snacks too.

Prep: 15 minutes
Bake: 38 minutes
Oven: 325°F
Makes: 5 servings

Nonstick cooking spray
2½ **cups regular rolled oats**
1 **cup whole bran cereal**
½ **cup toasted wheat germ**
¼ **cup sliced almonds**
½ **cup raspberry applesauce**
⅓ **cup honey**
¼ **teaspoon ground cinnamon**
⅓ **cup dried cranberries, blueberries, and/or cherries**
Vanilla low-fat yogurt or fat-free milk (optional)

❶ Lightly coat a 15×10×1-inch baking pan with nonstick cooking spray; set aside. In a large bowl stir together rolled oats, bran cereal, wheat germ, and almonds. In a small bowl stir together applesauce, honey, and cinnamon. Pour applesauce mixture over cereal mixture; stir until combined.

❷ Spread cereal mixture evenly in the prepared baking pan. Bake in a 325° oven for 35 minutes, stirring occasionally. Carefully stir in dried cranberries. Bake for 3 to 5 minutes more or until golden brown.

❸ Turn out onto a large piece of foil to cool completely. To store, place in an airtight container for up to 2 weeks. If desired, serve with vanilla yogurt or fat-free milk.

Nutrition Facts per serving: 216 cal., 4 g total fat (1 g sat. fat), 0 mg chol., 18 mg sodium, 41 g carbo., 6 g fiber, 7 g pro.
Daily Values: 4% vit. A, 6% vit. C, 6% calcium, 14% iron

breakfast & brunch

streusel FRENCH TOAST

Crushed, shredded wheat biscuits add a slightly crunchy topping to this make-ahead, nutrition-packed breakfast. Fresh strawberries make it even more special.

Prep: 20 minutes
Chill: 2 to 24 hours
Bake: 30 minutes
Makes: 6 servings

Nonstick spray coating

¾ **cup refrigerated or frozen egg product, thawed, or 3 eggs, slightly beaten**

1 **cup evaporated fat-free milk**

3 **tablespoons sugar**

2 **teaspoons vanilla**

½ **teaspoon ground cinnamon**

¼ **teaspoon ground nutmeg**

6 **1-inch slices Italian bread (3 to 4 inches in diameter)**

1 **large shredded wheat biscuit, crushed (⅔ cup)**

1 **tablespoon butter or margarine, melted**

2 **cups sliced strawberries**

3 **tablespoons sugar, or sugar substitute equal to 3 tablespoons sugar**

½ **teaspoon ground cinnamon**

1 Spray a 2-quart rectangular baking dish with nonstick coating; set aside. In a medium bowl beat together the egg product or eggs, evaporated milk, 3 tablespoons sugar, vanilla, ½ teaspoon cinnamon, and nutmeg. Arrange the bread slices in a single layer in prepared baking dish. Pour egg mixture evenly over slices. Cover and chill for 2 to 24 hours, turning bread slices once with a wide spatula.

2 Combine crushed biscuit and melted butter or margarine; sprinkle evenly over the bread slices. Bake, uncovered, in a 375° oven about 30 minutes until lightly browned.

3 Meanwhile, in a small bowl combine the strawberries, 3 tablespoons sugar or sugar substitute, and ½ teaspoon cinnamon. Serve with French toast.

Nutrition facts per serving: 244 cal., 5 g total fat (2 g sat. fat), 7 mg chol., 300 mg sodium, 41 g carbo., 1 g fiber, 10 g pro.
Daily values: 14% vit. A, 48% vit. C, 15% calcium, 14% iron

Using sugar substitute option: 220 cal. and 35 g carbo.

stuffed FRENCH TOAST

The cream cheese-and-fruit stuffing creates a delicious surprise with every bite. To save time in the morning, fill the pockets the night before, covering the bread tightly with plastic wrap and storing it in the refrigerator.

breakfast & brunch

Prep: 15 minutes
Bake: 8 minutes
Makes: 4 servings

- **4 1-inch-thick diagonally cut slices French bread**
- **¼ of an 8-ounce tub light cream cheese**
- **½ cup finely chopped fruit, such as nectarines or peeled peaches, pears, or apricots**
- **1 teaspoon sugar-free apricot, apricot-pineapple, orange marmalade, or peach spread**
- **Nonstick spray coating**
- **¼ cup refrigerated or frozen egg product, thawed**
- **¼ cup fat-free milk**
- **⅛ teaspoon ground cinnamon**
- **½ cup sugar-free apricot, apricot-pineapple, orange marmalade, or peach spread**

1 Cut a pocket in the top of each bread slice; set aside. In a small bowl stir together the cream cheese, chopped fruit, and the 1 teaspoon fruit spread. Fill each pocket with a rounded tablespoon of the cream cheese mixture.

2 Spray a foil-lined baking sheet with nonstick coating; set aside. In a shallow bowl stir together the egg product, milk, and cinnamon. Dip the stuffed slices into the egg mixture, coating both sides.

3 Arrange bread slices on the prepared baking sheet. Bake in a 450° oven for 8 to 10 minutes or until heated through.

4 Meanwhile, in a small saucepan heat the remaining ½ cup fruit spread over medium heat just until melted. Invert the French toast onto serving plates. Top with melted spread.

Nutrition facts per serving: 196 cal., 6 g total fat (1 g sat. fat), 18 mg chol., 355 mg sodium, 28 g carbo., 0 g fiber, 6 g pro.
Daily values: 13% vit. A, 1% vit. C, 5% calcium, 8% iron

oat PANCAKES

Pancakes always are a treat for a leisurely weekend breakfast or brunch. But these wheat and oat pancakes are exceptionally good. The pear sauce with a hint of maple adds the crowning touch.

Prep: 30 minutes
Stand: 15 to 30 minutes
Cook: 4 minutes per batch
Makes: 8 (¼-cup) servings

1¼ cups regular rolled oats

¾ cup all-purpose flour

½ cup whole wheat flour

1 tablespoon baking powder

¼ teaspoon salt

3 slightly beaten egg whites

2¼ cups buttermilk

2 tablespoons cooking oil

2 tablespoons honey (optional)

1 teaspoon vanilla

1 recipe Maple-Pear Sauce
    Nonstick spray coating

1 In a large bowl combine the oats, all-purpose flour, whole wheat flour, baking powder, and salt. Make a well in the center of mixture; set aside. In a medium bowl combine the egg whites, buttermilk, oil, honey (if desired), and vanilla. Add egg white mixture all at once to flour mixture. Stir just until moistened (batter should be lumpy). Cover batter; allow to stand at room temperature for 15 to 30 minutes. Meanwhile, prepare Maple-Pear Sauce; keep warm.

2 Spray a griddle or heavy skillet with nonstick coating. Preheat over medium-high heat. For each pancake, pour about ¼ cup of the batter onto the hot griddle or skillet. Spread batter into a circle about 4 inches in diameter. Cook over medium heat about 2 minutes on each side or until the pancakes are golden, turning to cook second sides when pancakes have bubbly surfaces and edges are slightly dry. Serve with Maple-Pear Sauce. Makes 8 servings (16 pancakes).

Maple-Pear Sauce: Peel and core 4 large pears; cut pears into ¼-inch slices. Toss with 1 tablespoon lemon juice; set aside. In a large heavy saucepan combine ½ cup unsweetened apple juice, ½ cup sugar-free pancake and waffle syrup product, and 3 inches stick cinnamon. Bring to boiling. Add pear slices; reduce heat. Simmer, uncovered, for 3 to 5 minutes or until the pears are tender. Stir together 2 tablespoons unsweetened apple juice and 1 tablespoon cornstarch; stir into pear mixture along with ¼ cup dried cranberries. Cook and stir until bubbly. Cook and stir for 2 minutes more. Remove from heat and discard cinnamon.

Nutrition facts per serving: 257 cal., 5 g total fat (1 g sat. fat), 3 mg chol., 320 mg sodium, 46 g carbo., 3 g fiber, 8 g pro.
Daily values: 0% vit. A, 6% vit. C, 18% calcium, 12% iron

pancakes WITH BERRY SAUCE

A fresh strawberry sauce drizzled over feathery-light whole wheat pancakes is sure to open sleepy eyes.

Start to Finish: 25 minutes
Makes: 5 (2-pancake) servings

½ **cup whole wheat flour**

½ **cup all-purpose flour**

1 **tablespoon sugar**

2 **teaspoons baking powder**

¼ **teaspoon salt**

¾ **cup fat-free milk**

1 **teaspoon cooking oil**

2 **egg whites**

Nonstick cooking spray

2 **cups fresh or frozen unsweetened strawberries, thawed**

1 **tablespoon sugar**

1 **teaspoon vanilla**

Quartered fresh strawberries (optional)

1 In a medium bowl combine whole wheat flour, all-purpose flour, sugar, baking powder, and salt. Stir in milk and oil. In another bowl, beat egg whites until stiff (tips stand straight). Fold egg whites into flour mixture.

2 Lightly coat a griddle with nonstick cooking spray. Heat griddle over medium heat. For each pancake pour about ¼ cup batter onto the hot griddle. Cook over medium heat until pancakes are golden brown (1 to 2 minutes per side); turn to second sides when pancakes have bubbly surfaces and slightly dry edges.

3 Meanwhile, in a blender container or food processor bowl combine strawberries, sugar, and vanilla. Cover and blend or process until smooth. In a small saucepan heat sauce until warm. If desired, top pancakes with quartered strawberries. Serve pancakes with sauce.

Nutrition Facts per serving: 148 cal., 2 g total fat, 1 mg chol., 319 mg sodium, 28 g carbo., 3 g fiber, 6 g pro.
Daily Values: 2% vit. A, 55% vit. C, 16% calcium, 7% iron

breakfast & brunch

toasted walnut WAFFLES

Why go out for waffles when you can make these great-tasting ones at home? Ground walnuts provide a light crunch and nutty flavor to make these waffles more special.

breakfast & brunch

Prep: 25 minutes
Cook: per waffle iron directions
Makes: 8 (2-waffle) servings

1   recipe Blueberry Sauce
1   cup all-purpose flour
1   cup whole wheat flour
¼   cup toasted coarsely ground walnuts
2   teaspoons baking powder
1   teaspoon baking soda
4   egg whites
2¼ cups buttermilk
2   tablespoons cooking oil

① Prepare Blueberry Sauce. Set aside.

② For waffles, stir together all-purpose flour, whole wheat flour, walnuts, baking powder, and baking soda. In a large bowl beat the egg whites with an electric mixer on medium speed until very foamy. Stir in buttermilk and oil. Gradually add flour mixture, beating by hand until smooth.

③ Pour 1 cup of the batter onto grids of a preheated, lightly greased waffle iron. Close lid quickly; do not open lid until waffle is done. Bake according to manufacturer's directions. When done, use a fork to lift waffle off grid. Repeat with remaining batter. Serve waffles with Blueberry Sauce.

Blueberry Sauce: In a saucepan combine 1 cup blueberries, ¼ cup white grape juice, and 1 tablespoon honey. Heat just until bubbles form around edges. Let cool for 1 to 2 minutes. Transfer to a blender container. Cover and blend until smooth. Transfer sauce to a serving bowl. Stir in 1 cup blueberries. Makes 1⅔ cups sauce.

Nutrition facts per 2 waffles with about 3 tablespoons sauce: 227 cal., 7 g total fat (1 g sat. fat), 3 mg chol., 352 mg sodium, 35 g carbo., 3 g fiber, 8 g pro.
Daily values: 0% vit. A, 8% vit. C, 14% calcium, 10% iron

mushroom-FONTINA STRATA

Using mostly egg whites—rather than whole eggs—helps lighten up this strata. If fontina cheese is unavailable, the dish tastes great using part-skim mozzarella cheese or Swiss cheese.

Prep: 25 minutes
Chill: 4 to 24 hours
Bake: 35 minutes
Makes: 6 servings

Nonstick spray coating

3 **cups assorted sliced fresh mushrooms, such as shiitake, button, white, and/or cremini**

½ **cup chopped onion**

1 **clove garlic, minced**

2 **ounces Canadian-style bacon, finely chopped**

8 **½-inch-thick slices French bread**

½ **cup shredded fontina cheese**

2 **tablespoons assorted snipped fresh herbs (such as basil, oregano, marjoram, or thyme) or 2 teaspoons assorted dried herbs, crushed**

1 **cup fat-free cottage cheese**

1 **cup evaporated fat-free milk**

3 **egg whites**

1 **egg**

1 **tablespoon Dijon-style mustard**

⅛ **teaspoon pepper**

1 **small tomato, seeded and chopped**

1 Spray a medium skillet with nonstick coating. Cook the mushrooms, onion, and garlic in skillet until tender. Drain off any liquid. Stir in Canadian-style bacon.

2 Spray a 2-quart rectangular baking dish with nonstick coating. Arrange the bread slices in the prepared baking dish, cutting as necessary to fit. Sprinkle mushroom mixture over bread. In a small bowl toss together fontina cheese and desired herbs. Sprinkle over mushroom mixture.

3 In a blender container or food processor bowl combine cottage cheese, evaporated milk, egg whites, egg, mustard, and pepper. Cover and blend or process until smooth; pour evenly over ingredients in baking dish. Lightly press bread down with the back of a spoon. Cover; chill for 4 to 24 hours.

4 Bake, uncovered, in a 350° oven about 35 minutes or until a knife inserted near the center comes out clean. Sprinkle with chopped tomato. Let stand for 5 minutes before serving.

Nutrition facts per serving: 227 cal., 6 g total fat (2 g sat. fat), 56 mg chol., 543 mg sodium, 24 g carbo., 1 g fiber, 20 g pro.
Daily values: 12% vit. A, 11% vit. C, 18% calcium, 11% iron

breakfast & brunch

cheddar-POLENTA PUFF

With an airy, soufflé like texture, this side dish works as well for dinner as it does for brunch. Extra-sharp cheddar cheese gives an extra-rich flavor to this puff.

Prep: 40 minutes
Bake: 25 minutes
Makes: 4 servings

- **4 egg whites**
- **1½ cups fat-free milk**
- **2 tablespoons finely chopped red sweet pepper**
- **1 tablespoon thinly sliced green onion**
- **¼ teaspoon salt**
- **⅛ teaspoon ground red pepper**
- **⅓ cup cornmeal**
- **1 egg yolk, slightly beaten**
- **¼ cup grated Parmesan cheese**
- **¼ cup shredded extra-sharp cheddar cheese (1 ounce)***
- **Nonstick spray coating**

1 Allow egg whites to stand at room temperature for 30 minutes. Meanwhile, in a large heavy saucepan combine milk, sweet pepper, green onion, salt, and red pepper. Cook and stir over medium heat until mixture just begins to bubble. Slowly add cornmeal, stirring constantly. Cook and stir over medium heat about 5 minutes or until mixture begins to thicken. Remove from heat. Stir half of the cornmeal mixture into the egg yolk. Return mixture to the saucepan. Stir in Parmesan cheese and cheddar cheese until melted.

2 Lightly spray a 1½-quart soufflé dish with nonstick coating; set aside. In a large mixing bowl beat egg whites with an electric mixer on medium to high speed until stiff peaks form (tips stand straight). Gently fold about half of the beaten egg whites into the cheese mixture. Gradually pour cheese mixture over remaining beaten egg whites, folding to combine. Pour into prepared soufflé dish.

3 Bake in a 375° oven about 25 minutes or until a knife inserted in center comes out clean and top is golden brown. Serve immediately.

*Note: This recipe calls for regular cheddar cheese—not reduced-fat cheddar. The baking time may cause reduced-fat cheese to toughen.

Nutrition facts per serving: 168 cal., 6 g total fat (4 g sat. fat), 69 mg chol., 397 mg sodium, 14 g carbo., 1 g fiber, 13 g pro.
Daily values: 20% vit. A, 10% vit. C, 21% calcium, 5% iron

spring-fresh FRITTATA

Spring is prime time for fresh asparagus and new potatoes. Both are showcased here in a frittata, the classic Italian omelet. Use a broiler-proof skillet, as the frittata finishes cooking under the broiler.

breakfast & brunch

Start to Finish: 25 minutes
Makes: 4 servings

¼ **pound whole tiny new potatoes, coarsely chopped (about 1 cup)**

1 **cup water**

¼ **pound asparagus spears, trimmed and cut into 1-inch lengths (about ½ cup)**

1½ **cups refrigerated or frozen egg product, thawed***

¼ **cup fat-free milk**

1 **tablespoon snipped fresh rosemary or 1 teaspoon dried rosemary, crushed**

⅛ **teaspoon pepper**

Dash salt

2 **teaspoons olive oil**

1 **small onion, thinly sliced and separated into rings**

1 **clove garlic, minced**

⅓ **cup crumbled basil-and-tomato feta cheese**

1 **small tomato, seeded and chopped**

1 In a medium saucepan combine potatoes and water. Bring to boiling; reduce heat. Simmer, covered, for 10 minutes. Add the asparagus; return to simmering. Simmer, covered, for 4 to 6 minutes more or until vegetables are just tender. Drain the vegetables well.

2 Meanwhile, beat together the egg product, milk, rosemary, pepper, and salt; set aside. In a 10-inch broiler-proof skillet heat olive oil; cook onion and garlic in hot oil until tender. Stir in potatoes and asparagus.

3 Pour egg mixture into skillet over vegetables. Cook over medium heat. As mixture sets, run a spatula around edge of skillet, lifting egg mixture so the uncooked portion flows underneath. Continue cooking and lifting edges until egg mixture is almost set (surface will be moist). Sprinkle with the feta cheese.

4 Place broiler-proof skillet under the broiler 4 to 5 inches from the heat. Broil about 1 minute or until the top is just set. Sprinkle with tomato. Cut into wedges.

*Note: If desired, omit egg product; use 4 whole eggs and 3 egg whites.

Nutrition facts per serving: 191 cal., 9 g total fat (3 g sat. fat), 15 mg chol., 393 mg sodium, 12 g carbo., 1 g fiber, 16 g pro.
Daily values: 26% vit. A, 24% vit. C, 13% calcium, 19% iron

breakfast CASSEROLE

To make ahead, cook the potatoes and leeks. Layer the cooked mixture, ham, and cheese in the baking dish. Cover and refrigerate. In the morning, combine the remaining ingredients, pour over the casserole, and bake.

Prep: 25 minutes
Bake: 35 minutes
Makes: 6 servings

- 1 **pound whole tiny new potatoes, cut into ¼-inch slices**
- ⅓ **cup thinly sliced leek**
  Nonstick spray coating
- ¾ **cup chopped lower-fat and lower-sodium cooked ham**
- 3 **ounces reduced-fat Swiss cheese, cut into small pieces**
- 1¼ **cups fat-free milk**
- 1 **tablespoon all-purpose flour**
- ¾ **cup refrigerated or frozen egg product, thawed**
- 2 **teaspoons snipped fresh thyme or ½ teaspoon dried thyme, crushed**
- ¼ **teaspoon pepper**

1 In a large saucepan cook sliced potatoes in a small amount of lightly salted boiling water about 10 minutes or just until tender, adding leeks during the last 5 minutes of cooking. Drain potato and leek mixture.

2 Spray a 2-quart rectangular baking dish with nonstick coating. Layer cooked potatoes and leeks in bottom of dish. Sprinkle ham and Swiss cheese over potatoes.

3 In a medium bowl stir the milk into the flour until smooth. Stir in the egg product, thyme, and pepper. Pour the egg mixture over the potatoes.

4 Bake, uncovered, in a 350° oven for 35 to 40 minutes or until a knife inserted near center comes out clean. Serve immediately.

Nutrition facts per serving: 180 cal., 4 g total fat (1 g sat. fat), 16 mg chol., 445 mg sodium, 23 g carbo., 1 g fiber, 13 g pro.
Daily values: 10% vit. A, 26% vit. C, 14% calcium, 16% iron

breakfast & brunch

breakfast TORTILLA WRAP

This bacon and egg burrito makes a tidy on-the-go breakfast that you can wrap up in about 10 minutes.

Start to Finish: 10 minutes
Makes: 1 serving

1 **strip turkey bacon, chopped**

2 **tablespoons chopped green sweet pepper**

⅛ **teaspoon ground cumin**

⅛ **teaspoon salt (optional)**

⅛ **teaspoon crushed red pepper (optional)**

¼ **cup refrigerated egg product or 2 slightly beaten egg whites**

2 **tablespoons chopped tomato**

3 **dashes bottled hot pepper sauce (optional)**

1 **8-inch fat-free flour tortilla, warmed**

1 In a medium nonstick skillet cook bacon until crisp. Add green pepper, cumin, and, if desired, salt and crushed red pepper. Cook for 3 minutes. Add egg product; cook for 2 minutes. Stir in tomato and, if desired, hot pepper sauce. Spoon onto tortilla and roll up.

Nutrition Facts per serving: 185 cal., 3 g total fat (1 g sat. fat), 10 mg chol., 643 mg sodium, 27 g carbo., 2 g fiber, 11 g pro.
Daily Values: 5% vit. A, 31% vit. C, 1% calcium, 6% iron

breakfast & brunch

breakfast BAKE

Put all your eggs in one basket (or dish, in this case) along with ham and your favorite cheese such as cheddar, Swiss, American, or Monterey Jack with jalapeño peppers.

Prep: 15 minutes
Bake: 30 minutes
Stand: 10 minutes
Chill: 2 hours
Oven: 325°F
Makes: 4 servings

Nonstick cooking spray

4 **slices bread**

½ **cup diced cooked lean ham**

⅓ **cup reduced-fat shredded cheddar cheese**

4 **eggs**

⅔ **cup fat-free milk**

⅛ **teaspoon black pepper**

❶ Lightly coat two 16- to 20-ounce casseroles with nonstick cooking spray. Tear bread into bite-size pieces; place half of the bread in the prepared dishes. Sprinkle ham and cheese over bread. Top with remaining torn bread.

❷ In a medium mixing bowl beat together eggs, milk, and pepper with a rotary beater or a fork. Pour egg mixture evenly over bread; press lightly with the back of a spoon to thoroughly moisten bread. Cover and chill for 2 to 24 hours.

❸ Bake in a 325° oven about 30 minutes or until a knife inserted near centers comes out clean. Let stand for 10 minutes before serving.

Nutrition Facts per serving: 235 cal., 12 g total fat (5 g sat. fat), 237 mg chol., 546 mg sodium, 15 g carbo., 1 g fiber, 16 g pro.
Daily Values: 10% vit. A, 1% vit. C, 18% calcium, 10% iron

eggs and more PITA POCKETS

Creamy scrambled eggs and Canadian bacon pack these pita breads with protein. It's the ideal breakfast to eat at home or on the go.

Start to Finish: 15 minutes
Makes: 4 servings

- 2 **eggs**
- 4 **egg whites**
- 3 **ounces Canadian-style bacon, finely chopped**
- 3 **tablespoons water**
- 2 **tablespoons snipped fresh chives (optional)**
- ⅛ **teaspoon salt**
- **Nonstick cooking spray**
- 2 **large pita bread rounds**
- ½ **cup shredded cheddar cheese (2 ounces)**

1 In a medium mixing bowl beat together eggs, egg whites, Canadian-style bacon, water, chives (if desired), and salt with a rotary beater or a fork.

2 Lightly coat a large nonstick skillet with cooking spray. Heat skillet over medium heat. Add egg mixture to skillet. Cook without stirring until egg mixture begins to set. Run a spatula around the edge of the skillet, lifting egg mixture so the uncooked portion flows underneath. Continue cooking until egg mixture is cooked through but is still glossy and moist.

3 Cut pita rounds in half crosswise. Fill pita halves with egg mixture. Sprinkle with cheese.

Nutrition Facts per serving: 233 cal., 9 g total fat (4 g sat. fat), 133 mg chol., 734 mg sodium, 18 g carbo., 1 g fiber, 18 g pro.
Daily Values: 6% vit. A, 14% calcium, 8% iron

breakfast & brunch

the casual OMELET

The indulgence of breakfast in bed is yours to savor with a ready-in-minutes omelet. If you like, round out the meal with fresh fruit.

Start to Finish: 18 minutes
Makes: 2 servings

Nonstick cooking spray

8 **ounces refrigerated or frozen egg product, thawed**

1 **tablespoon snipped fresh chives, Italian parsley, or chervil**

Dash salt

Dash cayenne pepper

¼ **cup shredded reduced-fat sharp cheddar cheese (1 ounce)**

1 **cup spinach leaves**

1 **recipe Red Pepper Relish**

Fresh fruit (optional)

① Lightly coat an 8-inch nonstick skillet with flared sides or a crepe pan with nonstick cooking spray. Heat skillet over medium heat.

② In a mixing bowl combine egg product, chives, salt, and cayenne pepper. Beat with an electric mixer on medium speed or a rotary beater until frothy.

③ Pour mixture into the prepared skillet. Cook over medium heat. As egg mixture sets, run a spatula around edge of skillet, lifting eggs so uncooked portion flows underneath. When eggs are set but still shiny, sprinkle with cheese. Top with ¾ cup spinach and 2 tablespoons Red Pepper Relish. Fold one side of omelet partially over filling. Top with remaining spinach and 1 tablespoon Red Pepper Relish. Reserve remaining relish for another use. Cut omelet in half; transfer omelet halves to plates. If desired, serve with fresh fruit.

Red Pepper Relish: In a bowl combine ⅔ cup chopped red sweet pepper, 2 tablespoons finely chopped onion, 1 tablespoon cider vinegar, and ¼ teaspoon black pepper.

Nutrition Facts per serving: 122 cal., 3 g total fat (2 g sat. fat), 10 mg chol., 404 mg sodium, 7 g carbo., 3 g fiber, 16 g pro.
Daily Values: 103% vit. A, 167% vit. C, 16% calcium, 19% iron

turkey-APPLE SAUSAGE

A nice change of pace from pork sausage, these turkey patties have a hint of apple. If you like, try the Mexican-style version, which substitutes green chile peppers for the apple.

Prep: 15 minutes
Broil: 10 minutes
Makes: 4 servings

½ cup shredded peeled apple

2 tablespoons soft bread crumbs

1½ teaspoons snipped fresh sage or ½ teaspoon dried sage, crushed

¼ teaspoon black pepper

⅛ teaspoon salt

⅛ teaspoon paprika

⅛ teaspoon ground red pepper
   Dash ground nutmeg

8 ounces ground raw turkey
   Nonstick spray coating

1 In a large bowl combine the shredded apple, bread crumbs, sage, black pepper, salt, paprika, red pepper, and nutmeg. Add the turkey; mix well. Shape mixture into four ½-inch-thick patties.

2 Spray the unheated rack of a broiler pan with nonstick coating. Arrange patties on rack. Broil 4 to 5 inches from the heat about 10 minutes or until no longer pink, turning once. (Or, spray large skillet with nonstick coating. Preheat over medium heat. Add sausage and cook for 8 to 10 minutes or until no longer pink.)

Nutrition facts per serving: 89 cal., 5 grams total fat (1 g sat. fat), 21 mg chol., 99 mg sodium, 4 g carbo., 0 g fiber, 8 g pro.
Daily values: 0% vit. A, 2% vit. C, 1% calcium, 4% iron

Mexican-Style Turkey Sausage: Prepare as directed above, except substitute one 4½-ounce can diced green chile peppers for the apple, and omit the sage, paprika, and nutmeg. Add 1 large clove garlic, minced; ¼ teaspoon ground cumin; and ¼ teaspoon dried oregano, crushed, to the turkey mixture. Continue as directed.

Nutrition facts per serving: 83 cal., 5 g total fat (1 g sat. fat), 21 mg chol., 179 mg sodium, 2 g carbo., 0 g fiber, 8 g pro.
Daily values: 0% vit. A, 15% vit. C, 4% calcium, 6% iron

The Turkey Grind

You can purchase ground turkey at the supermarket, but you may want to check whether the meat also includes the skin (which adds a considerable amount of fat). If you like, purchase skinless, boneless turkey breasts and grind them in your food processor. This ensures that the turkey has the lowest possible fat content and is more healthful.

apricot COFFEE CAKE

A member of the ginger family, cardamom is an aromatic spice used in Scandinavian and Indian cooking. It has a sweet-spicy flavor that pairs nicely with fruits, such as apricots, pears, or peaches.

Prep: 20 minutes
Rise: 50 minutes
Bake: 30 minutes
Makes: 12 servings

Nonstick spray coating

2 cups all-purpose flour

1 package active dry yeast

½ teaspoon ground cardamom
   or nutmeg

½ cup water

2 tablespoons sugar

2 tablespoons butter or
   margarine

¼ teaspoon salt

⅓ cup refrigerated or frozen
   egg product, thawed

⅓ cup finely snipped dried
   apricots

   Sugar-free apricot spread
   (optional)

1 Generously spray a 1-quart casserole or soufflé dish with nonstick coating; set aside. In a large bowl combine 1 cup of the flour, the yeast, and cardamom or nutmeg. In a saucepan heat and stir the water, sugar, butter or margarine, and salt just until warm (120° to 130°) and butter or margarine almost melts; add to flour mixture along with the egg product. Beat with an electric mixer on low speed for 30 seconds, scraping the bowl constantly. Beat on high speed for 3 minutes.

2 Using a wooden spoon, stir in apricots and remaining flour (batter will be stiff). Spoon the batter into prepared casserole. Cover and let rise in a warm place until nearly double (50 to 60 minutes).

3 Bake in a 375° oven for 30 minutes. (If necessary, cover the cake loosely with foil the last 10 minutes of baking to prevent overbrowning.) Remove coffee cake from casserole or soufflé dish. Cool slightly on a wire rack. If desired, serve warm cake with apricot spread.

Nutrition facts per serving: 111 cal., 2 g total fat (1 g sat. fat), 5 mg chol., 77 mg sodium, 19 g carbo., 1 g fiber, 3 g pro.
Daily values: 5% vit. A, 0% vit. C, 0% calcium, 8% iron

breakfast & brunch

tropical COFFEE CAKE

Mango and coconut give this delicious coffee cake an island flair. Yogurt and just a small amount of oil help keep the cake moist. If you can't find mangoes, substitute nectarines or peaches.

Prep: 25 minutes
Bake: 35 minutes
Makes: 8 servings

1¼ cups all-purpose flour
 ¼ cup sugar plus 4 packets heat-stable sugar substitute, or ½ cup sugar
 ½ teaspoon baking powder
 ½ teaspoon baking soda
 ¼ teaspoon salt
 ¼ teaspoon ground nutmeg
 1 beaten egg
 ⅔ cup plain fat-free yogurt
 2 tablespoons cooking oil
 ½ teaspoon vanilla
 1 medium mango, peeled, seeded, and finely chopped (about 1 cup)
 1 tablespoon all-purpose flour
 2 tablespoons flaked coconut

1 Lightly grease and flour a 9×1½-inch round baking pan; set aside. In a large bowl stir together the 1¼ cups flour, the sugar plus sugar substitute or the sugar, baking powder, baking soda, salt, and nutmeg. Make a well in the center of the flour mixture; set aside.

2 In a small mixing bowl stir together the egg, yogurt, oil, and vanilla. Add the egg mixture all at once to flour mixture. Stir just until moistened (batter should be slightly lumpy). Toss chopped mango with the 1 tablespoon flour; gently fold into batter. Spread batter into prepared pan.

3 Sprinkle coconut over batter in pan. Bake in a 350° oven for 35 minutes. Serve warm.

Nutrition facts per serving: 169 cal., 5 g total fat (1 g sat. fat), 27 mg chol., 194 mg sodium, 28 g carbo., 1 g fiber, 4 g pro.
Daily values: 11% vit. A, 12% vit. C, 5% calcium, 7% iron

Using the ½ cup sugar option: 193 cal. and 34 g carbo.

banana CRUNCH POPS

Remember the frozen bananas of your childhood? These cinnamon-spiced bananas with a crisp coating taste even better.

Prep: 15 minutes
Freeze: 2 hours
Stand: 10 minutes
Makes: 4 servings

⅔ **cup fat-free yogurt (any flavor)**

¼ **teaspoon ground cinnamon**

1 **cup crisp rice cereal or chocolate-flavor crisp rice cereal**

2 **bananas, cut in half crosswise**

4 **wooden sticks**

1 Place yogurt in a small shallow dish; stir in cinnamon. Place cereal in another small shallow dish. Insert a wooden stick into each banana piece. Roll banana pieces in yogurt mixture, covering the entire piece of banana. Roll in cereal to coat. Place on a baking sheet lined with waxed paper. Freeze about 2 hours or until firm.

2 When frozen, wrap each banana pop in freezer wrap. Store pops in the freezer. Before serving, let stand at room temperature for 10 to 15 minutes.

Nutrition Facts per serving: 99 cal., 0 g total fat (0 g sat. fat), 1 mg chol., 94 mg sodium, 23 g carbo., 2 g fiber, 3 g pro.
Daily Values: 4% vit. A, 21% vit. C, 7% calcium, 4% iron

breakfast & brunch

iced ESPRESSO

Pour tall glasses of this refreshing, low-fat coffee drink for brunch or in place of dessert.

Prep: 20 minutes
Chill: 3 hours
Makes: 6 (6-ounce) servings

½ **cup ground espresso coffee or French roast coffee**

1 **teaspoon finely shredded orange peel**

4 **cups water**

3 **tablespoons sugar**

1½ **cups fat-free milk**

Ice cubes

Orange peel strips (optional)

1 **teaspoon grated semisweet chocolate (optional)**

❶ In a drip coffee maker or percolator prepare coffee with shredded orange peel and water according to manufacturer's directions. Pour coffee into a heatproof pitcher; stir in sugar and milk. Chill at least 3 hours or until serving time.

❷ To serve, fill 6 glasses with ice cubes; pour coffee mixture over ice. If desired, garnish with orange peel strips and grated chocolate.

Nutrition Facts per serving: 48 cal., 0 g total fat (0 g sat. fat), 1 mg chol., 36 mg sodium, 10 g carbo., 0 g fiber, 2 g pro.
Daily Values: 2% vit. A, 1% vit. C, 8% calcium, 1% iron

breakfast & brunch

fruit and soy SMOOTHIES

Whip up a grab-and-go smoothie. To keep it interesting play around with fruit combos such as mango-blueberry, banana-grape, or other duets that suit your personal taste.

breakfast & brunch

Start to Finish: 5 minutes
Makes: 3 (1-cup) servings

- **1 cup vanilla-flavor soy milk**
- **½ cup orange juice**
- **1 cup chopped papaya**
- **½ cup frozen unsweetened whole strawberries**
- **2 tablespoons soy protein powder (optional)**
- **1 tablespoon honey (optional)**

1 In a blender container combine soy milk, orange juice, fruit, and, if desired, protein powder and honey. Cover and blend until mixture is smooth. Immediately pour into glasses.

Nutrition Facts per serving: 97 cal., 1 g total fat (0 g sat. fat), 0 mg chol., 47 mg sodium, 18 g carbo., 2 g fiber, 3 g pro.
Daily Values: 8% vit. A, 108% vit. C, 12% calcium, 5% iron

berry-banana SMOOTHIES

Keep the ingredients for this recipe on hand to make healthful after-school snacks.

Start to Finish: 10 minutes
Makes: 2 servings

- **1 cup orange juice**
- **1 small banana, peeled, cut up, and frozen**
- **¼ cup assorted fresh or frozen berries, such as raspberries, blackberries, and/or strawberries**
- **3 tablespoons vanilla low-fat yogurt**
- **Fresh mint (optional)**
- **Fresh berries (optional)**

1 In a blender container combine orange juice, frozen banana pieces, desired berries, and yogurt. Cover and blend until smooth.

2 To serve, pour into 2 glasses. If desired, garnish with fresh mint and additional fresh berries.

Nutrition Facts per serving: 123 cal., 1 g total fat (0 g sat. fat), 2 mg chol., 19 mg sodium, 28 g carbo., 2 g fiber, 3 g pro.
Daily Values: 6% vit. A, 116% vit. C, 6% calcium, 3% iron

breakfast & brunch

To Caffeine or Not to Caffeine

Several studies have looked at caffeine intake and its effect, or lack thereof, on health. So far there has been little evidence that moderate amounts of caffeine increase the risk of any diseases or conditions. However, excessive caffeine intake could cause jitters and insomnia. How much is too much varies from person to person based on usual caffeine habits and individual sensitivity. In general 200 to 300 milligrams, the amount of caffeine in about two to three cups of coffee, is a safe daily amount.

lunches
& LIGHT MEALS

If you're bored by the typical ham-sandwich-and-chips lunch, break out of your rut and try something different, like Peppery Artichoke Pitas or Ginger-Lime Chicken Salad. Add fresh fruit and sparkling water for a lunch you'll look forward to. These recipes also make a great light dinner.

Lahvosh Roll, *recipe page 72*

lahvosh ROLL

Lahvosh looks and feels like a giant crisp cracker, and you must soften it before using. (You may be able to find the presoftened variety and skip Step 1.)

Prep: 15 minutes
Stand: 1 hour
Chill: 2 hours
Makes: 6 servings

- 1 **15-inch sesame seed lahvosh (Armenian cracker bread) or two 10-inch tortillas**
- ½ **of an 8-ounce tub cream cheese with chives and onion**
- ¼ **cup chopped, drained marinated artichoke hearts**
- 2 **tablespoons diced pimiento**
- 1 **teaspoon dried oregano, crushed**
- 6 **ounces thinly sliced prosciutto or cooked ham**
- 4 **ounces sliced provolone cheese**
- 2 **large romaine lettuce leaves, ribs removed**

1 Dampen both sides of lahvosh by holding it briefly under gently running cold water. Place lahvosh, seeded side down, between 2 damp, clean kitchen towels. Let stand about 1 hour or until soft.

2 In a bowl stir together cream cheese, artichoke hearts, pimiento, and oregano. Remove top towel from lahvosh. Spread lahvosh with cream cheese filling. Arrange prosciutto over cream cheese. Place provolone slices in center and lettuce next to provolone. Roll from lettuce edge, using the towel to lift and roll the bread. (Or, if using tortillas, spread tortillas with cream cheese mixture. Divide remaining ingredients between the tortillas. Roll up tortillas.)

3 Wrap roll in plastic wrap and chill seam side down for at least 2 hours. To serve, cut roll into 1-inch slices.

Make-ahead directions: Prepare Lahvosh Roll as directed through Step 2. Wrap roll in plastic wrap and chill in the refrigerator seam side down for up to 24 hours. To serve, cut roll into 1-inch slices.

Nutrition Facts per serving: 300 cal., 16 g total fat (8 g sat. fat), 51 mg chol., 1,226 mg sodium, 22 g carbo., 0 g fiber, 17 g pro.
Daily Values: 18% vit. A, 17% vit. C, 18% calcium, 9% iron

lunches

deli GREEK-STYLE PITAS

Pita bread rounds are great for lunches on the go because they make tidy, no-leak sandwiches that stay fresh and dry longer than sliced bread or rolls.

Prep: 10 minutes
Chill: 1 hour
Makes: 2 servings

½ **cup deli creamy cucumber and onion salad or Homemade Creamy Cucumber Salad**

¼ **cup chopped roma tomato**

½ **teaspoon snipped fresh dillweed**

2 **whole wheat or white pita bread rounds**

6 **ounces thinly sliced cooked deli roast beef, turkey, or chicken**

❶ In a bowl combine cucumber and onion salad, tomato, and dill. Cover and chill for 1 hour. Cut pita rounds in half crosswise. Line pita halves with roast beef. Spoon some salad mixture into each pita half.

Homemade Creamy Cucumber Salad: Combine 2 tablespoons plain low-fat yogurt, 1 teaspoon vinegar, ¼ teaspoon sugar, and a dash of salt. Add ½ cup thinly sliced cucumber and one-fourth of a small red onion, thinly sliced. Toss gently to coat.

Nutrition Facts per serving: 400 cal., 15 g total fat (5 g sat. fat), 67 mg chol., 703 mg sodium, 39 g carbo., 6 g fiber, 30 g pro.
Daily Values: 4% vit. A, 10% vit. C, 3% calcium, 27% iron

lunches

seasoned TUNA SANDWICHES

Tired of the same brown-bag lunch? This recipe combines an old favorite—tuna—with fruity olive oil, fresh lemon juice, and capers for a taste of the Mediterranean.

Start to Finish: 15 minutes
Makes: 4 servings

- 2 **6-ounce cans solid white tuna (water-pack), drained**
- 2 **tablespoons olive oil**
- 2 **teaspoons lemon juice**
- 1 **teaspoon capers, drained**
- ⅛ **teaspoon freshly ground black pepper**
- 2 **tablespoons fat-free mayonnaise dressing or salad dressing**
- 8 **slices whole wheat bread**
- 4 **lettuce leaves (optional)**
- 4 **tomato slices**

1 In a small bowl combine tuna, oil, lemon juice, capers, and pepper.

2 To assemble each sandwich, spread ½ tablespoon of the mayonnaise dressing on a slice of bread. Top with a lettuce leaf (if desired), tomato slice, and one-fourth of the tuna mixture. Top with a second slice of bread.

Nutrition Facts per serving: 309 cal., 11 g total fat (2 g sat. fat), 36 mg chol., 669 mg sodium, 26 g carbo., 2 g fiber, 25 g pro.
Daily Values: 3% vit. A, 8% vit. C, 7% calcium, 15% iron

lunches

GREAT FOR
KIDS

turkey-tomato WRAPS

A cool idea for meals on the move, wraps are easy to pack and neat to eat.

Prep: 20 minutes
Chill: 2 hours
Makes: 6 servings

1 **7-ounce container prepared hummus**

3 **8- to 10-inch tomato-basil flour tortillas or plain flour tortillas**

8 **ounces thinly sliced, cooked peppered turkey breast**

6 **romaine lettuce leaves, ribs removed**

3 **small tomatoes, thinly sliced**

3 **thin slices red onion, separated into rings**

1 Spread hummus evenly over tortillas. Layer turkey breast, romaine, tomatoes, and onion on top of each tortilla. Roll up each tortilla into a spiral. Cut each roll in half and wrap with plastic wrap. Chill for 2 to 4 hours. Tote in an insulated cooler with ice packs.

Nutrition Facts per serving: 236 cal., 6 g total fat (1 g sat. fat), 32 mg chol., 458 mg sodium, 29 g carbo., 4 g fiber, 19 g pro.
Daily Values: 27% vit. A, 35% vit. C, 6% calcium, 13% iron

lunches

Brown-Bagging It

Packing your own lunches for work is an easy way to eat healthier and saves money. Pack your lunch the night before so you can grab-and-go in the a.m. Be creative when putting your midday meal together. Wraps are great alternatives to sandwiches. Or skip the bread altogether and make roll-ups with lean meats and cheese. Try sprinkling dried cranberries into a salad with some slices of smoked turkey. Whatever you choose to put in your brown bag, be sure to use cold packs, if necessary, to keep your lunch at the correct temperature.

egg and vegetable WRAPS

Need a lunchtime energy boost? High-protein eggs wrapped with crisp, refreshing veggies with a light dressing are the perfect solution.

Start to Finish: 30 minutes
Makes: 6 servings

- 4 **hard-cooked eggs, chopped**
- 1 **cup chopped cucumber**
- 1 **cup chopped zucchini or yellow summer squash**
- ½ **cup finely chopped red onion**
- ½ **cup shredded carrot**
- ¼ **cup fat-free or light mayonnaise dressing or salad dressing**
- 2 **tablespoons Dijon-style mustard**
- 1 **tablespoon fat-free milk**
- 1 **teaspoon snipped fresh tarragon or basil**
- ⅛ **teaspoon paprika**
- 6 **lettuce leaves**
- 6 **10-inch whole wheat, spinach, or vegetable flour tortillas**
- 2 **roma tomatoes, thinly sliced**

❶ In a large bowl combine eggs, cucumber, zucchini, red onion, and carrot. For dressing, in a small bowl stir together mayonnaise dressing, Dijon mustard, milk, tarragon, and paprika. Pour dressing over the egg mixture; toss gently to coat.

❷ For each sandwich, place a lettuce leaf on a tortilla. Place 3 or 4 tomato slices on top of the lettuce, slightly off center. Spoon about ⅔ cup of the egg mixture on top of the tomato slices. Fold in two opposite sides of the tortilla; roll up from the bottom. Cut the rolls in half diagonally.

Nutrition Facts per serving: 265 cal., 7 g total fat (2 g sat. fat), 141 mg chol., 723 mg sodium, 40 g carbo., 4 g fiber, 11 g pro.
Daily Values: 78% vit. A, 27% vit. C, 8% calcium, 14% iron

curried chicken SALAD

Curry powder, used in small doses, really perks up a recipe like this one. The celery and apples lend crunch, while the wild rice adds a satisfying chewiness to this delicious salad.

Prep: 30 minutes
Chill: 1 to 4 hours
Makes: about 6 (1-cup) servings

12 **ounces skinless, boneless chicken breast halves**

1 **cup water**

¼ **teaspoon salt**

⅔ **cup light or fat-free mayonnaise dressing or salad dressing**

¼ **cup fat-free milk**

2 **teaspoons curry powder**

¼ **teaspoon salt**

2 **cups chopped red apples**

2 **cups cooked wild rice, chilled**

1½ **cups sliced celery**

½ **cup golden raisins**

Romaine or spinach leaves (optional)

❶ In a medium skillet combine the chicken, water, and ¼ teaspoon salt. Bring to boiling; reduce heat. Simmer, covered, for 12 to 14 minutes or until the chicken is tender and no longer pink. Drain well; let cool. Cut the chicken into bite-size pieces.

❷ Meanwhile, for the dressing, in a small bowl stir together the mayonnaise dressing or salad dressing, milk, curry powder, and ¼ teaspoon salt.

❸ In a large bowl stir together cooked chicken, apples, cooked wild rice, celery, and raisins; stir in the dressing. Cover and chill for 1 to 4 hours. If desired, serve on romaine or spinach leaves.

Nutrition facts per serving: 281 cal., 11 g total fat (2 g sat. fat), 30 mg chol., 436 mg sodium, 33 g carbo., 3 g fiber, 14 g pro.
Daily values: 1% vit. A, 7% vit. C, 3% calcium, 8% iron

lunches

ginger-lime CHICKEN SALAD

Yogurt serves as a healthy alternative to mayonnaise in this tangy, quick-to-prepare chicken salad.

Prep: 10 minutes
Chill: 30 minutes
Makes: 4 servings

¼ **cup fat-free plain yogurt**
2 **tablespoons lime juice**
2 **teaspoons grated fresh ginger**
2 **cups chopped, cooked chicken breast**
1 **cup snow pea pods, bias-cut lengthwise**
1 **cup thinly sliced celery**
1 **tablespoon thinly sliced red onion**

1 In a medium bowl combine yogurt, lime juice, and ginger. Add chicken, stirring to coat. Cover and chill at least 30 minutes. In a medium bowl toss together pea pods, celery, and onion. Place the vegetable mixture in 4 salad bowls. Top with the chicken mixture.

Nutrition Facts per serving: 147 cal., 3 g total fat (1 g sat. fat), 60 mg chol., 86 mg sodium, 5 g carbo., 1 g fiber, 23 g pro.
Daily Values: 2% vit. A, 28% vit. C, 6% calcium, 6% iron

lunches

mango salad WITH TURKEY

To save time prepare the Lime Vinaigrette ahead and cover and chill up to 4 hours. Shake the dressing before drizzling over salad. For an extra burst of citrus flavor, serve the salad with lime wedges.

Start to Finish: 30 minutes
Makes: 4 servings

- ¼ **cup salad oil**
- ¼ **teaspoon finely shredded lime peel**
- 2 **tablespoons lime juice**
- ¼ **teaspoon grated fresh ginger**
- 6 **cups torn mixed greens**
- 4 **mangoes, seeded, peeled, and cut into thin slices**
- 8 **ounces cooked smoked turkey or chicken, cut into thin bite-size strips**
- 1 **green onion, thinly sliced**
- ¼ **cup snipped fresh cilantro**
  Lime wedges (optional)

① In a screw-top jar combine salad oil, lime peel, lime juice, and ginger. Cover and shake well. Divide greens among 4 salad plates. Arrange one-fourth of the mango, smoked turkey, and green onion on each plate of greens. Sprinkle with cilantro. Drizzle vinaigrette over salad. If desired, serve with lime wedges on the side.

Nutrition Facts per serving: 321 cal., 15 g total fat (2 g sat. fat), 25 mg chol., 417 mg sodium, 39 g carbo., 5 g fiber, 12 g pro.
Daily Values: 181% vit. A, 119% vit. C, 7% calcium, 6% iron

lunches

chicken and VEGETABLE SALAD

Remember this salad when it's too hot to cook. All you need are breadsticks, iced tea, and a fresh fruit dessert to complete the meal.

Start to Finish: 25 minutes
Makes: 4 servings

½ cup low-fat cottage cheese or fat-free cottage cheese

1 tablespoon catsup

1 hard-cooked egg, chopped (optional)

1 green onion, thinly sliced

1 tablespoon sweet pickle relish

⅛ teaspoon salt

1½ cups chopped cooked chicken (about 8 ounces)

½ cup sliced celery

½ cup chopped red or green sweet pepper

Lettuce leaves

2 tablespoons sliced almonds, toasted

❶ For dressing, in a food processor bowl combine cottage cheese and catsup. Cover and process until smooth; transfer to a small bowl. Stir in egg (if desired), green onion, pickle relish, and salt. Set aside.

❷ In a medium bowl combine chicken, celery, and sweet pepper. Add dressing and gently toss to mix.

❸ To serve, divide salad among 4 lettuce-lined dinner plates. Sprinkle with almonds.

Nutrition Facts per serving: 164 cal., 6 g total fat (1 g sat. fat), 49 mg chol., 322 mg sodium, 6 g carbo., 1 g fiber, 20 g pro.
Daily Values: 25% vit. A, 64% vit. C, 5% calcium, 7% iron

lunches

85

fruit & chicken SALAD

Frozen juice concentrates are ideal ingredients for making low-fat dressings. Because concentrates deliver a lot of punch in a small amount, you don't need to use much. Here, concentrate also lends body to the dressing.

Prep: 25 minutes
Chill: 2 to 4 hours
Makes: 4 servings

½ **cup fat-free dairy sour cream**

½ **cup fat-free mayonnaise dressing or salad dressing**

1 **tablespoon frozen orange juice concentrate, thawed**

⅛ **teaspoon ground ginger**
   Dash ground red pepper

3 **green onions, sliced (⅓ cup)**

2 **cups thinly sliced celery**

1½ **cups seedless red or green grapes, halved**

1½ **cups chopped cooked chicken**

½ **cup dried apricots, cut into slivers**

4 **lettuce leaves**

2 **plum tomatoes, thinly sliced**

1 **cucumber, thinly sliced**

❶ For dressing, stir together the sour cream, mayonnaise dressing or salad dressing, orange juice concentrate, ginger, and red pepper. Stir in green onions.

❷ In a large bowl toss together celery, grapes, chicken, and apricots; stir in the dressing. Cover and chill for 2 to 4 hours.

❸ To serve, line 4 salad plates with lettuce leaves. Arrange tomatoes and cucumber on top of lettuce. Top with chicken mixture.

Nutrition facts per serving: 264 cal., 3 g total fat (1 g sat. fat), 44 mg chol., 511 mg sodium, 40 g carbo., 5 g fiber, 21 g pro.
Daily values: 23% vit. A, 50% vit. C, 9% calcium, 15% iron

lunches

apricot chicken SALAD

The sweetness of dried apricots and apricot nectar contrasts tastefully with the pungency of mustard in the dressing for this grilled salad. A small amount of sugar helps to cut the sharpness of the vinegar and mustard.

lunches

Start to Finish: 30 minutes
Makes: 4 servings

- ½ **cup apricot nectar or peach nectar**
- 3 **tablespoons finely chopped dried apricots or peaches**
- 3 **tablespoons snipped parsley**
- 3 **tablespoons balsamic vinegar, red wine vinegar, or cider vinegar**
- 1 **tablespoon olive oil**
- 1 **tablespoon brown mustard**
- 1 **teaspoon sugar**
- 1 **clove garlic, minced**
- 4 **skinless, boneless chicken breast halves (about 12 ounces total)**
- ¼ **teaspoon onion salt**
- ¼ **teaspoon pepper**
- 4 **cups torn mixed salad greens**
- 1 **cup sliced yellow summer squash**
- 1 **cup cherry tomatoes, halved**
- 1 **cup sliced fresh mushrooms**

1 For dressing, in a small mixing bowl stir together the nectar, apricots or peaches, parsley, vinegar, olive oil, brown mustard, sugar, and garlic. Cover and chill until serving time or up to 24 hours.

2 Rinse chicken; pat dry. Sprinkle the onion salt and pepper over both sides of chicken. Grill the chicken on the lightly greased rack of an uncovered grill directly over medium coals for 12 to 15 minutes or until tender and no longer pink, turning once. (Or, place the chicken on the unheated lightly greased rack of a broiler pan. Broil 4 to 5 inches from the heat for 12 to 15 minutes or until chicken is tender and no longer pink, turning once.) Cut chicken breasts into bite-size strips.

3 Meanwhile, in a large bowl toss together greens, summer squash, tomatoes, and mushrooms. Stir dressing; pour about half of the dressing over greens mixture. Toss to coat.

4 To serve, divide greens and vegetables among 4 salad plates. Top with chicken. Drizzle each serving with 1 to 2 tablespoons of the remaining dressing.

Nutrition facts per serving: 202 cal., 6 g total fat (1 g sat. fat), 45 mg chol., 207 mg sodium, 18 g carbo., 2 g fiber, 19 g pro.
Daily values: 16% vit. A, 54% vit. C, 3% calcium, 17% iron

Shed the Skin

It's OK to leave the skin on chicken during cooking because it adds flavor and keeps moistness in, yet the meat doesn't absorb much of the fat. However, because skin contains a lot of fat, removing it before eating chicken significantly lowers the fat. Compare the difference between a 3-ounce serving of roasted chicken served with and without skin:

Light meat with skin	8 g fat	193 calories
Light meat without skin	3 g fat	142 calories

turkey-pear SALAD

Fruit, turkey, and nuts are a tasty trio, especially when combined with a tangy buttermilk dressing. This salad is a great way to use any leftover turkey or chicken.

Start to Finish: 25 minutes
Makes: 4 servings

½ **cup buttermilk**

2 **tablespoons light mayonnaise dressing or salad dressing**

1 **tablespoon frozen apple juice concentrate or frozen orange juice concentrate, thawed**

1 **teaspoon Dijon-style mustard**

6 **cups torn mixed salad greens**

2 **medium pears or apples, thinly sliced**

8 **ounces cooked turkey or chicken, cut into bite-size strips (1½ cups)**

¼ **cup toasted, broken walnuts (optional)**

1 For dressing, in a small bowl stir together buttermilk, mayonnaise dressing or salad dressing, apple or orange juice concentrate, and mustard. Cover and chill for up to 24 hours.

2 To serve, divide salad greens among 4 salad plates. Arrange the pear or apple slices and turkey or chicken on the greens; drizzle each serving with about 3 tablespoons dressing. If desired, sprinkle with walnuts.

Nutrition facts per serving: 225 cal., 9 g total fat (2 g sat. fat), 47 mg chol., 121 mg sodium, 18 g carbo., 3 g fiber, 18 g pro.
Daily values: 4% vit. A, 21% vit. C, 5% calcium, 9% iron

lunches

turkey and FRUIT PASTA SALAD

For a slightly smoky flavor, use the turkey ham option. For additional variety and color, use fresh blueberries or raspberries in place of the strawberries.

Prep: 25 minutes
Chill: 4 hours
Makes: 4 servings

1 **cup dried gemelli pasta or
   1⅓ cups dried rotini pasta**

1½ **cups chopped cooked turkey,
   chicken, or turkey ham
   (about 8 ounces)**

2 **green onions, sliced**

⅓ **cup lime juice or lemon juice**

¼ **cup salad oil**

1 **tablespoon honey**

2 **teaspoons snipped fresh
   thyme or ½ teaspoon dried
   thyme, crushed**

2 **medium nectarines or large
   plums, sliced**

1 **cup halved strawberries**

1 Cook pasta according to package directions; drain. Rinse with cold water; drain again.

2 In a large bowl combine cooked pasta, turkey, and green onions; toss gently to combine.

3 For dressing, in a screw-top jar combine lime juice, oil, honey, and thyme. Cover and shake well. Pour dressing over pasta mixture; toss gently to coat. Cover and chill for 4 to 24 hours.

4 Just before serving, add the nectarines and strawberries; toss gently to combine.

Nutrition Facts per serving: 382 cal., 17 g total fat (3 g sat. fat), 40 mg chol., 40 mg sodium, 37 g carbo., 3 g fiber, 20 g pro.
Daily Values: 11% vit. A, 54% vit. C, 4% calcium, 12% iron

lunches

ham and CANTALOUPE SALAD

To tote this lush salad for lunch either at your desk or in the park, pack the sliced melon, dressing, and greens mixture in separate containers.

Prep: 25 minutes
Chill: 1 hour
Makes: 4 servings

1   small cantaloupe, halved and seeded

4   cups torn romaine lettuce

1   cup torn spinach

8   ounces lean cooked ham, cut into bite-size strips (1½ cups)

2   green onions, thinly sliced

¼   cup unsweetened pineapple juice

1   tablespoon white wine vinegar

1   tablespoon salad oil

1½ teaspoons snipped fresh mint or ½ teaspoon dried mint, crushed

¼   cup sliced almonds, toasted

❶ Coarsely chop half of the melon; slice remaining melon. In a large bowl combine the chopped melon, lettuce, spinach, ham, and green onions.

❷ In a screw-top jar combine pineapple juice, white wine vinegar, salad oil, and mint. Cover and shake well.

❸ Arrange melon slices on 4 plates. Pour dressing over greens mixture; toss lightly to coat. Divide salad among plates; sprinkle with almonds.

Nutrition Facts per serving: 230 cal., 11 g total fat (2 g sat. fat), 27 mg chol., 839 mg sodium, 20 g carbo., 4 g fiber, 15 g pro.
Daily Values: 141% vit. A, 144% vit. C, 8% calcium, 14% iron

Nutrition by Color

Cantaloupe is grouped nutritionally with other orange fruits and vegetables like apricots, papayas, butternut squash, and carrots. These orange foods are important to add to your diet for the high amounts of antioxidants they contain, including vitamin C, carotenoids, and bioflavonoids. These nutrients are shown to reduce the risk of heart disease and some cancers. They also help keep the eyes and immune system healthy.

spinach PASTA SALAD

The basil, prosciutto, and pine nuts—classic Italian favorites—keep this cool pasta salad packed with interesting flavors.

Prep: 25 minutes
Chill: 4 hours
Makes: 6 servings

- 8 **ounces dried ziti or other medium pasta**
- 1 **cup lightly packed spinach leaves**
- ¼ **cup lightly packed basil leaves**
- 2 **cloves garlic, quartered**
- 2 **tablespoons finely shredded Parmesan cheese**
- ⅛ **teaspoon salt**
- ⅛ **teaspoon black pepper**
- 1 **tablespoon olive oil**
- 1 **tablespoon water**
- ½ **cup fat-free or light mayonnaise dressing or salad dressing**
- 6 **spinach leaves**
- 6 **radicchio leaves (optional)**
- 1 **ounce chopped prosciutto or ham**
- 2 **tablespoons toasted pine nuts**

1 Cook pasta according to package directions; drain. Rinse with cold water; drain again. Set aside.

2 Meanwhile, in a blender container or food processor bowl combine the 1 cup spinach, the basil, garlic, cheese, salt, and pepper. Add oil and water; cover and blend or process until nearly smooth and mixture forms a paste, scraping down sides of container frequently. Combine mayonnaise dressing and spinach mixture. Add to pasta and toss until well coated. Cover and chill for 4 to 24 hours.

3 To serve, line a salad bowl with spinach leaves and, if desired, radicchio leaves. Spoon salad into lined bowl. Sprinkle with chopped prosciutto and pine nuts.

Nutrition Facts per serving: 304 cal., 15 g total fat (4 g sat. fat), 18 mg chol., 494 mg sodium, 32 g carbo., 2 g fiber, 12 g pro.
Daily Values: 14% vit. A, 5% vit. C, 17% calcium, 13% iron

lunches

pork & MANGO SALAD

Mango chutney supplies the flavor for this exotic vinaigrette, which is a natural for complementing the flavor of pork. Look for the chutney next to the jams and jellies at the supermarket.

Start to Finish: 30 minutes
Makes: 4 servings

- 3 tablespoons mango chutney
- 2 tablespoons white wine vinegar or rice wine vinegar
- 1 tablespoon Dijon-style mustard or brown mustard
- 1 clove garlic, minced
- ⅛ teaspoon pepper
- 1 tablespoon olive oil
- 1 tablespoon water
- 8 ounces pork tenderloin
  Nonstick spray coating
- 6 cups torn mixed salad greens
- ½ of an 8-ounce can sliced water chestnuts, drained
- 1 medium mango, peeled, seeded, and sliced; or 2 medium nectarines, sliced
- 2 tablespoons snipped chives

① For vinaigrette, in a blender container or food processor bowl combine chutney, vinegar, mustard, garlic, and pepper. Cover and blend or process until smooth. In a small bowl combine olive oil and water. With blender or food processor running, add oil mixture in a thin steady stream to chutney mixture; blend or process for 15 seconds more.

② Trim any fat from the pork; cut into ¼-inch slices. Spray a large skillet with nonstick coating. Preheat the skillet over medium-high heat. Cook pork in hot skillet for 3 to 4 minutes or until pork is no longer pink, turning once. Remove pork from skillet; keep warm.

③ In a large bowl toss together the salad greens and water chestnuts. Pour about half of the vinaigrette over the greens mixture. Toss to coat.

④ To serve, divide greens mixture among 4 salad plates. Arrange some of the mango or nectarine slices and pork on the greens mixture. Drizzle each serving with about 1 tablespoon of the remaining vinaigrette. Sprinkle with the snipped chives.

Nutrition facts per serving: 192 cal., 6 g total fat (1 g sat. fat), 40 mg chol., 137 mg sodium, 21 g carbo., 2 g fiber, 14 g pro.
Daily values: 24% vit. A, 32% vit. C, 2% calcium, 9% iron

lunches

caribbean PORK SALAD

Pork tenderloin, one of the leanest pork cuts available, works tasty wonders in this grilled salad. The marinade adds a soy-pineapple flavor to the meat, which is carried through in the dressing.

Prep: 30 minutes
Marinate: 4 to 24 hours
Grill: 30 minutes
Makes: 4 servings

12 ounces pork tenderloin
½ cup unsweetened pineapple juice
3 tablespoons reduced-sodium soy sauce
3 tablespoons vinegar
2 cloves garlic, minced
½ teaspoon ground red pepper
1 tablespoon olive oil
2 medium red, yellow, or green sweet peppers, cut into 1-inch-wide strips
8 ½-inch-thick slices fresh or canned pineapple
8 romaine leaves

1 Trim fat from pork. Place pork in a plastic bag set in a shallow dish. For marinade, in a screw-top jar, combine pineapple juice, soy sauce, vinegar, garlic, and ground red pepper; cover and shake well. Pour ½ cup of the marinade over pork. Close the bag. Marinate in the refrigerator for 4 to 24 hours, turning bag occasionally.

2 Meanwhile, for salad dressing, combine the remaining marinade with the olive oil. Cover and chill until serving time.

3 Drain pork, discarding marinade. In a grill with a cover arrange preheated coals around a drip pan. Test for medium heat above pan. Place meat on grill rack directly over drip pan. Cover and grill about 30 minutes or until no pink remains and juices run clear. During the last 10 minutes of grilling, place the sweet peppers and pineapple on the grill rack over the coals. Grill until sweet peppers are tender and pineapple is heated through, turning occasionally.

4 To serve, cut pork into thin slices. Line 4 salad plates with romaine. Arrange pork, sweet pepper, and pineapple on the romaine. Shake dressing; drizzle each serving with about 2 tablespoons of the dressing.

Nutrition facts per serving: 204 cal., 7 g total fat (2 g sat. fat), 60 mg chol., 446 mg sodium, 15 g carbo., 2 g fiber, 21 g pro.
Daily values: 57% vit. A, 156% vit. C, 3% calcium, 15% iron

Lunches

spiced BEEF SALAD

This Southwestern-style salad includes a corn relish, deli roast beef, a chili-flavored dressing, and crispy, baked tortilla chips. It's a fun, out-of-the-ordinary salad.

Start to Finish: 30 minutes
Makes: 4 servings

Nonstick spray coating

1 **9- to 10-inch fat-free flour tortilla or jalapeño-flavored flour tortilla**

⅓ **cup bottled reduced-calorie ranch salad dressing**

2 **teaspoons chili powder**

1 **large red sweet pepper, chopped**

1 **cup frozen whole kernel corn, thawed**

4 **green onions, sliced (½ cup)**

6 **cups torn romaine**

6 **1-ounce slices lean cooked beef**

½ **of a medium red onion, thinly sliced**

1 **cup cherry tomatoes, halved**

½ **cup shredded reduced-fat Monterey Jack cheese**

1 Spray a baking sheet with nonstick coating; set aside. Cut tortilla in half; cut each half crosswise into ¼-inch-wide strips. Arrange strips in a single layer on prepared baking sheet. Bake in 350° oven for 5 to 10 minutes or until strips are crisp and brown. Set aside to cool.

2 Meanwhile, for dressing, in a bowl combine bottled salad dressing and chili powder; set aside. In another bowl combine the sweet pepper, corn, and green onions; pour 2 tablespoons of the dressing over the vegetable mixture. Toss to coat.

3 To serve, divide romaine among 4 salad plates. Spoon the vegetable mixture onto the romaine. Cut beef slices in half crosswise. Roll each half-slice of beef into a cone shape; arrange 3 rolls on each plate. Arrange the onion slices and tomatoes around vegetable mixture; sprinkle with cheese. Drizzle each serving with about 1 tablespoon of the remaining dressing. Top with tortilla strips.

Nutrition facts per serving: 281 cal., 11 g total fat (3 g sat. fat), 47 mg chol., 378 mg sodium, 26 g carbo., 4 g fiber, 22 g pro.
Daily values: 121% vit. A, 295% vit. C, 15% calcium, 23% iron

lunches

fajita BEEF SALAD

Lime does double duty in this recipe, both in the marinade and the dressing. Its tart flavor enhances the grilled beef and honey-kissed dressing.

Prep: 35 minutes
Marinate: 24 hours
Grill: 12 minutes
Makes: 4 servings

½ **teaspoon finely shredded lime peel**

⅓ **cup lime juice**

3 **tablespoons water**

4 **teaspoons olive oil**

¼ **cup chopped onion**

1 **clove garlic, minced**

12 **ounces beef flank steak**

3 **tablespoons water**

2 **tablespoons powdered fruit pectin**

2 **tablespoons honey**

6 **cups torn mixed salad greens**

2 **small red and/or yellow tomatoes, cut into wedges**

1 **small avocado, halved, seeded, peeled, and chopped (optional)**

1 In a screw-top jar combine the lime peel, lime juice, 3 tablespoons water, and olive oil. Cover and shake well. Pour half of the lime juice mixture into a small bowl; stir in onion and garlic. Reserve remaining lime juice mixture.

2 Score the beef by making shallow diagonal cuts at 1-inch intervals in a diamond pattern. Repeat on other side. Place beef in a plastic bag set in a shallow dish. Pour the lime juice-and-onion mixture over the beef. Close bag. Marinate in the refrigerator for 24 hours, turning occasionally.

3 For dressing, in a small bowl gradually stir 3 tablespoons water into fruit pectin; stir in reserved lime juice mixture and honey. Cover and chill for 24 hours.

4 Drain beef, discarding marinade. Grill beef on the rack of an uncovered grill directly over medium coals to desired doneness, turning once. Allow 12 to 14 minutes for medium. (Or, place beef on the unheated rack of a broiler pan. Broil 3 to 4 inches from the heat to desired doneness, turning once. Allow 12 to 14 minutes for medium.)

5 To serve, thinly slice beef across grain. Arrange the greens, tomatoes, and, if desired, the avocado on 4 salad plates. Top with beef. Drizzle each serving with about 2 tablespoons of the dressing.

Nutrition facts per serving: 224 cal., 9 g total fat (3 g sat. fat), 40 mg chol., 72 mg sodium, 20 g carbo., 2 g fiber, 18 g pro.
Daily values: 5% vit. A, 26% vit. C, 2% calcium, 15% iron

lunches

beef & PASTA SALAD

The intense flavor of blue cheese proves that a little bit goes a long way to deliver great taste. Using a medley of vegetables and beef, this do-ahead salad is ideal for a quick midweek dinner.

Prep: 30 minutes
Chill: 2 to 24 hours
Makes: 4 servings

- **4 ounces dried radiatore or medium shell macaroni**
- **⅓ cup bottled reduced-calorie creamy Italian or ranch salad dressing**
- **2 tablespoons snipped fresh basil or 2 teaspoons dried basil, crushed**
- **2 tablespoons crumbled blue cheese**
- **¼ teaspoon pepper**
- **1 small zucchini, halved lengthwise and sliced (1 cup)**
- **1 green onion, sliced (2 tablespoons)**
- **3 small plum tomatoes, halved and sliced**
- **4 cups torn fresh spinach**
- **4 ounces thinly sliced lean cooked beef, cut into strips**

1 In a large saucepan cook the pasta according to package directions, except omit any oil or salt; drain. Rinse with cold running water; drain again.

2 Meanwhile, for dressing, in a bowl stir together salad dressing, basil, blue cheese, and pepper; set aside.

3 In a large bowl toss together pasta, zucchini, and green onion. Drizzle dressing over pasta mixture. Toss to coat. Cover and chill for 2 to 24 hours.

4 To serve, gently stir tomato into the salad. Divide the spinach among 4 salad plates. Top with pasta mixture and beef.

Nutrition facts per serving: 237 cal., 7 g total fat (2 g sat. fat), 30 mg chol., 285 mg sodium, 29 g carbo., 3 g fiber, 16 g pro.
Daily values: 42% vit. A, 44% vit. C, 8% calcium, 26% iron

Cheese, Please

Fortunately, many cheeses, such as Monterey Jack, cheddar, mozzarella, American, Swiss, and Parmesan, are readily available in lower-fat versions. But some highly flavored cheeses, such as blue cheese, feta, and Asiago cheese, aren't.

However, these cheeses have very pungent flavors. So a little goes a long way. Just use them sparingly, then you can have your favorite cheese and eat it, too.

lunches

shrimp TABBOULEH SALAD

Middle Eastern tabbouleh lends an exotic touch to this salad, which begins with a convenient packaged salad mix. Traditional tabbouleh combines bulgur wheat with tomato, onion, parsley, mint, lemon, and olive oil.

Prep: 20 minutes
Chill: 1½ hours
Makes: 4 servings

1   5¼-ounce package tabbouleh wheat salad mix

8   ounces peeled, deveined, cooked small shrimp or cooked bay scallops

1   cup frozen peas, thawed

1   cup chopped tomatoes

4   green onions, sliced (½ cup)

3   tablespoons snipped cilantro

3   tablespoons lemon juice

1   tablespoon olive oil

4   lettuce leaves

1 Prepare salad mix according to package directions; stir in the shrimp or scallops, peas, tomatoes, green onions, cilantro, lemon juice, and olive oil. Cover and chill for 1½ hours.

2 To serve, arrange lettuce leaves on 4 salad plates. Top with salad mixture.

Nutrition facts per serving: 235 cal., 4 g total fat (1 g sat. fat), 11 mg chol., 507 mg sodium, 37 g carbo., 9 g fiber, 18 g pro.
Daily values: 12% vit. A, 65% vit. C, 3% calcium, 23% iron

lunches

shrimp SALAD

This salad has the makings of an elegant meal and deserves to be included on a special celebration menu. The flavors of asparagus and shrimp flourish with the addition of a balsamic vinaigrette.

Prep: 25 minutes
Chill: 4 to 24 hours
Makes: 4 servings

- 2 **tablespoons dried tomato pieces (not oil-packed)**
- ¼ **cup balsamic vinegar**
- 2 **tablespoons olive oil**
- 1 **tablespoon snipped fresh basil**
- 2 **teaspoons Dijon-style mustard**
- 2 **cloves garlic, minced**
- ¼ **teaspoon sugar**
- ⅛ **teaspoon pepper**
- 12 **ounces fresh or frozen peeled shrimp**
- 4 **cups water**
- 1 **clove garlic**
- 8 **ounces asparagus, cut into 2-inch lengths**
- 6 **cups torn mixed salad greens**
- 2 **medium pears, thinly sliced**

1 In a small bowl pour boiling water over tomato pieces to cover; let stand for 2 minutes. Drain.

2 For dressing, in a screw-top jar combine tomato pieces, vinegar, the olive oil, basil, mustard, the 2 cloves garlic, sugar, and pepper. Cover and shake well. If desired, cover and chill for up to 24 hours.

3 Thaw shrimp, if frozen. In a large saucepan bring the water and the 1 clove garlic to boiling; add asparagus. Return to boiling. Simmer, uncovered, for 4 minutes. Add shrimp. Return to boiling. Simmer, uncovered, for 1 to 3 minutes more or until shrimp are opaque. Drain, discarding garlic. Rinse under cold running water; drain well. Cover and chill for 4 to 24 hours.

4 To serve, divide greens and pears among 4 salad plates. Top each with some of the shrimp and asparagus. Shake dressing; drizzle each serving with about 2 tablespoons of the dressing.

Nutrition facts per serving: 221 cal., 8 g total fat (1 g sat. fat), 131 mg chol., 260 mg sodium, 21 g carbo., 4 g fiber, 17 g pro.
Daily values: 11% vit. A, 37% vit. C, 5% calcium, 23% iron

lunches

marinated SEAFOOD SALAD

When it's too hot to cook, a chilled seafood salad will help keep you—and the kitchen—cool. Feta cheese, the crowning touch, adds a distinctive flavor to this salad.

lunches

Prep: 30 minutes
Marinate: 2 to 3 hours
Makes: 6 servings

12 **ounces fresh or frozen peeled shrimp**

8 **ounces fresh or frozen bay scallops**

6 **cups water**

½ **teaspoon salt**

3 **tablespoons lemon juice**

2 **tablespoons olive oil**

2 **teaspoons snipped fresh oregano or tarragon or ½ teaspoon dried oregano or tarragon, crushed**

¼ **teaspoon dry mustard**

¼ **teaspoon salt**

⅛ **teaspoon pepper**

6 **cups torn mixed salad greens**

¼ **cup crumbled feta cheese**

1 Thaw shrimp and scallops, if frozen. In a large saucepan bring water and the ½ teaspoon salt to boiling; add shrimp and scallops. Return to boiling. Simmer, uncovered, for 1 to 3 minutes or until shrimp and scallops are opaque. Drain. Rinse under cold running water; drain well. Place shrimp and scallops in a plastic bag set in a shallow dish.

2 For dressing, combine lemon juice, olive oil, oregano or tarragon, mustard, the ¼ teaspoon salt, and the pepper. Pour over shrimp and scallops in bag. Close bag. Marinate in the refrigerator for 2 to 3 hours, turning bag occasionally.

3 To serve, divide the greens among 6 salad plates. Spoon seafood and dressing over the greens. Sprinkle each serving with feta cheese.

Nutrition facts per serving: 156 cal., 8 g total fat (2 g sat. fat), 109 mg chol., 372 mg sodium, 4 g carbo., 1 g fiber, 18 g pro.
Daily values: 14% vit. A, 22% vit. C, 8% calcium, 14% iron

salmon salad NIÇOISE

Based on the classic French niçoise salad, this salad has all the essential ingredients: red potatoes, green beans, tomato, eggs, and capers. Instead of using the traditional tuna, this version calls for salmon.

Start to Finish: 30 minutes
Makes: 4 servings

12 ounces fresh or frozen salmon steaks, 1 inch thick

1½ cups water

2 tablespoons lemon juice

1 pound small round red potatoes, cut into thin slices

½ pound green beans

¼ cup lemon juice

2 tablespoons olive oil

2 tablespoons water

2 teaspoons snipped dill

1 clove garlic, minced

¼ teaspoon salt

¼ teaspoon pepper

2 medium tomatoes, cut into wedges

2 hard-cooked eggs, quartered

2 teaspoons capers, rinsed and drained

1 Thaw salmon, if frozen. Rinse salmon; pat dry. In a large skillet bring the 1½ cups water and the 2 tablespoons lemon juice to boiling; add salmon. Return to boiling; reduce heat. Simmer, covered, for 8 to 12 minutes or until salmon flakes easily when tested with a fork. Remove salmon from skillet, discarding liquid. Cover and chill salmon.

2 Meanwhile, in a large saucepan cook potatoes in boiling water about 12 minutes or until tender, adding green beans the last 6 minutes of cooking time. Drain; set aside to cool.

3 For dressing, in a small bowl stir together the ¼ cup lemon juice, the olive oil, the 2 tablespoons water, the dill, garlic, salt, and pepper.

4 To serve, cut cooked salmon into 4 equal portions; arrange on 4 salad plates. Toss about half of the dressing with the potatoes and beans. Arrange potatoes and beans, tomato wedges, and eggs on the plates. Sprinkle each serving with capers. Drizzle each serving with about 1 tablespoon of the remaining dressing.

Nutrition facts per serving: 325 cal., 13 g total fat (2 g sat. fat), 122 mg chol., 256 mg sodium, 35 g carbo., 4 g fiber, 20 g pro.
Daily values: 13% vit. A, 70% vit. C, 5% calcium, 25% iron

lunches

salmon SALAD

This salad will remind you of a Caesar salad—without the raw eggs, anchovies, high fat, and calories. Plain yogurt adds the creamy texture to the garlic and lemon dressing.

Prep: 20 minutes
Chill: 30 minutes
Broil: 8 to 12 minutes
Makes: 4 servings

2 tablespoons olive oil
5 cloves garlic, thinly sliced
2 tablespoons lemon juice
1 tablespoon Worcestershire sauce
1 tablespoon Dijon-style mustard
1 tablespoon water
½ teaspoon pepper
⅓ cup plain fat-free yogurt
12 ounces fresh or frozen skinless, boneless salmon fillets, 1 inch thick
Nonstick spray coating
10 cups torn romaine
½ cup thinly sliced red onion
¼ cup freshly grated Parmesan cheese
1 cup cherry tomatoes, halved
½ cup pitted ripe olives, halved (optional)

① In a small saucepan heat olive oil over medium-low heat. Cook and stir garlic in hot oil for 1 to 2 minutes or until garlic is lightly golden. Transfer garlic to a blender container. Add lemon juice, Worcestershire sauce, mustard, water, and pepper. Cover; blend until combined. Reserve 2 tablespoons of garlic mixture; set aside. Add yogurt to remaining garlic mixture in blender. Cover and blend until smooth. Chill until serving time.

② Thaw salmon, if frozen. Rinse salmon; pat dry. Brush the reserved garlic mixture evenly over salmon. Cover and chill for 30 minutes.

③ Spray the unheated rack of a broiler pan with nonstick coating. Place the salmon on the rack. Broil 4 to 5 inches from heat for 8 to 12 minutes or until salmon flakes easily when tested with a fork, turning once.

④ Meanwhile, in a large bowl toss romaine, onion, and Parmesan cheese with the chilled yogurt mixture. Divide romaine mixture among 4 salad plates. Place one salmon fillet on each salad. Top with tomatoes and, if desired, olives.

Nutrition facts per serving: 234 cal., 13 g total fat (3 g sat. fat), 21 mg chol., 331 mg sodium, 12 g carbo., 4 g fiber, 19 g pro.
Daily values: 43% vit. A, 95% vit. C, 16% calcium, 19% iron

lunches

italian bread & FISH SALAD

Panzanella is a traditional Italian bread-and-tomato side salad. Here, it's transformed into a main dish by adding fish. A generous sprinkling of fresh basil enhances the flavor—don't be tempted to leave it off.

Start to Finish: 30 minutes
Makes: 4 servings

- 3   slices Italian or wheat bread, cut into 1-inch cubes
- 12 ounces fresh or frozen skinless, boneless fish fillets (salmon, halibut, or swordfish), 1 inch thick
- 1½ cups water
- 3   slices lemon
- 1   bay leaf
- 3   tablespoons white wine vinegar or white balsamic vinegar
- 2   tablespoons olive oil
- 2   cloves garlic, minced
- ¼   teaspoon salt
- ⅛   teaspoon pepper
- 6   cups torn mixed salad greens
- 3   medium tomatoes, seeded and coarsely chopped
- ½   of a medium red onion, cut into thin wedges and separated
- ½   of a medium cucumber, cut into chunks
- ¼   cup shredded fresh basil

1 To dry bread cubes, spread cubes in a single layer in a shallow baking pan. Bake in 350° oven about 10 minutes or until crisp, stirring once.

2 Meanwhile, thaw fish, if frozen. Rinse fish; pat dry. To poach fish, in a large skillet bring water, lemon slices, and bay leaf to boiling; add fish fillets. Return to boiling; reduce heat. Simmer, covered, for 8 to 12 minutes or until fish flakes easily when tested with a fork. Remove fish from skillet, discarding poaching liquid. Cut fish into bite-size pieces.

3 For dressing, in a screw-top jar combine the vinegar, olive oil, garlic, salt, and pepper. Cover and shake well. In a large bowl combine dried bread cubes and salad greens; drizzle with dressing. Toss to coat.

4 To serve, divide salad greens and bread cubes among 4 salad plates. Arrange tomatoes, onion, and cucumber on top of greens. Top with fish and basil.

Nutrition facts per serving: 240 calories, 11 g total fat (2 g saturated fat), 15 mg cholesterol, 327 mg sodium, 21 g carbohydrate, 3 g fiber, 16 g protein
Daily values: 12% vit. A, 46% vit. C, 5% calcium, 15% iron

lunches

dilled TUNA SALAD

Turn ho-hum tuna salad into something special by tossing it with a lemon-dill dressing. Serving the salad with pita chips offers an alternative to a standard tuna salad sandwich.

Start to Finish: 25 minutes
Makes: 4 servings

1   **recipe Pita Crisps**

⅓   **cup bottled reduced-calorie creamy cucumber or ranch salad dressing**

1   **tablespoon Dijon-style mustard**

1   **tablespoon snipped fresh dill or 1 teaspoon dried dillweed**

½   **teaspoon finely shredded lemon peel**

1½ **cups chopped, seeded cucumber**

6   **ounces cooked tuna fillets* or one 9¼-ounce can chunk white tuna (water pack), drained and flaked**

½   **cup shredded carrot**

4   **cups torn lettuce**

1   **medium tomato, cut into wedges**

¼   **teaspoon pepper**

① Prepare Pita Crisps.

② Meanwhile, for dressing, in a bowl stir together salad dressing, mustard, dill, and lemon peel; set aside.

③ In a medium bowl gently toss together cucumber, tuna, and carrot; drizzle dressing over tuna mixture. Toss to coat.

④ To serve, divide lettuce among 4 salad plates. Spoon tuna mixture on top of lettuce. Place tomato and Pita Crisps on salad. Sprinkle salad with pepper.

Pita Crisps: Split 2 pita bread rounds horizontally. Spray the cut side of the pita rounds with butter- or olive oil-flavored nonstick coating; sprinkle with ⅛ teaspoon garlic powder. Cut each pita half into 4 wedges. Spread wedges in a single layer in a 15x10x1-inch baking pan. Bake in a 350° oven for 8 to 10 minutes or until crisp.

***Note:** To cook fresh tuna, in a medium skillet bring 1 cup of water to boiling; add the tuna. Cover and simmer for 8 to 10 minutes or until fish flakes easily with a fork. Break into small chunks. Cover and chill until needed.

Nutrition facts per serving: 236 cal., 8 g total fat (1 g sat. fat), 21 mg chol., 464 mg sodium, 25 g carbo., 2 g fiber, 17 g pro.
Daily values: 77% vit. A, 23% vit. C, 5% calcium, 13% iron

lunches

109

scallops & PASTA SALAD

The fat content in this seafood pasta salad is minimal because the dressing is made without any oil. Pectin provides body to this dressing. Look for it with the jelly-making supplies or baking products at the supermarket.

Prep: 30 minutes
Chill: 3 to 24 hours
Makes: 5 (2-cup) servings

- 1 **teaspoon finely shredded orange peel**
- ⅓ **cup orange juice**
- ¼ **cup white wine vinegar**
- 2 **tablespoons powdered fruit pectin**
- 1 **tablespoon sugar**
- 6 **ounces dried medium shell macaroni**
- 8 **ounces fresh or frozen sea scallops**
- 2 **cups water**
- 4 **cups torn fresh spinach**
- 1 **cup frozen peas**
- ½ **cup coarsely chopped red onion**
- ½ **cup thinly sliced celery**
- ⅓ **cup chopped red sweet pepper**

❶ For dressing, in a small bowl stir together the orange peel, orange juice, vinegar, pectin, and sugar until smooth. Cover and chill at least 3 hours or up to 24 hours.

❷ Cook macaroni according to package directions; drain. Rinse with cold water; drain again.

❸ Meanwhile, thaw scallops, if frozen. Cut any large scallops in half. Bring water to boiling; add scallops. Return to boiling. Simmer, uncovered, for 1 to 3 minutes or until scallops are opaque. Drain. Rinse under cold running water.

❹ For salad, in a large bowl toss together cooked macaroni, cooked scallops, spinach, peas, onion, celery, and sweet pepper. Stir dressing; pour over salad. Toss to coat.

Nutrition facts per serving: 227 cal., 1 g total fat (0 g sat. fat), 14 mg chol., 142 mg sodium, 42 g carbo., 4 g fiber, 13 g pro.
Daily values: 40% vit. A, 66% vit. C, 98% calcium, 26% iron

lunches

green bean & RICE SALAD

This salad contains two types of beans: green beans and black beans. The rice and bean combo makes it hearty enough for a light main-dish salad for four. Or, if you like, it can serve 8 to 10 people as a side dish.

lunches

Prep: 15 minutes
Cook: 10 minutes
Chill: 2 to 8 hours
Makes: about 4 (1¼-cup) servings

1¼ **cups water**

1 **cup quick-cooking brown rice**

1 **cup fresh green beans or frozen cut green beans**

¼ **cup finely chopped onion**

2 **cloves garlic, minced**

½ **teaspoon instant chicken bouillon granules**

1 **15-ounce can light-sodium black beans, rinsed and drained**

½ **cup chopped red sweet pepper**

½ **cup chopped, seeded cucumber**

3 **tablespoons rice wine vinegar or white wine vinegar**

2 **tablespoons olive oil**

1 **tablespoon snipped fresh oregano or 1 teaspoon dried oregano, crushed**

¼ **teaspoon black pepper**

4 **lettuce leaves**

1 In a medium saucepan combine the water, uncooked rice, green beans, onion, garlic, and bouillon granules. Bring to boiling; reduce heat. Simmer, covered, about 10 minutes or until the rice and beans are tender and liquid is absorbed. Remove from heat. Transfer to a large bowl. Gently stir in black beans, sweet pepper, and cucumber.

2 Meanwhile, for dressing, in a screw-top jar combine the vinegar, olive oil, oregano, and black pepper. Cover; shake well. Drizzle over rice mixture. Toss to coat. Cover and chill for 2 to 8 hours.

3 To serve, line 4 salad plates with lettuce. Top with rice mixture.

Nutrition facts per serving: 210 cal., 7 g total fat (1 g sat. fat), 0 mg chol., 225 mg sodium, 31 g carbo., 5 g fiber, 7 g pro.
Daily values: 11% vit. A, 43% vit. C, 3% calcium, 11% iron

black bean & RICE SALAD

Fiber-rich black beans help pack nutrition into this Mexican-style salad. It's great for brown bag lunches. Baked tortilla chips, fresh fruit, and milk make this salad a meal to look forward to.

Start to Finish: 30 minutes
Makes: 6 (1-cup) servings

1 cup cooked long-grain rice, chilled

4 ounces Monterey Jack cheese with jalapeño peppers, cut into ¼-inch cubes

1 cup chopped tomatoes

1 cup chopped yellow or red sweet pepper

½ of a medium cucumber, halved lengthwise and thinly sliced

¾ cup canned reduced-sodium black beans, rinsed and drained

¾ cup frozen whole kernel corn

2 green onions, thinly sliced (¼ cup)

¾ cup picante sauce or salsa

6 romaine leaves

½ cup fat-free dairy sour cream

❶ In a large mixing bowl stir together the cooked rice, cheese, tomatoes, sweet pepper, cucumber, black beans, corn, and green onions; add picante sauce or salsa. Toss to coat.

❷ To serve, line 6 salad plates with romaine leaves. Top with rice mixture. Serve with sour cream.

Nutrition facts per serving: 189 cal., 7 g total fat (4 g sat. fat), 17 mg chol., 374 mg sodium, 25 g carbo., 3 g fiber, 11 g pro.
Daily values: 20% vit. A, 87% vit. C, 17% calcium, 11% iron

Good Fats?

Fats and oils have a place in every diet. Without them, we couldn't absorb vitamins A, D, E, and K. Our nervous system couldn't function without fat and the cells of our body would fall apart. Monounsaturated fats, the fats in most vegetable oils—for example, olive oil—have added benefits. They help prevent heart disease by actively raising the levels of the desirable HDL-cholesterol in the blood. Fat (or oil) is nothing to be afraid of, but remember, at 9 calories per gram—120 calories per tablespoon—enjoy it sparingly.

lunches

113

tortellini SALAD

Fruit pectin, the same ingredient used for making jams and jellies, provides body to the dressing without using oil. Supermarkets usually stock pectin with the baking goods.

Prep: 40 minutes
Chill: 2 to 24 hours
Makes: 4 (2-cup) servings

- 2 **tablespoons snipped fresh basil or 1 teaspoon dried basil, crushed**
- 4 **teaspoons powdered fruit pectin**
- 1 **tablespoon Dijon-style mustard**
- 2 **cloves garlic, minced**
- 1 **teaspoon sugar**
- ¼ **teaspoon pepper**
- ⅓ **cup water**
- 2 **tablespoons white wine vinegar or rice wine vinegar**
- 1 **9-ounce package refrigerated light garlic-and-cheese tortellini or one 9-ounce package light cheese ravioli**
- 3 **cups broccoli flowerets**
- 1 **cup sliced carrots**
- 2 **green onions, sliced (¼ cup)**
- 1 **large tomato, chopped**
- 1 **cup fresh pea pods, halved**
- 4 **lettuce leaves**

1 For dressing, in a small mixing bowl stir together basil, pectin, mustard, garlic, sugar, and pepper. Stir in water and vinegar. Cover and chill for 30 minutes.

2 Meanwhile, cook tortellini or ravioli according to package directions, except omit any oil or salt. Add the broccoli and carrots during the last 3 minutes of cooking. Drain. Rinse with cold running water; drain again.

3 In a large bowl combine the pasta mixture and green onions; drizzle with dressing. Toss to coat. Cover and chill for 2 to 24 hours.

4 To serve, gently stir tomato and pea pods into salad. Line 4 salad plates with lettuce leaves. Top with pasta mixture.

Nutrition facts per serving: 253 cal., 4 g total fat (2 g sat. fat), 43 mg chol., 398 mg sodium, 42 g carbo., 7 g fiber, 14 g pro.
Daily values: 102% vit. A, 141% vit. C, 10% calcium, 17% iron

lunches

super
SUPPERS

What to have for dinner is an age-old dilemma. These tantalizing entrées, including Chicken with Fruit Salsa, Asian Flank Steak, Spice-Rubbed Pork Chops, or Fish with Cherry Relish, are sure to please you, your family, and dinner guests.

Herbed Beef Tenderloin, *recipe page 118*

herbed BEEF TENDERLOIN

Stir fresh parsley, rosemary, and thyme into Dijon mustard to create a flavorful herb rub for roast beef. Mustard-spiked sour cream makes a refreshing condiment.

Prep: 5 minutes
Roast: 30 minutes
Stand: 15 minutes
Oven: 325°F
Makes: 8 servings

1 **2-pound beef tenderloin roast**

¼ **cup snipped fresh parsley**

2 **tablespoons Dijon-style mustard**

1 **tablespoon snipped fresh rosemary**

2 **teaspoons snipped fresh thyme**

1 **teaspoon olive oil or cooking oil**

½ **teaspoon coarsely ground black pepper**

2 **cloves garlic, minced**

½ **cup light dairy sour cream**

2 **teaspoons Dijon-style mustard**

   Coarsely ground black pepper

❶ Trim fat from meat. In small bowl stir together parsley, the 2 tablespoons mustard, the rosemary, thyme, oil, pepper, and garlic. Rub over top and sides of meat.

❷ Place meat on a rack in a shallow roasting pan. Insert an oven-going meat thermometer into center of meat. Roast in a 325° oven for 30 to 45 minutes or until meat thermometer registers 135°F. Cover with foil and let stand 15 minutes. (The meat's temperature will rise 10°F while it stands.)

❸ Meanwhile, for sauce, stir together sour cream and the 2 teaspoons mustard. Thinly slice meat. Serve with sauce. If desired, sprinkle with additional pepper.

Nutrition Facts per serving: 215 cal., 11 g total fat (4 g sat. fat), 75 mg chol., 178 mg sodium, 2 g carbo., 0 g fiber, 25 g pro.
Daily Values: 4% vit. A, 5% vit. C, 4% calcium, 18% iron

super suppers

mustard STEAK SANDWICHES

Save calories by serving this sandwich with just the bottom half of the roll. Use a knife and fork for easier eating.

Prep: 10 minutes
Broil: 15 minutes
Makes: 6 servings

2 **tablespoons Dijon-style mustard**

1 **teaspoon brown sugar**

½ **teaspoon cracked black pepper**

1 **clove garlic, minced**

1 **pound beef flank steak, trimmed of separable fat**

3 **hoagie rolls, split and toasted**

1 **cup shredded lettuce**

Thinly sliced tomato

Dijon-style mustard (optional)

❶ In a small bowl stir together mustard, brown sugar, pepper, and garlic. Set aside.

❷ Place meat on the unheated rack of a broiler pan. Score steak on both sides by making shallow cuts at 1-inch intervals in a diamond pattern. Brush steak with some of the mustard mixture. Broil steak 4 to 5 inches from the heat for 7 minutes. Turn and brush steak with remaining mustard mixture. Broil until done as desired, allowing 8 to 11 minutes more for medium (160°F).

❸ To serve, thinly slice meat diagonally across the grain. Top each hoagie half with some of the lettuce and sliced tomato. Layer meat slices on each sandwich. If desired, serve with additional mustard.

Nutrition Facts per serving: 333 cal., 9 g total fat (3 g sat. fat), 30 mg chol., 500 mg sodium, 38 g carbo., 2 g fiber, 22 g pro.
Daily Values: 7% vit. A, 11% vit. C, 6% calcium, 19% iron

Fatless Flavor

It's no secret that fat, salt, and sugar give food flavor, so when it comes to eating healthfully, replacing these things with other ingredients is important. Certainly ingredients like mustard, pepper, vinegar, and salsa are great low-cal, fat-free flavorings. And there are so many varieties of each of these that the possibilities are endless. Consider hot or honey mustard, balsamic or raspberry vinegar, and tomato or black bean salsa. The list goes on. As long as you're willing to experiment, you'll never run out of variations.

super suppers

beef WITH MUSHROOM SAUCE

For a more elegant dinner, broil beef tenderloin instead of eye round steaks and make the sauce using ⅓ cup dry red wine and ⅓ cup water in place of the vegetable juice.

Prep: 20 minutes
Broil: 10 minutes
Makes: 4 servings

⅛ teaspoon black pepper

4 3-ounce beef eye round steaks, trimmed of separable fat

1 cup sliced fresh mushrooms

½ cup sliced green onions

2 cloves garlic, minced

2 teaspoons butter or margarine

2 teaspoons cornstarch

⅔ cup low-sodium vegetable juice

½ teaspoon instant beef bouillon granules

1 Rub pepper over meat. Place meat on the unheated rack of a broiler pan. Broil 4 to 5 inches from the heat until done as desired, turning once. Allow 10 to 12 minutes for medium rare (145°F) or 12 to 15 minutes for medium (160°F).

2 Meanwhile, in a saucepan cook mushrooms, onions, and garlic in hot butter until vegetables are tender. Stir in cornstarch. Add vegetable juice and beef bouillon granules. Cook and stir until thickened and bubbly. Cook and stir 2 minutes more. Keep warm while cooking meat. Serve the sauce over meat.

Nutrition Facts per serving: 170 cal., 7 g total fat (3 g sat. fat), 51 mg chol., 181 mg sodium, 5 g carbo., 1 g fiber, 20 g pro.
Daily Values: 11% vit. A, 21% vit. C, 2% calcium, 10% iron

roast with SPICY POTATOES

Tri-tip roast is a boneless cut of beef from the bottom sirloin. Because of its shape, it's also sometimes called triangular roast. This versatile cut tastes wonderful roasted, grilled, or broiled, and it's low in calories.

Prep: 25 minutes
Roast: 30 minutes
Stand: 15 minutes
Oven: 425°F
Makes: 6 to 8 servings

1½ **pounds tiny new potatoes (15 to 18), halved**

1½ **teaspoons chili powder**

½ **teaspoon ground cumin**

¼ **teaspoon garlic powder**

¼ **teaspoon salt**

¼ **teaspoon dried oregano, crushed**

⅛ **teaspoon cayenne pepper**

3 **tablespoons lemon juice**

1 **tablespoon cooking oil**

1 **1½- to 2-pound boneless tri-tip roast**

1 In a covered medium saucepan cook potatoes in a small amount of boiling salted water about 10 minutes or until nearly tender. Drain well.

2 Meanwhile, in a small bowl combine chili powder, cumin, garlic powder, salt, oregano, and cayenne pepper. Gently toss potatoes with 2 tablespoons of the lemon juice and the oil. Sprinkle with 1½ teaspoons of the chili powder mixture. Toss again to coat potatoes evenly. Arrange potatoes in a single layer in a lightly greased 15×10×1-inch baking pan; set aside.

3 Brush both sides of roast with remaining 1 tablespoon lemon juice. Sprinkle with remaining chili powder mixture. Place roast on a rack set in a shallow roasting pan. Insert a meat thermometer into center of roast. Roast, uncovered, in a 425° oven until done as desired. Allow 30 to 35 minutes for medium rare (140°F) or 40 to 45 minutes for medium (155°F). Remove roast from oven. Cover with foil and let stand for 15 minutes. (The meat's temperature will rise 5°F while it stands.)

4 Meanwhile, while roast is standing, place the potatoes in the 425° oven. Bake, uncovered, 15 minutes or until potatoes are tender and brown, carefully turning potatoes once.

5 To serve, thinly slice roast across the grain. Serve potatoes with roast.

Nutrition Facts per serving: 265 cal., 8 g total fat (2 g sat. fat), 54 mg chol., 175 mg sodium, 20 g carbo., 2 g fiber, 28 g pro.
Daily Values: 5% vit. A, 34% vit. C, 2% calcium, 22% iron

super suppers

spinach-stuffed FLANK STEAK

Dried tomatoes have a sweet, tart flavor. To save on calories and fat, choose those that are not packed in oil. Soften the tomatoes in hot water for 10 minutes before using.

Prep: 20 minutes
Broil: 10 minutes
Makes: 4 servings

- ¼ **cup dried tomatoes (not oil packed)**
- 1 **1-pound beef flank steak or top round steak, trimmed of separable fat**
- ⅛ **teaspoon salt**
- ⅛ **teaspoon black pepper**
- 1 **10-ounce package frozen chopped spinach, thawed and well drained**
- 2 **tablespoons grated Parmesan cheese**
- 2 **tablespoons snipped fresh basil**

1 In a small bowl soak the dried tomatoes in enough hot water to cover for 10 minutes. Drain. Snip into small pieces.

2 Meanwhile, score both sides of steak in a diamond pattern by making shallow diagonal cuts at 1-inch intervals. Place meat between 2 pieces of plastic wrap. Working from center to edges, pound with the flat side of a meat mallet into a 12×8-inch rectangle. Remove plastic wrap. Sprinkle with the salt and pepper.

3 Spread the spinach over the steak. Sprinkle with the softened tomatoes, Parmesan cheese, and basil. Roll the steak up from a short side. Secure with wooden toothpicks at 1-inch intervals, starting ½ inch from an end. Cut between the toothpicks into eight 1-inch slices.

4 Place slices cut side down on the unheated rack of a broiler pan. Broil 3 to 4 inches from the heat until done as desired, turning once. Allow 10 to 12 minutes for medium rare (145°F) or 12 to 16 minutes for medium (160°F). Before serving, remove the toothpicks.

Nutrition Facts per serving: 214 cal., 9 g total fat (4 g sat. fat), 47 mg chol., 348 mg sodium, 4 g carbo., 2 g fiber, 28 g pro.
Daily Values: 207% vit. A, 11% vit. C, 10% calcium, 14% iron

super suppers

spiced beef STIR-FRY

This is no ordinary stir-fry! The aromatic blend of five spices infuses bold flavors into this dish. Fresh mint and cilantro add further intrigue to the mix.

Start to Finish: 40 minutes
Makes: 5 servings

- 1 teaspoon ground cumin
- ½ teaspoon garlic powder
- ½ teaspoon ground ginger
- ½ teaspoon ground allspice
- ½ teaspoon paprika
- ¼ teaspoon salt
- ¼ teaspoon pepper
- 1 pound boneless beef sirloin steak, cut into ¾-inch cubes
- 1 14½-ounce can reduced-sodium chicken broth
- 1¼ cups couscous
- 3 plum tomatoes, chopped
- ½ of a medium cucumber, halved lengthwise and sliced
- 2 tablespoons snipped cilantro or parsley
- 1 tablespoon snipped mint
  Nonstick spray coating
- 8 green onions, bias-sliced into 1-inch lengths (1 cup)
- 2 teaspoons cooking oil

1 In a plastic bag combine cumin, garlic powder, ginger, allspice, paprika, salt, and pepper. Add beef. Close bag. Toss to coat beef with spice mixture; set aside.

2 In a medium saucepan bring the chicken broth to boiling. Stir in the couscous. Remove from heat. Cover; let stand for 5 minutes. Stir in tomato, cucumber, cilantro or parsley, and mint. Cover to keep warm.

3 Spray a large nonstick skillet with nonstick coating. Preheat over medium-high heat. Add green onions. Stir-fry for 2 to 3 minutes or until crisp-tender. Remove green onions from skillet.

4 Carefully add 1 teaspoon of the oil to the skillet. Add half of the beef. Stir-fry for 2 to 3 minutes or to desired doneness. Remove from the skillet. Repeat with the remaining oil and beef. Return all beef to skillet; heat through.

5 To serve, divide couscous mixture among 5 plates. Top each with some of the beef and green onions.

Nutrition facts per serving: 378 cal., 11 g total fat (4 g sat. fat), 60 mg chol., 394 mg sodium, 40 g carbo., 8 g fiber, 28 g pro.
Daily values: 9% vit. A, 23% vit. C, 3% calcium, 26% iron

super suppers

asian FLANK STEAK

Sweet and spicy Szechwan-style cooking promises palate-pleasing diversity for your taste buds. Preparing and marinating the steak the day before allows you to pop it under the broiler and have it on the table in short order.

Prep: 15 minutes
Marinate: 4 to 24 hours
Broil: 12 minutes
Makes: 6 servings

1   1¼-pounds beef flank steak
½   cup beef broth
⅓   cup hoisin sauce
¼   cup reduced-sodium soy sauce
¼   cup sliced green onions
3   tablespoons dry sherry or apple, orange, or pineapple juice
1   tablespoon sugar
1   teaspoon grated fresh ginger
4   cloves garlic, minced
    Nonstick spray coating

1 Trim fat from beef. Place beef in a plastic bag set in a shallow dish. For marinade, in a small bowl stir together beef broth, hoisin sauce, soy sauce, green onions, sherry or juice, sugar, ginger, and garlic. Pour over beef. Close bag. Marinate in refrigerator for 4 to 24 hours, turning bag occasionally.

2 Drain beef, discarding the marinade. Spray the unheated rack of a broiler pan with nonstick coating. Place beef on the prepared rack. Broil 4 to 5 inches from the heat to desired doneness, turning once. Allow 12 to 14 minutes for medium. (Or, grill the beef on the rack of an uncovered grill directly over medium coals to desired doneness, turning once. Allow 12 to 14 minutes for medium.) To serve, thinly slice beef across the grain.

Nutrition facts per serving: 144 cal., 7 g total fat (3 g sat. fat), 44 mg chol., 113 mg sodium, 1 g carbo., 0 g fiber, 18 g pro.
Daily values: 0% vit. A, 0% vit. C, 0% calcium, 11% iron

No Beef With Beef

Protein is a vital nutrient that our bodies need for a variety of functions, such as building tissue and keeping the immune system strong. Many people enjoy meat as their primary source of protein in the diet. Red meat is one of the best sources of iron and zinc—two minerals in short dietary supply for many people. Today's beef comes from cattle that are raised to be leaner, with some cuts—such as flank and tenderloin steak—having less fat than dark meat poultry. Beef also is closely trimmed of fat by butchers. All of this makes beef a viable participant in a healthful diet.

ginger BEEF STIR-FRY

When you crave steak but not the high fat and calories that go with it, try this stir-fry. Lean beef and crispy spring vegetables make up a full-flavored dinner you can toss together in minutes.

Start to Finish: 30 minutes
Makes: 4 servings

- 8 ounces beef top round steak
- ½ cup reduced-sodium beef broth
- 3 tablespoons reduced-sodium soy sauce
- 2½ teaspoons cornstarch
- 1 teaspoon sugar
- 1 teaspoon grated fresh ginger
  Nonstick cooking spray
- 1¼ pounds fresh asparagus spears, trimmed and cut into 2-inch pieces (3 cups), or 3 cups small broccoli florets
- 1½ cups sliced fresh mushrooms
- 4 green onions, bias-sliced into 2-inch pieces
- 1 tablespoon cooking oil
- 2 cups hot cooked rice

1. If desired, partially freeze beef for easier slicing. Trim fat from beef. Thinly slice beef across the grain into bite-size strips. Set aside. For sauce, in a small bowl stir together beef broth, soy sauce, cornstarch, sugar, and ginger; set aside.

2. Lightly coat an unheated wok or large skillet with nonstick cooking spray. Heat over medium-high heat. Add asparagus, mushrooms, and green onions. Stir-fry for 3 to 4 minutes or until vegetables are crisp-tender. Remove from wok or skillet.

3. Carefully add the oil to wok or skillet. Add beef; stir-fry for 2 to 3 minutes or until brown. Push the beef from center of the wok or skillet. Stir sauce. Add sauce to center of wok or skillet. Cook and stir until thickened and bubbly.

4. Return vegetables to wok or skillet. Stir all ingredients together to coat with sauce; heat through. Serve immediately over hot cooked rice.

Nutrition Facts per serving: 258 cal., 7 g total fat (2 g sat. fat), 25 mg chol., 523 mg sodium, 31 g carbo., 3 g fiber, 19 g pro.
Daily Values: 10% vit. A, 20% vit. C, 5% calcium, 18% iron

horseradish FLANK STEAK

A classic at British clubs, this supper works well as a salad, too. Serve thin strips of this grilled flank steak cold on a bed of mixed greens. Top with the mustard sauce or dress with bottled fat-free Italian dressing.

Prep: 20 minutes
Marinate: 6 to 24 hours
Grill: 12 minutes
Makes: 4 servings

1 **1-pound beef flank steak**

3 **tablespoons Dijon-style mustard**

3 **tablespoons lemon juice**

4½ **teaspoons reduced-sodium Worcestershire sauce**

⅓ **cup fat-free dairy sour cream or fat-free mayonnaise or salad dressing**

1 **green onion, finely chopped (2 tablespoons)**

1 **to 2 teaspoons prepared horseradish**

1 Trim fat from beef. Use a sharp knife to score beef by making shallow diagonal cuts at 1-inch intervals in a diamond pattern. Repeat on other side. Place beef in a plastic bag set in a shallow dish.

2 For marinade, in a small bowl combine 2 tablespoons of the Dijon-style mustard, the lemon juice, and Worcestershire sauce. Pour over beef. Close the bag. Marinate beef in the refrigerator for 6 to 24 hours, turning the bag occasionally.

3 In a small bowl combine the remaining Dijon-style mustard; the sour cream, mayonnaise, or salad dressing; green onion; and horseradish. Cover and refrigerate. Remove from refrigerator 30 minutes before serving time.

4 Drain the beef, discarding the marinade. Grill on the rack of an uncovered grill directly over medium coals to desired doneness, turning once. Allow 12 to 14 minutes for medium.

5 To serve, thinly slice beef across the grain. Serve with sour cream mixture.

Nutrition facts per serving: 208 cal., 9 g total fat (3 g sat. fat), 53 mg chol., 398 mg sodium, 6 g carbo., 0 g fiber, 24 g pro.
Daily values: 3% vit. A, 26% vit. C, 3% calcium, 16% iron

super suppers

deviled ROAST BEEF

For the mustard lover in your midst, here's a "deviled" beef dish that is sinfully delicious. One taste and you may be willing to barter anything for another helping.

Prep: 25 minutes
Roast: 1½ hours
Stand: 15 minutes
Makes: 8 to 10 servings

1 2- to 2½-pounds beef eye of round roast

¼ cup Dijon-style mustard

¼ teaspoon coarsely ground pepper

2 cups sliced fresh mushrooms

1 cup beef broth

1 small onion, cut into thin wedges

¼ cup water

2 cloves garlic, minced

1 teaspoon Worcestershire sauce

¼ teaspoon dried thyme, crushed

½ cup fat-free milk

3 tablespoons all-purpose flour

1 Trim fat from beef. In a small bowl stir together 2 tablespoons of the Dijon-style mustard and the pepper; rub onto the beef. Place the beef on a rack in a shallow roasting pan. Insert a meat thermometer. Roast beef in a 325° oven until thermometer registers 140° for medium-rare (1½ to 2 hours) or 155° for medium (1¾ to 2¼ hours). Cover with foil; let stand for 15 minutes before carving. (The temperature of the meat will rise 5° during standing.)

2 Meanwhile, for sauce, in a medium saucepan combine the mushrooms, beef broth, onion, water, garlic, Worcestershire sauce, and thyme. Bring to boiling; reduce heat. Simmer, covered, about 5 minutes or until vegetables are tender. In a small bowl stir together milk and remaining Dijon-style mustard; gradually stir into flour. Add to mushroom mixture in saucepan. Cook and stir over medium heat until thickened and bubbly. Cook and stir for 1 minute more.

3 To serve, thinly slice beef across the grain. Arrange on a serving platter. Spoon some of the sauce over beef. Pass remaining sauce.

Nutrition facts per serving: 217 cal., 9 g total fat (3 g sat. fat), 78 mg chol., 342 mg sodium, 5 g carbo., 0 g fiber, 28 g pro.
Daily values: 0% vit. A, 4% vit. C, 2% calcium, 22% iron

italian BEEF SKILLET

The preparation for this beef and vegetable dish takes about 35 minutes. Then sit back and you can relax while it simmers.

Prep: 35 minutes
Cook: 1¼ hours
Makes: 4 servings

1 **pound boneless beef round steak**

Nonstick cooking spray

2 **cups sliced fresh mushrooms**

1 **cup chopped onion**

1 **cup coarsely chopped green sweet pepper**

½ **cup chopped celery**

2 **cloves garlic, minced**

1 **14½-ounce can diced tomatoes, undrained**

½ **teaspoon dried basil, crushed**

¼ **teaspoon dried oregano, crushed**

⅛ **to ¼ teaspoon crushed red pepper**

2 **tablespoons grated Parmesan cheese**

Hot cooked pasta (optional)

1️⃣ Trim fat from meat. Cut meat into 4 serving-size pieces. Lightly coat a large skillet with cooking spray. Heat over medium heat. Add meat and cook until brown, turning to brown evenly. Remove meat from skillet; set aside.

2️⃣ Add mushrooms, onion, sweet pepper, celery, and garlic to skillet. Cook until vegetables are nearly tender. Stir in undrained tomatoes, basil, oregano, and crushed red pepper. Return meat to skillet, spooning vegetable mixture over meat. Cover and simmer about 1¼ hours or until meat is tender, stirring occasionally.

3️⃣ Transfer meat to a serving platter. Spoon vegetable mixture over meat and sprinkle with Parmesan cheese. If desired, serve with hot cooked pasta.

Nutrition Facts per serving: 212 cal., 4 g total fat (1 g sat. fat), 51 mg chol., 296 mg sodium, 14 g carbo., 3 g fiber, 30 g pro.
Daily Values: 6% vit. A, 74% vit. C, 11% calcium, 20% iron

Cooking with Herbs

Using herbs is a great way to add flavor to foods, especially when you're trying to control salt and fat. Some recipes call for fresh herbs; others call for dried. What's the difference? Fresh herbs add more flavor, but they have a less concentrated taste that fades quickly. When substituting one for the other, you can replace 1 tablespoon of fresh herbs with 1 teaspoon of dried herbs. Crush dried herbs in your hands before using to bring out the essential oils. If using fresh herbs wait until near the end of the cooking time to add them to avoid losing the flavor.

super suppers

saucy beef AND ONIONS

With the variety of fat-free and reduced-fat products available in grocery stores, low-fat cooking is easier than ever. Here light sour cream and a jar of fat-free gravy create a saucy hamburger stroganoff.

Start to Finish: 35 minutes
Makes: 4 servings

- 12 **ounces lean ground beef**
- 2 **cups sliced fresh mushrooms**
- 2 **medium onions, cut into thin wedges**
- 1 **clove garlic, minced**
- 1 **12-ounce jar fat-free beef gravy**
- ⅔ **cup light dairy sour cream**
- 1 **tablespoon Worcestershire sauce**
- ¾ **teaspoon snipped fresh thyme or sage or ¼ teaspoon dried thyme or sage, crushed**
- ⅛ **teaspoon black pepper**
- 2 **cups hot cooked rice or noodles**
- 2 **tablespoons snipped fresh parsley**

❶ In a large skillet cook ground beef, mushrooms, onions, and garlic until meat is brown and onions are tender. Drain off fat.

❷ In a medium bowl stir together beef gravy, sour cream, Worcestershire sauce, thyme, and pepper. Stir into meat mixture. Cook and stir until heated through.

❸ Serve meat mixture over hot cooked rice. Sprinkle with fresh parsley.

Nutrition Facts per serving: 396 cal., 15 g total fat (6 g sat. fat), 83 mg chol., 972 mg sodium, 35 g carbo., 1 g fiber, 32 g pro.
Daily Values: 7% vit. A, 9% vit. C, 10% calcium, 22% iron

super suppers

131

steak RÉMOULADE SANDWICHES

Served in France as an accompaniment to cold meats, fish, and seafood, the classic mayonnaise-based sauce called a rémoulade brings something new to the steak sandwich.

Prep: 15 minutes
Grill: 11 minutes
Makes: 4 servings

¼ cup light mayonnaise dressing or salad dressing

1½ teaspoons finely minced cornichons or gherkins

1 teaspoon drained capers, chopped

¼ teaspoon lemon juice
   Black pepper

2 8-ounce boneless beef top loin steaks, cut 1 inch thick

2 teaspoons prepared garlic spread or 2 teaspoons bottled minced garlic (4 cloves)

1 large yellow sweet pepper, cut lengthwise into 8 strips

4 kaiser or French-style rolls, split and toasted

1 cup arugula or fresh spinach leaves

① For rémoulade, in a small bowl combine mayonnaise dressing, cornichons, capers, lemon juice, and several dashes black pepper. Cover and refrigerate until ready to serve.

② Pat steaks dry with a paper towel. Using your fingers, rub garlic spread over steaks. Sprinkle with additional black pepper.

③ For a charcoal grill, place steaks and sweet pepper strips on the rack of an uncovered grill directly over medium coals. Grill until meat is done as desired and sweet pepper strips are crisp-tender, turning once halfway through grilling. Allow 11 to 15 minutes for medium rare (145°F) or 14 to 18 minutes for medium (160°F). (For a gas grill, preheat grill. Reduce heat to medium. Place steaks and sweet pepper strips on grill rack over heat. Cover and grill as above.) Transfer cooked steaks and sweet pepper strips to a cutting board; cut steaks into ¼-inch slices.

④ If desired, grill rolls directly over medium heat about 1 minute or until toasted. Spread rémoulade on cut sides of toasted rolls. Fill rolls with arugula, steak slices, and sweet pepper strips. Add roll tops.

Nutrition Facts per serving: 416 cal., 15 g total fat (4 g sat. fat), 62 mg chol., 517 mg sodium, 37 g carbo., 2 g fiber, 32 g pro.
Daily Values: 6% vit. A, 162% vit. C, 8% calcium, 23% iron

flank steak WITH CHILI SAUCE

A hint of honey sweetens the spicy tomato sauce. Reduce the chili powder if you don't want so much heat.

Prep: 20 minutes
Grill: 17 minutes
Makes: 6 servings

- ½ **cup water**
- 1 **cup chopped onion**
- 4 **cloves garlic, minced**
- 2 **teaspoons chili powder**
- 1 **8-ounce can low-sodium tomato sauce**
- ⅓ **cup vinegar**
- 2 **tablespoons honey**
- ½ **teaspoon salt**
- ¼ **teaspoon black pepper**
- 1¼ **pounds beef flank steak**

❶ For sauce, in a medium saucepan bring water to boiling. Add onion, garlic, and chili powder. Reduce heat. Simmer, covered, for 5 minutes or until tender. Stir in tomato sauce, vinegar, honey, salt, and pepper. Return to boiling, stirring constantly. Boil for 5 minutes or until slightly thickened.

❷ Meanwhile, trim fat from meat. Score both sides of steak in a diamond pattern by making shallow diagonal cuts at 1-inch intervals. Brush lightly with some of the sauce. For a charcoal grill, place steak on the rack of an uncovered grill directly over medium coals. Grill for 17 to 21 minutes or until medium doneness (160°F), turning once halfway through grilling and brushing with the sauce during the last 5 minutes of grilling. (For a gas grill, preheat grill. Reduce heat to medium. Place steak on grill rack over heat. Cover and grill as above.)

❸ In a small saucepan reheat the remaining sauce until bubbly. To serve, thinly slice steak across grain. Pass warmed sauce.

Nutrition Facts per serving: 194 cal., 7 g total fat (3 g sat. fat), 38 mg chol., 262 mg sodium, 12 g carbo., 1 g fiber, 22 g pro.
Daily Values: 10% vit. A, 12% vit. C, 3% calcium, 12% iron

super suppers

feta-stuffed BURGERS

Just a little bit of feta cheese adds a rich, tangy flavor to these stuffed burgers. Feta is sometimes referred to as pickled cheese because it is stored in a salty brine similar to pickles.

Prep: 30 minutes
Grill: 12 minutes
Chill: 4 to 24 hours
Makes: 6 servings

¼ **cup refrigerated or frozen egg product, thawed**

2 **tablespoons water**

⅓ **cup rolled oats**

¼ **teaspoon black pepper**

⅛ **teaspoon salt**

1 **pound lean ground beef**

2 **teaspoons Dijon-style mustard**

⅓ **cup crumbled feta cheese**

3 **English muffins, split and toasted**

1 **recipe Tomato-Basil Relish**
   Fresh basil (optional)

① In a bowl stir together egg product and water. Stir in oats, pepper, and salt. Add beef; mix well. Shape mixture into twelve ¼-inch-thick patties. Spread mustard on one side of 6 patties. Top with crumbled cheese. Place remaining patties on top of cheese, pressing edges to seal.

② For charcoal grill, place patties on the rack of an uncovered grill directly over medium coals. Grill for 12 to 14 minutes or until meat is done (160°F). (For a gas grill, preheat grill. Reduce heat to medium. Place patties on grill rack over heat. Cover and grill as above.)

③ Serve patties on toasted English muffin halves. Top with Tomato-Basil Relish. If desired, garnish with fresh basil.

Tomato-Basil Relish: In a small bowl stir together 2 chopped roma tomatoes; ⅓ cup chopped seeded cucumber; 2 tablespoons thinly sliced green onion; 1 tablespoon red wine vinegar; 1 tablespoon snipped, fresh basil or 1 teaspoon dried basil, crushed; and ⅛ teaspoon black pepper. Cover and chill for at least 4 hours or up to 24 hours.

Nutrition Facts per serving: 239 cal., 10 g total fat (4 g sat. fat), 55 mg chol., 353 mg sodium, 18 g carbo., 2 g fiber, 19 g pro.
Daily Values: 8% vit. A, 10% vit. C, 10% calcium, 15% iron

super suppers

135

pizza BURGERS

Pack all your favorite pizza flavors into a bun: grilled pepper strips, mozzarella cheese, and spaghetti sauce.

Prep: 25 minutes
Grill: 10 minutes
Makes: 8 servings

1 **egg**

1¼ **cups purchased meatless
     spaghetti sauce**

½ **cup fine dry bread crumbs**

⅓ **cup chopped onion (1 small)**

1 **teaspoon dried basil or
    oregano, crushed**

2 **cloves garlic, minced**

2 **pounds lean ground beef**

2 **medium green, yellow, and/
    or red sweet peppers, cut
    into rings and halved**

1 **tablespoon olive oil or
    cooking oil**

8 **kaiser rolls, split and toasted**

1 **cup shredded mozzarella
    cheese (4 ounces)**

① In a large bowl beat egg and ¼ cup of the spaghetti sauce with a whisk. Stir in bread crumbs, onion, basil, and garlic. Add beef; mix well. Shape meat mixture into eight ½-inch-thick patties.

② Tear off an 18×12-inch piece of heavy foil. Place sweet pepper pieces in center of foil; drizzle with oil. Bring up 2 opposite edges of foil and seal with a double fold; fold in remaining edges to enclose the peppers, leaving space for steam to build.

③ For a charcoal grill, place patties and foil packet on the grill rack directly over medium coals. Grill for 10 to 13 minutes or until meat is done (160°F) and peppers are tender, turning patties and foil packet once halfway through grilling. (For a gas grill, preheat grill. Reduce heat to medium. Place patties and packet on grill rack over heat. Cover and grill as above.)

④ Meanwhile, heat remaining 1 cup spaghetti sauce. Serve patties on rolls with pepper pieces and cheese. Spoon some of the heated spaghetti sauce over burgers. Pass any remaining spaghetti sauce.

Nutrition Facts per serving: 460 cal., 18 g total fat (6 g sat. fat), 106 mg chol., 742 mg sodium, 42 g carbo., 0 g fiber, 32 g pro.
Daily Values: 6% vit. A, 43% vit. C, 18% calcium, 27% iron

super suppers

roasted GARLIC STEAK

Roasting the garlic with fresh or dried basil and rosemary boosts the flavor to a great new level.

Prep: 15 minutes
Grill: 30 minutes
Makes: 6 servings

1 or 2 whole garlic bulb(s)

3 to 4 teaspoons snipped fresh basil or 1 teaspoon dried basil, crushed

1 tablespoon snipped fresh rosemary or 1 teaspoon dried rosemary, crushed

2 tablespoons olive oil or cooking oil

1½ pounds boneless beef ribeye steaks or sirloin steak, cut 1 inch thick

1 to 2 teaspoons cracked black pepper

½ teaspoon salt

super suppers

1 Using a sharp knife, cut off the top ½ inch from each garlic bulb to expose the ends of the individual cloves. Leaving garlic bulb(s) whole, remove any loose, papery outer layers.

2 Fold a 20×18-inch piece of heavy foil in half crosswise. Trim into a 10-inch square. Place garlic bulb(s) cut side up in center of foil square. Sprinkle garlic with basil and rosemary and drizzle with oil. Bring up 2 opposite edges of foil and seal with a double fold. Fold remaining edges together to enclose garlic, leaving space for steam to build.

3 For a charcoal grill, place garlic packet on the rack of an uncovered grill directly over medium coals. Grill about 30 minutes or until garlic feels soft when packet is squeezed, turning garlic occasionally.

4 Meanwhile, trim fat from steaks. Sprinkle pepper and salt evenly over both sides of steaks; rub in with your fingers. While garlic is grilling, add steaks to grill. Grill until done as desired, turning once halfway through grilling. For ribeye steaks, allow 11 to 15 minutes for medium rare (145°F) and 14 to 18 minutes for medium (160°F). For sirloin steak, allow 14 to 18 minutes for medium rare (145°F) and 18 to 22 minutes for medium (160°F). (For a gas grill, preheat grill. Reduce heat to medium. Place garlic, then steaks on grill rack over heat. Cover and grill as above.)

5 To serve, cut steaks into 6 serving-size pieces. Remove garlic from foil, reserving the oil mixture. Squeeze garlic pulp from each clove onto steaks. Mash pulp slightly with a fork; spread over steaks. Drizzle with the reserved oil mixture.

Nutrition Facts per serving: 189 cal., 9 g total fat (2 g sat. fat), 52 mg chol., 139 mg sodium, 4 g carbo., 0 g fiber, 22 g pro.
Daily Values: 1% vit. A, 6% vit. C, 3% calcium, 14% iron

fennel-cumin LAMB CHOPS

You can make the spice rub in advance and store it in an airtight jar for up to 1 week. You'll like it with pork chops or a pork roast too.

Prep: 15 minutes
Marinate: 30 minutes
Grill: 10 minutes
Makes: 2 servings

1 large clove garlic, minced
¾ teaspoon fennel seed, crushed
¾ teaspoon ground cumin
¼ teaspoon ground coriander
¼ teaspoon salt
⅛ teaspoon black pepper
4 lamb rib chops, cut about 1 inch thick

1 For rub, combine garlic, fennel, cumin, coriander, salt, and pepper. Sprinkle mixture over both sides of chops; rub in with your fingers. Place chops on a plate; cover with plastic wrap and chill for 30 minutes to 24 hours.

2 For a charcoal grill, place chops on the rack of an uncovered grill directly over medium coals. Grill until done as desired. Allow 10 to 14 minutes for medium rare (145°F) and 14 to 16 minutes for medium (160°F). (For a gas grill, preheat grill. Reduce heat to medium. Place chops on grill rack over heat. Cover and grill as above.)

Nutrition Facts per serving: 208 cal., 11 g total fat (4 g sat. fat), 80 mg chol., 368 mg sodium, 1 g carbo., 0 g fiber, 25 g pro.
Daily Values: 1% vit. C, 4% calcium, 14% iron

What's Fennel?

Fennel, a vegetable that originated in the Mediterranean area, has a big white bulb with green leaves and stalks growing out of it. Its mildly sweet taste is similar to that of anise or licorice. When buying fennel be sure to choose bulbs that are firm and fragrant, and use it within a week for the best flavor and quality. Nutritionally speaking, fennel is a good source of potassium and also contains vitamin C and folic acid.

veal SCALOPPINE

Serve this fat- and calorie-trimmed classic with hot cooked broccoli and whole wheat dinner rolls.

Start to Finish: 30 minutes
Makes: 4 servings

12 ounces boneless veal leg round steak, veal leg sirloin steak, or beef top round steak, cut ¼ inch thick and trimmed of separable fat

Salt

Black pepper

½ cup chopped onion

¼ cup water

2 cloves garlic, minced

1 14½-ounce can diced tomatoes, undrained

3 tablespoons dry white wine

1 tablespoon snipped fresh oregano or 1 teaspoon dried oregano, crushed

1 tablespoon capers, drained (optional)

⅛ teaspoon black pepper

Nonstick cooking spray

2 cups hot cooked noodles

1 Cut meat into 8 pieces. Place each piece of meat between 2 pieces of plastic wrap. Working from center to edges, pound with flat side of a meat mallet to about ⅛-inch thickness. Remove plastic wrap. Sprinkle meat lightly with salt and pepper to taste. Set aside.

2 For sauce, in a medium covered saucepan combine onion, water, and garlic. Cook until onion is tender. Stir in undrained tomatoes, wine, oregano, capers (if desired), and ⅛ teaspoon pepper. Bring to boiling; reduce heat. Simmer, uncovered, about 15 minutes or until desired consistency. Keep warm.

3 Meanwhile, lightly coat a large skillet with nonstick cooking spray. Heat over medium-high heat. Cook meat, half at a time, for 2 to 4 minutes or until done as desired, turning once. Transfer meat to a serving platter. Keep warm.

4 To serve, spoon the sauce over meat. Serve with hot cooked noodles.

Nutrition Facts per serving: 235 cal., 3 g total fat (1 g sat. fat), 93 mg chol., 279 mg sodium, 27 g carbo., 2 g fiber, 23 g pro.
Daily Values: 13% vit. A, 27% vit. C, 5% calcium, 14% iron

super suppers

veal with APPLE-MARSALA

Veal may be labeled "scaloppine" in your supermarket meat section. Scaloppine technically describes a thin scallop of meat that is quickly sautéed. It's generally cut ⅛ inch thick, and you don't have to pound it.

Start to Finish: 25 minutes
Makes: 4 servings

Nonstick cooking spray

12 **ounces veal scaloppine or boneless veal leg round steak or beef top round steak,* cut ¼ inch thick and trimmed of separable fat**

1 **apple, thinly sliced**

1 **clove garlic, minced**

½ **cup dry Marsala**

⅓ **cup reduced-sodium chicken broth**

1 **tablespoon snipped fresh parsley**

❶ Lightly coat an unheated large skillet with nonstick cooking spray. Heat over medium-high heat. Cook meat, half at a time, for 4 to 5 minutes or until no pink remains, turning once. Transfer to a serving platter. Keep warm.

❷ Add sliced apple and garlic to skillet. Stir in Marsala and chicken broth. Bring to boiling; reduce heat. Boil gently, uncovered, for 4 to 5 minutes or until mixture is reduced by half. Spoon over meat. Sprinkle with parsley.

*Note: If using round or beef steak, cut steak into 8 pieces. Place 1 piece of the cut steak between 2 pieces of plastic wrap. Working from center to edges, pound with flat side of meat mallet to ⅛-inch thickness. Remove plastic wrap. Repeat with remaining meat.

Nutrition Facts per serving: 133 cal., 2 g total fat (0 g sat. fat), 66 mg chol., 97 mg sodium, 6 g carbo., 1 g fiber, 19 g pro.
Daily Values: 1% vit. A, 6% vit. C, 1% calcium, 4% iron

Picking the Best Apple for the Job

There are more than 7,500 known varieties of apples. Certainly personal preference is important when choosing apples, but you must also consider what you'll be doing with them. Are they for baking, for applesauce, or for eating out of hand? For baking, the best apples are those that keep their shape and don't get too mushy, such as Rome Beauty and Idared. When making applesauce choose apples that don't turn brown easily such as Cortland and McIntosh. For eating as is, firm, juicy, tasty apples are the ones to pick, such as Empire and Gala.

peppered PORK AND PILAF

This tantalizing pork-and-rice combo gets a quick start from vegetables culled at the salad bar.

Prep: 15 minutes
Cook: 17 minutes
Stand: 5 minutes
Makes: 4 servings

- **4 boneless pork loin chops, cut ¾ inch thick**
- **1 tablespoon herb-pepper seasoning**
- **2 tablespoons olive oil**
- **2 cups cut-up salad bar vegetables (such as sweet peppers, carrots, mushrooms, onion, and/or broccoli)**
- **1 14-ounce can chicken broth**
- **2 cups quick-cooking brown rice**
- **¼ cup chopped roasted red sweet pepper**

1 Sprinkle both sides of meat with 2 teaspoons of the herb-pepper seasoning. In a large skillet cook chops in 1 tablespoon of the olive oil for 5 minutes. Turn chops. Cook for 5 to 7 minutes more or until meat is done (160°F) and juices run clear.

2 Meanwhile, if necessary, cut vegetables into bite-size pieces. In a medium saucepan heat the remaining 1 tablespoon olive oil. Add the vegetables and cook for 2 minutes. Carefully add broth. Bring to boiling. Stir in the rice, roasted pepper, and the remaining 1 teaspoon herb-pepper seasoning. Return to boiling; cover and simmer 5 minutes. Remove from heat. Let stand 5 minutes. Serve chops with the rice mixture.

Nutrition Facts per serving: 431 cal., 20 g total fat (5 g sat. fat), 77 mg chol., 408 mg sodium, 34 g carbo., 5 g fiber, 31 g pro.
Daily Values: 48% vit. A, 99% vit. C, 2% calcium, 16% iron

super suppers

tangy STIR-FRIED PORK

When fresh kumquats are in season, use them to add flavor and interest to pork tenderloin. Other times of the year, substitute thinly sliced orange.

Start to Finish: 25 minutes
Makes: 4 servings

12 ounces pork tenderloin, cut into ½-inch slices

1 teaspoon cooking oil

¼ cup dry white wine or reduced-sodium chicken broth

6 kumquats, thinly sliced, or ¼ of an orange, thinly sliced

2 tablespoons bottled hoisin sauce

1 green onion, bias-sliced into ¼-inch pieces

1 teaspoon sesame seeds, toasted

2 cups hot cooked brown rice

1 In a wok or large nonstick skillet cook pork in hot oil over medium-high heat for 6 to 8 minutes or until cooked through. Remove from wok or skillet.

2 Add wine, kumquat slices, and hoisin sauce to wok or skillet. Cook and stir for 1 minute.

3 Return pork to wok or skillet. Heat through. Stir in green onion and sesame seeds. Serve over hot cooked rice.

Nutrition Facts per serving: 244 cal., 4 g total fat (1 g sat. fat), 50 mg chol., 126 mg sodium, 26 g carbo., 3 g fiber, 23 g pro.
Daily Values: 3% vit. A, 20% vit. C, 3% calcium, 9% iron

pork DIANE

Worcestershire sauce, Dijon mustard, and a double dose of lemon—fresh lemon juice and lemon-pepper seasoning—add zest to tender pork loin chops.

Start to Finish: 30 minutes
Makes: 4 servings

- **1 tablespoon white wine Worcestershire sauce**
- **1 tablespoon water**
- **1 teaspoon lemon juice**
- **1 teaspoon Dijon-style mustard**
- **4 boneless pork top loin chops, cut ¾ to 1 inch thick**
- **½ to 1 teaspoon lemon-pepper seasoning**
- **2 tablespoons butter or margarine**
- **1 tablespoon snipped fresh chives or parsley**

1 For sauce, in a small bowl stir together Worcestershire sauce, water, lemon juice, and mustard. Set sauce aside.

2 Sprinkle both sides of chops with lemon-pepper seasoning. In a large skillet cook chops in hot butter over medium heat for 8 to 12 minutes or until meat is done (160°F) and juices run clear, turning once. Remove skillet from heat. Transfer chops to a serving platter; keep warm.

3 Pour sauce into skillet. Cook and stir to loosen any browned bits in bottom of skillet. Spoon sauce over chops. Sprinkle with chives.

Nutrition Facts per serving: 178 cal., 11 g total fat (5 g sat. fat), 66 mg chol., 302 mg sodium, 1 g carbo., 0 g fiber, 18 g pro.
Daily Values: 6% vit. A, 2% vit. C, 2% calcium, 4% iron

cranberry PORK CHOPS

For a holiday or everyday dinner, the combination of tart cranberries and succulent pork chops is a winner worth celebrating. Complement this festive main dish with steamed Brussels sprouts and a wild rice mix.

Start to Finish: 30 minutes
Makes: 4 servings

½ **teaspoon pepper**

¼ **teaspoon celery salt**

4 **pork loin chops (about 12 ounces total)**

2 **teaspoons cooking oil**

1 **large onion, thinly sliced and separated into rings**

2 **tablespoons water**

¾ **cup cranberries**

¼ **cup sugar**

3 **tablespoons water**

2 **tablespoons frozen orange juice concentrate, thawed**

1 **teaspoon finely shredded orange peel**

½ **teaspoon ground sage**

¼ **teaspoon salt**

1 In a small bowl stir together pepper and celery salt; rub onto both sides of chops. In a medium skillet heat oil over medium-high heat. Cook chops and onion rings in hot oil until chops are browned, turning once. Carefully add the 2 tablespoons water to skillet. Cover and cook over medium heat for 15 to 20 minutes more or until no pink remains and juices run clear. Transfer chops to serving plates; keep warm. Remove onions from juices with a slotted spoon; set aside.

2 Meanwhile, for the sauce, in a medium saucepan combine the cranberries, sugar, the 3 tablespoons water, the orange juice concentrate, orange peel, sage, and salt. Cook and stir over medium heat about 10 minutes or until the cranberry skins pop and mixture thickens. Stir in the onions; heat through. Remove from heat.

3 To serve, spoon about ¼ cup sauce over each pork chop.

Nutrition facts per serving: 209 cal., 8 g total fat (2 g sat. fat), 38 mg chol., 264 mg sodium, 22 g carbo., 2 g fiber, 13 g pro.
Daily values: 0% vit. A, 31% vit. C, 1% calcium, 5% iron

super suppers

blue cheese 'N' CHOPS

Looking for something impressive to serve guests? Try these herb-rubbed pork chops. Pan-sizzled in their own juices, the chops are then baked along with rice. Fresh pear and blue cheese are the final touch.

Prep: 15 minutes
Bake: 30 minutes
Makes: 4 servings

Nonstick spray coating
2½ **cups cooked brown rice**
4 **green onions, sliced (½ cup)**
⅓ **cup apple juice**
¼ **cup chopped toasted walnuts (optional)**
¼ **teaspoon salt**
⅛ **teaspoon pepper**
1 **teaspoon dried thyme, crushed**
¼ **teaspoon salt**
¼ **to ½ teaspoon pepper**
4 **boneless pork loin chops, cut ½ to ¾ inch thick (about 12 ounces total)**
1 **red pear, cored and chopped**
¼ **cup crumbled blue cheese**

1 Spray a 2-quart square baking dish and a large skillet with nonstick coating; set aside. In a large bowl combine the cooked rice, green onions, 2 tablespoons of the apple juice, the walnuts (if desired), ¼ teaspoon salt, and the ⅛ teaspoon pepper. Spoon rice mixture into prepared baking dish.

2 In a small bowl stir together the thyme, ¼ teaspoon salt, and the ¼ to ½ teaspoon pepper. Rub onto both sides of chops. Cook chops in skillet over medium-high heat until browned, turning once. Arrange browned chops on top of rice mixture. Pour remaining apple juice over chops.

3 Bake, covered, in a 350° oven about 30 minutes or until no pink remains in chops and juices run clear. Transfer chops to serving plates. Stir chopped pear and blue cheese into hot rice mixture; serve with chops.

Nutrition facts per serving: 305 cal., 9 g total fat (5 g sat. fat), 45 mg chol., 416 mg sodium, 38 g carbo., 3 g fiber, 17 g pro.
Daily values: 2% vit. A, 7% vit. C, 3% calcium, 11% iron

onion-glazed PORK

Glazing the onions allows their natural sweetness to come through, forming a perfect partnership with the juicy pork tenderloin. For extra flavor, use a variety of sweet onions such as Maui, Walla Walla, or Vidalia.

Start to Finish: 35 minutes
Makes: 4 servings

1 **12-ounce pork tenderloin**
   Nonstick spray coating
1 **tablespoon olive oil**
2 **medium onions, sliced and separated into rings**
1 **tablespoon brown sugar**
⅓ **cup water**
3 **tablespoons balsamic vinegar or white wine vinegar**
2 **teaspoons cornstarch**
¼ **teaspoon salt**
¼ **teaspoon pepper**
2 **tablespoons snipped parsley**

1 Trim any fat from pork. Cut pork crosswise into ½-inch-thick slices. Spray a large nonstick skillet with nonstick coating. Preheat skillet over medium-high heat. Cook half of the pork in the hot skillet for 3½ to 4 minutes or until pork is slightly pink in the center and the juices run clear, turning once. Remove pork from skillet; keep warm. Repeat with remaining pork.

2 Carefully add oil to skillet; add the onions. Cook, covered, over medium-low heat for 13 to 15 minutes or until onions are tender. Uncover; stir in the brown sugar. Cook and stir over medium-high heat for 4 to 5 minutes or until onions are golden.

3 Meanwhile, in a small bowl stir together water, vinegar, cornstarch, salt, and pepper; carefully stir into onion mixture in skillet. Cook and stir until thickened and bubbly. Cook and stir for 2 minutes more. Return pork to skillet; heat through.

4 To serve, transfer the pork and onion mixture to a serving platter. Sprinkle with parsley.

Nutrition facts per serving: 179 cal., 7 g total fat (2 g sat. fat), 60 mg chol., 182 mg sodium, 10 g carbo., 1 g fiber, 19 g pro.
Daily values: 1% vit. A, 10% vit. C, 1% calcium, 11% iron

super suppers

Flavor Boosters

Many dishes rely on fat and sodium for flavoring, but there are other ways to get great taste without compromising a well-managed diet. Acidic flavors from citrus and vinegars stimulate the taste buds while adding few, if any, calories and no fat. Herbs pack a lot of concentrated punch into a recipe without adding fat and very few calories. When using fresh herbs, snip or mince them and toss them into the final dish just before serving.

peachy PORK TENDERLOIN

Fruit and pork have been a dynamic duet for centuries because of the way the fruit enhances the taste of the pork. This simple, five-ingredient recipe showcases the harmony of these two flavor notes.

Prep: 10 minutes
Marinate: 4 to 24 hours
Grill: 30 minutes
Makes: 4 servings

1 **12-ounce pork tenderloin**

⅓ **cup peach nectar**

3 **tablespoons light teriyaki sauce**

2 **tablespoons snipped fresh rosemary or 2 teaspoons dried rosemary, crushed**

1 **tablespoon olive oil**

① Trim any fat from pork. Place the pork in a plastic bag set in a shallow dish. For the marinade, in a small bowl combine peach nectar, teriyaki sauce, rosemary, and olive oil. Pour over pork. Close bag. Marinate in refrigerator for 4 to 24 hours, turning bag occasionally. Drain the pork, discarding marinade.

② In a grill with a cover arrange preheated coals around a drip pan. Test for medium heat above the pan. Place pork on grill rack directly over the drip pan. Cover and grill about 30 minutes or until no pink remains and the juices run clear.

Nutrition facts per serving: 162 cal., 7 g total fat (2 g sat. fat), 60 mg chol., 285 mg sodium, 6 g carbo., 0 g fiber, 19 g pro.
Daily values: 0% vit. A, 2% vit. C, 1% calcium, 8% iron

super suppers

Lean on Pork

Q: Can pork find a place in a healthful diet?
A: Definitely! Today's pork comes from hogs that are bred to be lean. Also, the visible fat is trimmed more closely from the meat than in the past. In fact, pork compares favorably to the white meat of chicken. A 3-ounce portion of roasted pork tenderloin, for example, has 139 calories and 4 grams of fat. The same portion of roasted chicken (breast meat with no skin) has 142 calories and 3 grams of fat.

spice-rubbed PORK CHOPS

Big, meaty pork chops pair well with full-flavored ingredients. This lime and chili powder marinade is just the ticket. Add more or less of the hot pepper sauce to suit your taste.

Prep: 15 minutes
Marinate: 4 to 24 hours
Broil: 6 minutes
Makes: 4 servings

4 **boneless pork loin chops, cut ½ inch thick (about 1 pound total)**

¼ **cup lime juice**

2 **tablespoons chili powder**

1 **tablespoon olive oil**

1 **clove garlic, minced**

1½ **teaspoons ground cumin**

1½ **teaspoons ground cinnamon**

½ **teaspoon bottled hot pepper sauce**

¼ **teaspoon salt**

① Place chops in a plastic bag set in a shallow dish. For the marinade, in a small bowl stir together the lime juice, chili powder, olive oil, garlic, cumin, cinnamon, hot pepper sauce, and salt. Pour over chops. Close bag. Marinate in refrigerator for 4 to 24 hours, turning the bag occasionally. Drain chops, discarding marinade.

② Place chops on the unheated rack of a broiler pan. Broil 3 to 4 inches from the heat for 6 to 8 minutes or until no pink remains and juices run clear, turning once.

Nutrition facts per serving: 163 cal., 10 g total fat (3 g sat. fat), 51 mg chol., 128 mg sodium, 3 g carbo., 1 g fiber, 17 g pro.
Daily values: 7% vit. A, 7% vit. C, 1% calcium, 10% iron

super suppers

mustard-maple PORK ROAST

Dijon mustard and maple syrup make a wonderful glaze for pork. Let the roast stand for 15 minutes before carving—this allows the temperature to rise to 160°F and makes the roast easier to slice.

Prep: 20 minutes
Roast: 1½ hours
Stand: 15 minutes
Oven: 325°F
Makes: 8 to 10 servings

1 **2- to 2½-pound boneless pork loin roast (single loin)**

2 **tablespoons Dijon-style mustard**

1 **tablespoon maple-flavor syrup**

2 **teaspoons dried sage, crushed**

1 **teaspoon finely shredded orange peel**

¼ **teaspoon salt**

¼ **teaspoon black pepper**

20 **to 24 tiny new potatoes (about 1¾ pounds)**

16 **ounces packaged, peeled baby carrots**

1 **tablespoon olive oil**

¼ **teaspoon salt**

① Trim fat from meat. Stir together mustard, syrup, sage, orange peel, the ¼ teaspoon salt, and the pepper. Spoon mixture onto meat. Place roast fat side up on a rack in a shallow roasting pan. Insert a meat thermometer. Roast, uncovered, in a 325° oven for 45 minutes.

② Meanwhile, peel a strip of skin from the center of each potato. Cook potatoes in boiling salted water for 5 minutes. Add carrots; cook 5 minutes more. Drain.

③ Toss together potatoes, carrots, olive oil, and ¼ teaspoon salt. Place in roasting pan around pork roast. Roast, uncovered, for 45 minutes to 1 hour more or until meat thermometer registers 155°F. Cover with foil and let stand for 15 minutes. (The meat's temperature will rise 5°F while it stands.)

Nutrition Facts per serving: 281 cal., 10 g total fat (3 g sat. fat), 51 mg chol., 309 mg sodium, 29 g carbo., 3 g fiber, 19 g pro.
Daily Values: 128% vit. A, 24% vit. C, 3% calcium, 17% iron

super suppers

153

jamaican pork WITH MELON

You'll find jerk seasoning in the spice aisle of the supermarket or in food specialty shops. You can also sprinkle it on skinless, boneless chicken breast halves before grilling.

Prep: 15 minutes
Grill: 12 minutes
Makes: 4 servings

1 **cup chopped honeydew melon**

1 **cup chopped cantaloupe**

1 **tablespoon snipped fresh mint**

1 **tablespoon honey**

4 **teaspoons Jamaican jerk seasoning**

4 **boneless pork top loin chops, cut ¾ to 1 inch thick**

Star anise (optional)

Fresh mint sprigs (optional)

1 For salsa, in a medium bowl combine honeydew, cantaloupe, snipped mint, and honey. Cover and chill until ready to serve or for up to 8 hours.

2 Sprinkle Jamaican jerk seasoning evenly over both sides of each chop; rub in with your fingers. For a charcoal grill, place chops on the rack of an uncovered grill directly over medium coals. Grill for 12 to 15 minutes or until meat juices run clear (160°F), turning once halfway through grilling. (For a gas grill, preheat grill. Reduce heat to medium. Place chops on grill rack over heat. Cover and grill as above.) Serve salsa with chops. If desired, garnish with star anise and/or mint sprigs.

Nutrition Facts per serving: 240 cal., 7 g total fat (2 g sat. fat), 77 mg chol., 366 mg sodium, 12 g carbo., 1 g fiber, 31 g pro.
Daily Values: 26% vit. A, 48% vit. C, 3% calcium, 7% iron

super suppers

154

margarita-glazed PORK CHOPS

You can use tequila or fresh lime juice to make the marinade. Either way the taste is reminiscent of Mexico's most beloved cocktail, the margarita.

Prep: 10 minutes
Grill: 12 minutes
Makes: 8 servings

8   boneless pork top loin chops, cut 1 inch thick (about 3 pounds total)

⅔ cup sugar-free orange marmalade

2   fresh jalapeño peppers, seeded and finely chopped*

¼ cup tequila or lime juice

2   teaspoons grated fresh ginger or 1 teaspoon ground ginger

Snipped fresh cilantro

Lime and orange wedges (optional)

1 Trim fat from the pork chops. For glaze, in a small bowl stir together orange marmalade, jalapeño peppers, tequila, and ginger.

2 For a charcoal grill, place chops on the rack of an uncovered grill directly over medium coals. Grill for 12 to 15 minutes or until meat juices run clear (160°F), turning once halfway through grilling and brushing frequently with glaze during the last 5 minutes of grilling. (For a gas grill, preheat grill. Reduce heat to medium. Place chops on grill rack over heat. Cover and grill as above.)

3 To serve, sprinkle with cilantro. If desired, garnish with lime and orange wedges.

*Note: Because chile peppers, such as jalapeños, contain volatile oils that can burn your skin and eyes, avoid direct contact with them as much as possible. When working with chile peppers, wear plastic or rubber gloves. If your bare hands do touch the chile peppers, wash your hands and nails well with soap and warm water.

Nutrition Facts per serving: 281 cal., 9 g total fat (3 g sat. fat), 93 mg chol., 62 mg sodium, 7 g carbo., 0 g fiber, 38 g pro.
Daily Values: 1% vit. A, 4% vit. C, 3% calcium, 7% iron

pork WITH PEACHY SALSA

Sliding the pork tenderloin slices onto skewers makes them easier to turn.

Prep: 30 minutes
Grill: 20 minutes
Makes: 6 servings

½ **cup chopped, peeled peaches
or unpeeled nectarines**

½ **cup chopped, seeded
cucumber**

⅓ **cup salsa**

1 **tablespoon snipped fresh
cilantro or parsley**

12 **slices bacon**

1½ **pounds pork tenderloin
(2 tenderloins)**

① For salsa, in a medium bowl combine peaches, cucumber, salsa, and cilantro. Toss gently. Cover and chill for up to 2 days or until serving time.

② In a large skillet over medium heat partially cook bacon. Bias-cut pork tenderloin into 1½-inch slices. Wrap a slice of bacon around each piece of pork. If desired, fasten bacon to meat with wooden toothpicks. Thread wrapped meat onto skewers.

③ For a charcoal grill, in a grill with a cover arrange medium-hot coals around a drip pan. Test for medium heat above pan. Place kabobs on grill rack directly over drip pan. Cover and grill for 20 to 22 minutes or until meat juices run clear (160°F), turning once. (For a gas grill, preheat grill. Reduce heat to medium. Place kabobs on grill rack over heat. Cover and grill as above.)

④ Remove meat from skewers. Serve with salsa.

Nutrition Facts per serving: 235 cal., 11 g total fat (4 g sat. fat), 87 mg chol., 338 mg sodium, 2 g carbo., 0 g fiber, 29 g pro.
Daily Values: 4% vit. A, 6% vit. C, 1% calcium, 8% iron

super suppers

pork with pear STUFFING

This dish is both elegant and easy to prepare. The stuffing makes a swirl of color in each slice and provides a sweet, nutty counterpoint to the tender pork.

Prep: 20 minutes
Roast: 35 minutes
Oven: 425°F
Makes: 4 servings

½ **cup chopped pear**

¼ **cup chopped hazelnuts (filberts) or almonds, toasted**

¼ **cup finely shredded carrot**

¼ **cup soft bread crumbs**

2 **tablespoons chopped onion**

1 **teaspoon grated fresh ginger**

¼ **teaspoon salt**

¼ **teaspoon black pepper**

1 **12-ounce pork tenderloin**

1 **teaspoon cooking oil**

2 **tablespoons sugar-free orange marmalade**

❶ For stuffing, in a small bowl combine pear, nuts, carrot, bread crumbs, onion, ginger, salt, and black pepper; set aside.

❷ Trim any fat from meat. Butterfly meat by making a lengthwise slit down the center to within ½ inch of the underside. Open flat; pound with the flat side of a meat mallet to about ¼-inch thickness.

❸ Spread stuffing over meat. Fold in ends. Starting from a long side, roll up meat. Secure with 100-percent-cotton string or wooden toothpicks. Place meat roll on a rack in a shallow roasting pan. Brush lightly with oil. Insert a meat thermometer into center of meat.

❹ Roast in a 425° oven for 30 to 40 minutes or until meat thermometer registers 155°F. Brush orange marmalade over top of meat. Roast about 5 minutes more or until meat thermometer registers 160°F.

Nutrition Facts per serving: 191 cal., 9 g total fat (1 g sat. fat), 55 mg chol., 193 mg sodium, 9 g carbo., 2 g fiber, 20 g pro.
Daily Values: 43% vit. A, 5% vit. C, 2% calcium, 9% iron

super suppers

Using Ginger

Often used in Asian cooking, fresh ginger adds a slightly peppery flavor to any kind of food. When buying ginger, look for pieces that are firm and mold-free. Once home simply pop it in the fridge where it will last two to three weeks, or freeze it to keep indefinitely. To use ginger, peel it first (no need to thaw if frozen), then slice, grate, mince, or julienne it. If you like a strong ginger flavor, add it near the end of cooking. For milder flavor add it near the beginning.

german-style CHICKEN

Germany's most famous mustard took its name from one of Germany's most famous cities—Düsseldorf. It's a dark, mild ingredient that harmonizes with the other flavors in this dish.

Prep: 5 minutes
Bake: 45 minutes
Oven: 375°F
Makes: 4 servings

- **4 medium chicken breast halves (2 pounds)**
- **¼ cup Düsseldorf or horseradish mustard**
- **2 tablespoons dry sherry**
- **½ teaspoon sweet Hungarian paprika or ¼ teaspoon hot Hungarian paprika**
- **½ cup soft rye bread crumbs**

1 Skin chicken breasts. In a small bowl combine mustard, sherry, and paprika. Brush 2 tablespoons of the mustard mixture evenly over top of chicken. Place chicken mustard side up in a 3-quart rectangular baking dish. Sprinkle with bread crumbs, patting lightly.

2 Bake, uncovered, in a 375° oven for 45 to 50 minutes or until chicken is no longer pink (170°F). Serve with remaining mustard mixture.

Nutrition Facts per serving: 232 cal., 9 g total fat (2 g sat. fat), 83 mg chol., 306 mg sodium, 4 g carbo., 0 g fiber, 31 g pro.
Daily Values: 4% vit. A, 3% calcium, 10% iron

super suppers

asian CHICKEN AND VEGGIES

Five-spice powder, a blend available on the grocery shelf, and a bottled cooking sauce give budget chicken pieces an Asian flair.

Prep: 10 minutes
Bake: 40 minutes
Oven: 400°F
Makes: 4 servings

- **8 chicken drumsticks and/or thighs, skinned (2 pounds)**
- **1 tablespoon cooking oil**
- **1½ teaspoons five-spice powder**
- **⅓ cup bottled plum sauce or sweet-and-sour sauce**
- **1 14-ounce package frozen loose-pack baby whole potatoes, broccoli, carrots, baby corn, and red pepper mix or one 16-ounce package frozen stir-fry vegetables (any combination)**

1 Arrange chicken pieces in a 13×9×2-inch baking pan, making sure pieces don't touch. Brush chicken pieces with cooking oil; sprinkle with 1 teaspoon of the five-spice powder. Bake, uncovered, in a 400° oven for 25 minutes.

2 Meanwhile, in a large bowl combine remaining ½ teaspoon five-spice powder and plum sauce. Add frozen vegetables; toss to coat.

3 Move chicken pieces to one side of the baking pan. Add vegetable mixture to the other side of the pan. Bake for 15 to 20 minutes more or until chicken is no longer pink (180°F), stirring vegetables once during baking. Using a slotted spoon, transfer chicken and vegetables to a serving platter.

Nutrition Facts per serving: 277 cal., 9 g total fat (2 g sat. fat), 98 mg chol., 124 mg sodium, 21 g carbo., 2 g fiber, 30 g pro.
Daily Values: 21% vit. A, 19% vit. C, 5% calcium, 11% iron

super suppers

chicken-broccoli STIR-FRY

Thirty minutes to a fresh, hot, homemade stir-fry—that beats takeout any day. Seasoned with hoisin sauce and sesame oil, this stir-fry isn't missing a thing.

Start to Finish: 30 minutes
Makes: 4 servings

½ **cup water**

2 **tablespoons soy sauce**

2 **tablespoons hoisin sauce**

2 **teaspoons cornstarch**

1 **teaspoon grated fresh ginger**

1 **teaspoon toasted sesame oil**

1 **pound broccoli**

1 **yellow sweet pepper**

2 **tablespoons cooking oil**

12 **ounces skinless, boneless chicken breasts or thighs, cut into bite-size pieces**

2 **cups chow mein noodles or hot cooked rice**

1 For sauce, in a small bowl stir together the water, soy sauce, hoisin sauce, cornstarch, ginger, and sesame oil. Set aside.

2 Cut florets from broccoli stems and separate florets into small pieces. Cut broccoli stems crosswise into ¼-inch slices. Cut pepper into short, thin strips.

3 In a wok or large skillet heat 1 tablespoon of the cooking oil over medium-high heat. Cook and stir broccoli stems in hot oil for 1 minute. Add broccoli florets and sweet pepper; cook and stir for 3 to 4 minutes or until crisp-tender. Remove from wok; set aside.

4 Add remaining oil to wok or skillet. Add chicken; cook and stir for 2 to 3 minutes or until no longer pink. Push chicken from center of wok. Stir sauce; pour into center of wok. Cook and stir until thickened and bubbly. Return cooked vegetables to wok; stir to coat with sauce. Cook and stir 1 minute more or until heated through. Serve with chow mein noodles.

Nutrition Facts per serving: 378 cal., 16 g total fat (3 g sat. fat), 49 mg chol., 877 mg sodium, 31 g carbo., 6 g fiber, 29 g pro.
Daily Values: 18% vit. A, 272% vit. C, 8% calcium, 13% iron

super suppers

162

keys-style citrus CHICKEN

The sunshine-inspired cooking of the Florida Keys draws on the best of both island and mainland. Here it combines fresh Florida citrus with the Caribbean penchant for fiery peppers.

Start to Finish: 20 minutes
Makes: 4 servings

4 medium skinless, boneless chicken breast halves (1 pound)

2 or 3 cloves garlic, peeled and thinly sliced

1 tablespoon butter or margarine

1 teaspoon finely shredded lime peel

2 tablespoons lime juice

¼ teaspoon ground ginger

⅛ teaspoon crushed red pepper

1 orange

1 In a large skillet cook chicken and garlic in butter over medium heat for 8 to 10 minutes or until chicken is no longer pink (170°F), turning chicken once and stirring garlic occasionally.

2 Meanwhile, in a small bowl combine lime peel, lime juice, ginger, and red pepper; set aside. Peel orange. Reserving juice, cut orange in half lengthwise, then cut crosswise into slices. Add reserved orange juice and the lime juice mixture to skillet. Place orange slices on top of chicken. Cover and cook for 1 to 2 minutes more or until heated through.

3 To serve, spoon any reserved drippings over chicken.

Nutrition Facts per serving: 202 cal., 5 g total fat (2 g sat. fat), 90 mg chol., 105 mg sodium, 5 g carbo., 1 g fiber, 33 g pro.
Daily Values: 4% vit. A, 37% vit. C, 3% calcium, 6% iron

Maximize Your Iron

The mineral iron carries oxygen throughout the body. It's primarily found in beef and other meats, as well as fortified breads and cereals. Vitamin C enhances iron absorption. So be sure to eat foods high in iron with foods high in vitamin C. In addition to oranges and orange juice, vitamin C is found in red peppers, strawberries, kiwifruits, and potatoes.

super suppers

163

chicken WITH WHITE BEANS

White kidney beans, also called cannellini beans, are popular in the Tuscany region of Italy. As American chefs become increasingly interested in Tuscan cooking, the beans are becoming much loved stateside too.

Start to Finish: 35 minutes
Makes: 6 servings

- 6 **skinless, boneless chicken thighs (1 pound)**
- 1 **tablespoon olive oil or cooking oil**
- ½ **cup dry white wine or water**
- 1 **teaspoon instant chicken bouillon granules**
- 2 **cloves garlic, minced**
- 1 **teaspoon dried oregano, crushed**
- ¾ **teaspoon dried thyme, crushed**
- ½ **teaspoon dried savory, crushed**
- ⅛ **teaspoon black pepper**
- 1 **pound banana, buttercup, or butternut squash, peeled, seeded, and cut into ½-inch pieces (about 2½ cups)**
- 1 **15-ounce can white kidney (cannellini) beans, rinsed and drained**
- 1 **14½-ounce can diced tomatoes, undrained**
- 2 **tablespoons snipped fresh parsley**

  Fresh parsley sprig (optional)

1 In a large skillet cook chicken in hot oil over medium-high heat until light brown, turning to brown evenly. Remove chicken from skillet. Drain off fat.

2 Add wine, bouillon granules, and garlic to skillet. Bring to boiling; reduce heat. Boil gently, uncovered, 3 minutes or until liquid is reduced by about half, scraping up any crusty browned bits from bottom of skillet.

3 Stir in oregano, thyme, savory, and pepper. Return chicken to skillet. Add squash. Bring to boiling; reduce heat. Cover and simmer for 15 to 20 minutes or until chicken is no longer pink (180°F) and squash is nearly tender. Stir in beans and undrained tomatoes. Simmer, uncovered, about 5 minutes more or until bean mixture is slightly thickened.

4 To serve, spoon the bean mixture into shallow bowls. Place chicken on top of bean mixture. Sprinkle with parsley. If desired, garnish with fresh parsley sprig.

Nutrition Facts per serving: 219 cal., 6 g total fat (1 g sat. fat), 60 mg chol., 462 mg sodium, 21 g carbo., 5 g fiber, 21 g pro.
Daily Values: 62% vit. A, 34% vit. C, 19% calcium, 16% iron

super suppers

pesto chicken AND SQUASH

Purchased pesto simplifies the preparation here. Look for jars of pesto near the spaghetti sauce in your grocery store.

Start to Finish: 20 minutes
Makes: 4 servings

- 4 skinless, boneless chicken breast halves (1 pound)
- 1 tablespoon olive oil
- 2 cups finely chopped yellow summer squash or zucchini
- 2 tablespoons purchased basil pesto
- 2 tablespoons finely shredded Asiago or Parmesan cheese

① In a large nonstick skillet cook chicken in hot oil over medium heat for 6 minutes.

② Turn chicken; add squash. Cook for 6 to 9 minutes more or until the chicken is no longer pink (170°F) and squash is crisp-tender, stirring squash gently once or twice. Transfer chicken and squash to 4 dinner plates. Spread pesto over chicken; sprinkle with cheese.

Nutrition Facts per serving: 186 cal., 10 g total fat (2 g sat. fat), 55 mg chol., 129 mg sodium, 2 g carbo., 1 g fiber, 23 g pro.
Daily Values: 4% vit. A, 10% vit. C, 7% calcium, 5% iron

fettuccine and SWEET PEPPERS

To make Romano cheese shavings, firmly pull a vegetable peeler or a cheese shaver over the edge of a block of Romano.

Start to Finish: 25 minutes
Makes: 4 servings

½ **cup chicken broth**

1 **teaspoon cornstarch**

1 **16-ounce package frozen sweet pepper stir-fry vegetables (yellow, green, and red sweet peppers and onion)**

1 **9-ounce package refrigerated fettuccine or linguine**

1 **tablespoon olive oil**

12 **ounces skinless, boneless chicken breasts, cut into bite-size pieces**

4 **cloves garlic, minced**

¼ **to ½ teaspoon crushed red pepper**

½ **cup chopped tomatoes**

¼ **cup snipped fresh basil**
Shaved Romano cheese

① In a small bowl stir together chicken broth and cornstarch; set aside.

② Bring a Dutch oven of salted water to boiling. Add frozen pepper mixture and pasta. Return to boiling and cook for 2 minutes or just until pasta is tender. Drain and return to Dutch oven. Toss with 1 teaspoon of the oil. Keep pasta warm.

③ Meanwhile, in a large skillet cook chicken, garlic, and crushed red pepper in remaining oil over medium-high heat for 2 to 3 minutes or until chicken is no longer pink, stirring often. Push chicken to side of skillet. Stir cornstarch mixture; add to center of skillet. Cook and stir until thickened and bubbly. Cook and stir for 2 minutes more. Stir in chicken to coat with sauce.

④ Remove chicken and sauce from heat; toss with cooked pasta mixture, tomatoes, and basil. Serve topped with shaved Romano cheese.

Nutrition Facts per serving: 397 cal., 9 g total fat (2 g sat. fat), 118 mg chol., 309 mg sodium, 44 g carbo., 5 g fiber, 33 g pro.
Daily Values: 25% vit. A, 38% vit. C, 11% calcium, 19% iron

Sweet Nutrition

As with most vegetables, sweet peppers are very low in calories and contain virtually no fat or salt. Available in a rainbow of colors including red, green, yellow, orange, and purple, they are loaded with nutrition. Each color represents a different set of phytochemicals such as anthocyanins, lutein, and lycopene. Put them all together and you have a mixture that can help lower the risk of some cancers, improve heart health, and help maintain eye health, memory, and urinary tract health.

cilantro chicken WITH NUTS

Served over shredded cabbage, this fabulous chicken dish is like a main-dish salad. Substitute rice if you want a more traditional Asian flavor.

Start to Finish: 25 minutes
Makes: 4 servings

1　pound skinless, boneless chicken breasts, cut into 1-inch strips

2　teaspoons roasted peanut oil

1　ounce honey-roasted peanuts

1　tablespoon soy sauce

2　teaspoons rice vinegar

1　teaspoon toasted sesame oil

1　cup fresh cilantro leaves

4　cups finely shredded napa cabbage or 2 cups hot cooked rice

　　Fresh cilantro sprigs (optional)

　　Lime wedges (optional)

1 In a heavy 10-inch skillet cook and stir chicken in hot peanut oil over high heat for 2 minutes. Add peanuts. Cook and stir for 3 minutes more or until chicken is no longer pink.

2 Add soy sauce, vinegar, and sesame oil. Cook and stir for 2 minutes more. Remove from heat. Stir in cilantro leaves.

3 To serve, spoon chicken mixture over cabbage or rice. If desired, garnish with cilantro sprigs and lime wedges.

Nutrition Facts per serving: 254 cal., 8 g total fat (1 g sat. fat), 49 mg chol., 322 mg sodium, 20 g carbo., 4 g fiber, 25 g pro.
Daily Values: 78% vit. A, 98% vit. C, 9% calcium, 13% iron

garlic-clove CHICKEN

Cooking garlic within the clove's casing imparts only a mild garlic flavor to foods cooked with it. That's why you'll never believe 25 cloves are used here.

Prep: 20 minutes
Bake: 45 minutes
Oven: 325°F
Makes: 4 servings

Nonstick cooking spray

2 **to 2½ pounds meaty chicken pieces (breasts, thighs, and drumsticks), skinned**

25 **cloves garlic (about ½ cup or 2 to 3 bulbs)**

¼ **cup dry white wine**

Salt

Cayenne pepper

① Lightly coat a large skillet with nonstick cooking spray. Heat skillet over medium heat. Add chicken and cook for 10 minutes, turning to brown evenly. Place chicken in a 2-quart square baking dish. Add unpeeled garlic cloves. Pour wine over chicken. Lightly sprinkle chicken with salt and cayenne pepper.

② Bake, covered, in a 325° oven for 45 to 50 minutes or until chicken is no longer pink (170°F for breasts, 180°F for thighs and drumsticks).

Nutrition Facts per serving: 194 cal., 3 g total fat (1 g sat. fat), 96 mg chol., 232 mg sodium, 6 g carbo., 0 g fiber, 31 g pro.
Daily Values: 1% vit. A, 14% vit. C, 5% calcium, 8% iron

roast tarragon CHICKEN

Tarragon's bold, aniselike flavor complements the sweetness of the roasted tomatoes and onions. You can also use rosemary or thyme.

Prep: 15 minutes
Roast: 45 minutes
Oven: 375°F
Makes: 6 servings

- **3 tablespoons olive oil**
- **2½ teaspoons dried tarragon, crushed**
- **2 cloves garlic, minced**
- **½ teaspoon coarsely ground black pepper**
- **¼ teaspoon salt**
- **1 pound cherry tomatoes**
- **8 small shallots**
- **2½ to 3 pounds meaty chicken pieces (breasts, thighs, and drumsticks)**

1 In a medium bowl stir together olive oil, tarragon, garlic, pepper, and salt. Add tomatoes and shallots; toss gently to coat. Use a slotted spoon to remove tomatoes and shallots from bowl, reserving the olive oil mixture.

2 If desired, skin chicken. Place chicken in a shallow roasting pan. Brush chicken with the reserved olive oil mixture.

3 Roast chicken in a 375° oven for 20 minutes. Add shallots; roast for 15 minutes. Add tomatoes; roast for 10 to 12 minutes more or until chicken is no longer pink (170°F for breasts; 180°F for thighs and drumsticks) and vegetables are tender.

Nutrition Facts per serving: 266 cal., 17 g total fat (4 g sat. fat), 66 mg chol., 166 mg sodium, 6 g carbo., 1 g fiber, 21 g pro.
Daily Values: 12% vit. A, 24% vit. C, 2% calcium, 8% iron

Roasting Vegetables

Finding ways to enhance foods' natural flavor in lieu of adding fat, salt, and sugar makes healthy eating easy. Roasting vegetables is only one of the ways to do this. Roasting (cooking with a high, dry heat) brings out the natural sugars in vegetables and concentrates their flavors. The natural flavor of the vegetables is good, but you can add any combination of dried herbs for variety.

super suppers

pizza WITH RED PEPPER SAUCE

Queso fresco's mild, salty flavor fares well as a topper for this chicken-and-roasted-pepper pizza.

Prep: 30 minutes
Bake: 10 minutes
Oven: 425°F
Makes: 6 servings

Nonstick cooking spray

2 **medium red sweet peppers**

1 **Anaheim pepper**

1 **tablespoon olive oil**

1 **clove garlic, cut up**

½ **teaspoon salt**

½ **teaspoon crushed cumin
   seeds**

1 **12-inch Italian bread shell**

6 **ounces coarsely shredded
   deli-roasted or rotisserie
   chicken (about 2 cups)**

2 **green onions, sliced**

2 **ounces crumbled or shredded
   queso fresco and/or
   Monterey Jack cheese
   (about ½ cup)**

3 **tablespoons dairy sour cream**

¼ **cup fresh cilantro leaves**

1 **small avocado, halved,
   seeded, peeled, and thinly
   sliced (optional)**

1 **serrano pepper or jalapeño
   pepper, thinly sliced
   (optional)**

① Line a baking sheet with foil; lightly coat foil with nonstick cooking spray. Set baking sheet aside. Cut sweet peppers and Anaheim pepper in half lengthwise. Remove seeds and membranes. Place pepper halves cut side down on prepared baking sheet. Roast in a 425° oven for 20 minutes or until skins are blistered. Wrap pepper halves in the foil; let stand for 10 minutes to steam. Peel and discard pepper skins. Coarsely chop peppers.

② In a blender container or food processor bowl combine peppers, oil, garlic, salt, and cumin seeds. Cover and blend or process until smooth. (Store sauce in a covered container in the refrigerator for up to 10 days.)

③ Place bread shell on a preheated baking stone or 12-inch pizza pan. Spread with the red pepper sauce. Bake in the 425° oven for 5 minutes. Top with chicken, green onions, and cheese. Bake 5 minutes more. Top with sour cream, cilantro, and, if desired, avocado and sliced pepper.

Nutrition Facts per serving: 299 cal., 9 g total fat (2 g sat. fat), 28 mg chol., 642 mg sodium, 38 g carbo., 1 g fiber, 18 g pro.
Daily Values: 60% vit. A, 190% vit. C, 16% calcium, 6% iron

super suppers

tortilla-crusted CHICKEN

Crushed tortillas make an irresistible coating for oven-fried chicken. Although chips have a reputation for being high in fat and calories, they lend lots of flavor and crunch, so you need to use only a few.

Prep: 10 minutes
Bake: 25 minutes
Oven: 375°F
Makes: 4 servings

Nonstick cooking spray

1 **cup finely crushed tortilla chips**

½ **teaspoon dried oregano, crushed**

¼ **teaspoon ground cumin**

¼ **teaspoon black pepper**

1 **egg**

4 **skinless, boneless chicken breast halves (1 pound)**

Salsa (optional)

1 Coat a 15×10×1-inch baking pan with nonstick cooking spray; set aside. In a shallow dish combine tortilla chips, oregano, cumin, and pepper. Place the egg in another shallow dish; beat slightly. Dip chicken in beaten egg and coat with tortilla chip mixture.

2 Arrange chicken in the prepared baking pan. Bake in a 375° oven about 25 minutes or until chicken is no longer pink (170°F). If desired, serve the chicken with salsa.

Nutrition Facts per serving: 305 cal., 10 g total fat (2 g sat. fat), 135 mg chol., 225 mg sodium, 16 g carbo., 2 g fiber, 36 g pro.
Daily Values: 3% vit. A, 2% vit. C, 7% calcium, 9% iron

super suppers

Turn Up the Heat with Salsa

Salsa is a lot more than a low-fat dip for chips or vegetables. There are countless varieties of salsa, each with its own unique flavor. In addition to the classic tomato–hot pepper salsa, you can try roasted corn, fruit, tomatillo, and many, many others. Adjust the heat level by carefully selecting the kind and amount of hot peppers you use. Consider using salsas as spreads on sandwiches, as garnishes for chicken or pork, or to add flavor to soups.

chicken with MOZZARELLA

This recipe requires that you pound the chicken breasts to flatten them, but take care not to pound them so hard that you tear the flesh, making holes through which the delicious filling can escape.

Prep: 40 minutes
Bake: 25 minutes
Oven: 400°F
Makes: 6 servings

- **6** skinless, boneless chicken breast halves (1½ pounds)
- Salt
- Black pepper
- **¼** cup finely chopped shallots or onion
- **1** clove garlic, minced
- **2** teaspoons olive oil
- **½** of a 10-ounce package frozen chopped spinach, thawed and well drained
- **3** tablespoons pine nuts or walnuts, toasted
- **¾** cup shredded smoked mozzarella cheese (3 ounces)
- **¼** cup seasoned fine dry bread crumbs
- **¼** cup grated Parmesan cheese
- **1** tablespoon olive oil

1 Place 1 chicken breast half between 2 pieces of plastic wrap. Pound lightly with the flat side of a meat mallet into a rectangle about ⅛ inch thick. Remove plastic wrap. Season with salt and pepper. Repeat with remaining chicken breasts.

2 For filling, in a medium skillet cook shallots and garlic in the 2 teaspoons hot oil until tender. Remove from heat; stir in spinach, nuts, and smoked mozzarella. In a shallow bowl combine bread crumbs and Parmesan cheese.

3 Place 2 to 3 tablespoons of filling on each chicken breast. Fold in the bottom and sides; then roll up. Secure with wooden toothpicks.

4 Lightly brush each roll with the 1 tablespoon olive oil; coat with bread crumb mixture. Place rolls seam side down in a shallow baking pan. Bake, uncovered, in a 400° oven about 25 minutes or until chicken is no longer pink (170°F). Remove toothpicks before serving.

Nutrition Facts per serving: 274 cal., 11 g total fat (3 g sat. fat), 77 mg chol., 368 mg sodium, 6 g carbo., 1 g fiber, 35 g pro.
Daily Values: 39% vit. A, 6% vit. C, 18% calcium, 8% iron

super suppers

pesto-stuffed CHICKEN

Fresh sorrel, a sour-tasting herb, looks like thin spinach. Remove any thick stems from the sorrel and spinach before making the homemade pesto. If sorrel isn't available, fill in with extra spinach.

Prep: 30 minutes
Bake: 25 minutes
Makes: 4 servings

1 recipe Sorrel Pesto

4 skinless, boneless chicken breast halves (about 1 pound total)

8 teaspoons soft goat cheese (chèvre)

Black pepper

Nonstick spray coating

1 7¼-ounce jar roasted red sweet peppers, drained and chopped (about 1 cup)

½ cup frozen artichoke hearts, thawed and chopped

2 teaspoons snipped fresh oregano or thyme

1 Prepare Sorrel Pesto. Rinse chicken; pat dry. Place one chicken breast half between 2 pieces of plastic wrap. Pound chicken lightly into a ⅛-inch-thick rectangle. Remove plastic wrap. Spread breast with 1 tablespoon of Sorrel Pesto and 2 teaspoons of goat cheese. Fold in long sides of chicken; roll up from short end. Secure with toothpicks. Season with pepper. Repeat with remaining chicken, pesto, and goat cheese.

2 Spray a large skillet and a 2-quart square baking dish with nonstick coating; set dish aside. Preheat skillet over medium heat. Place the chicken rolls in hot skillet, turning to brown evenly. Transfer browned chicken rolls to prepared baking dish. Bake in a 375° oven for 25 to 30 minutes or until chicken is tender and no longer pink.

3 Meanwhile, in a small saucepan combine roasted peppers, artichokes, and oregano or thyme. Cook and stir over medium heat until heated through. Serve over chicken.

Sorrel Pesto: In food processor bowl combine 1 cup firmly packed torn spinach leaves; ½ cup firmly packed torn sorrel leaves; 1 clove garlic, quartered; and ¼ cup finely shredded Asiago cheese. Cover; process with several on-off turns until a paste forms, stopping machine several times to scrape down sides. Combine 1 tablespoon walnut oil or olive oil and 1 tablespoon water. With machine running, gradually add oil mixture; process to consistency of soft butter. Reserve ¼ cup of pesto mixture. Cover and store remaining pesto in refrigerator for later use.

Nutrition facts per serving: 200 cal., 9 g total fat (3 g sat. fat), 70 mg chol., 164 mg sodium, 5 g carbo., 2 g fiber, 25 g pro.
Daily values: 27% vit. A, 178% vit. C, 4% calcium, 12% iron

super suppers

fruit & CHICKEN KABOBS

Bring the fresh style and bold flavors of the Caribbean to your backyard grill with these easy fruit-and-chicken kabobs, steeped in a sweet-and-fiery marinade.

Prep: 30 minutes
Marinate: 4 hours
Grill: 15 minutes
Makes: 4 servings

1 **pound skinless, boneless chicken breasts**

3 **tablespoons reduced-sodium soy sauce**

4 **teaspoons honey**

4 **teaspoons red wine vinegar**

½ **teaspoon curry powder**

½ **teaspoon ground allspice**

¼ **teaspoon bottled hot pepper sauce**

1 **medium red onion, cut into 1-inch wedges**

1 **nectarine, seeded and cut into 1-inch pieces, or 1 papaya, peeled, seeded, and cut into 1-inch pieces**

2 **cups hot cooked couscous or rice**

1 Rinse chicken; pat dry. Cut chicken into 1-inch pieces. Place chicken in a plastic bag set in a shallow dish. For marinade, in a small bowl stir together soy sauce, honey, vinegar, curry powder, allspice, and hot pepper sauce. Pour over chicken. Close the bag. Marinate chicken in the refrigerator for 4 hours, turning bag occasionally. Remove chicken from marinade, reserving the marinade.

2 In a saucepan cook the onion in a small amount of boiling water for 3 minutes; drain. Thread the chicken, nectarine or papaya pieces, and partially cooked onion alternately onto eight 6-inch metal skewers.

3 Grill the kabobs on the rack of an uncovered grill directly over medium-hot coals about 15 minutes or until chicken is tender and no longer pink, turning skewers occasionally. Place reserved marinade in a small saucepan. Bring to boiling. Cook, uncovered, for 1 minute. Pour marinade through a strainer, reserving liquid.

4 Before serving, brush kabobs with the strained marinade. Serve kabobs with hot cooked couscous or rice. Pass any remaining marinade.

Nutrition facts per serving: 374 cal., 4 g total fat (1 g sat. fat), 59 mg chol., 462 mg sodium, 54 g carbo., 9 g fiber, 30 g pro.
Daily values: 7% vit. A, 37% vit. C, 3% calcium, 12% iron

super suppers

177

italian CHICKEN

This dish contains all the best ingredients Italy has to offer—black olives, capers, garlic, basil, wine, olive oil, and tomatoes. Served with a salad and warm crusty bread, it's a memorable taste of Italy from your own kitchen.

Start to Finish: 40 minutes
Makes: 4 servings

- 4 skinless, boneless chicken breast halves (about 1 pound total)
- 2 tablespoons olive oil
- 1 large onion, halved and thinly sliced
- 2 cloves garlic, minced
- 3 large tomatoes, coarsely chopped
- ¼ cup Greek black olives or ripe olives, pitted and sliced
- 1 tablespoon capers, drained
- ¼ teaspoon salt
- ⅛ teaspoon pepper
- ¼ cup dry red wine or reduced-sodium chicken broth
- 2 teaspoons cornstarch
- ¼ cup snipped fresh basil
- 2 cups hot cooked couscous

❶ Rinse chicken; pat dry. In a large skillet heat 1 tablespoon of the olive oil over medium-high heat. Add chicken; cook for 4 to 5 minutes on each side or until chicken is tender and no longer pink. Remove from pan and keep warm.

❷ For sauce, add the remaining olive oil, onion, and garlic to hot skillet. Cook and stir for 2 minutes. Add the tomatoes, olives, capers, salt, and pepper to skillet. Bring to boiling; reduce heat. Simmer, covered, for 3 minutes. Stir together the wine or broth and cornstarch; add to the skillet. Cook and stir until thickened and bubbly. Cook and stir for 2 minutes more. Stir in basil. Pour sauce over chicken. Serve with couscous.

Nutrition facts per serving: 319 cal., 8 g total fat (2 g sat. fat), 59 mg chol., 289 mg sodium, 32 g carbo., 7 g fiber, 27 g pro.
Daily values: 8% vit. A, 42% vit. C, 3% calcium, 12% iron

super suppers

moroccan CHICKEN

The mystique of North Africa is captured in richly flavored recipes such as this one, which are abundant in fruits and aromatic spices. Serve this rich, slow-grilled chicken dish over fluffy couscous or saffron rice.

Prep: 20 minutes
Marinate: 4 to 24 hours
Grill: 50 minutes
Makes: 4 servings

- **2 pounds meaty chicken pieces (breasts, thighs, and drumsticks), skinned**
- **2 teaspoons finely shredded orange peel (set aside)**
- **½ cup orange juice**
- **1 tablespoon olive oil**
- **1 tablespoon grated fresh ginger**
- **1 teaspoon paprika**
- **1 teaspoon ground cumin**
- **½ teaspoon ground coriander**
- **¼ teaspoon crushed red pepper**
- **⅛ teaspoon salt**
- **2 tablespoons honey**
- **2 teaspoons orange juice**

1 Rinse chicken; pat dry. Place chicken in a plastic bag set in a deep dish. For the marinade, in a small bowl stir together the ½ cup orange juice, the olive oil, ginger, paprika, cumin, coriander, red pepper, and salt. Pour marinade over chicken. Close the bag. Marinate the chicken in the refrigerator for 4 to 24 hours, turning the bag occasionally.

2 Meanwhile, in a small bowl stir together the reserved orange peel, the honey, and the 2 teaspoons orange juice.

3 Drain the chicken, discarding the marinade. In a grill with a cover arrange preheated coals around a drip pan. Test for medium heat above pan. Place chicken, skinned side up, on lightly greased grill rack over drip pan.

4 Cover and grill for 50 to 60 minutes or until the chicken is tender and no longer pink. Occasionally brush chicken with honey mixture during the last 10 minutes of grilling. (Or, to bake, place chicken, skinned side up, in a shallow baking dish. Bake, uncovered, in a 375° oven for 45 to 55 minutes or until chicken is tender and no longer pink. Occasionally brush the chicken with the honey mixture during the last 10 minutes of baking.)

Nutrition facts per serving: 237 cal., 8 g total fat (2 g sat. fat), 92 mg chol., 98 mg sodium, 10 g carbo., 0 g fiber, 30 g pro.
Daily values: 2% vit. A, 9% vit. C, 1% calcium, 9% iron

super suppers

180

feta-stuffed CHICKEN

Feta cheese, popular in eastern Mediterranean countries such as Greece, Israel, and Lebanon, packs a simple chicken breast with tantalizing tang.

Start to Finish: 30 minutes
Makes: 4 servings

¼ **cup crumbled basil-and-tomato feta cheese***

2 **tablespoons fat-free cream cheese (1 ounce)**

4 **skinless, boneless chicken breast halves (about 1 pound total)**

¼ **to ½ teaspoon pepper**
Dash salt

1 **teaspoon olive oil or cooking oil**

¼ **cup chicken broth**

1 **10-ounce package prewashed fresh spinach, trimmed (8 cups)**

2 **tablespoons finely chopped toasted walnuts or pecans**

1 **tablespoon lemon juice**

❶ Combine feta cheese and cream cheese; set aside. Rinse the chicken; pat dry. Cut a horizontal slit through the thickest portion of each chicken breast half to form a pocket. Stuff pockets with the cheese mixture. If necessary, secure openings with wooden picks. Sprinkle chicken with pepper and salt.

❷ In a large nonstick skillet heat oil over medium-high heat. Cook chicken, uncovered, in hot oil about 12 minutes or until the chicken is tender and no longer pink, turning once (reduce heat to medium if chicken browns too quickly). Remove the chicken from skillet. Cover to keep chicken warm.

❸ Carefully add chicken broth to skillet. Bring to boiling; add half of the spinach. Cover and cook about 3 minutes or until spinach is just wilted. Remove spinach from skillet, reserving liquid in pan. Repeat with remaining spinach. Return all spinach to skillet. Stir in the walnuts or pecans and lemon juice. To serve, divide spinach mixture among 4 plates. Top with chicken breasts.

***Note:** If basil-and-tomato feta cheese is not available, add 1 teaspoon each of finely minced fresh basil and snipped oil-packed dried tomatoes, drained, to ¼ cup plain feta cheese.

Nutrition facts per serving: 199 cal., 8 g total fat (2 g sat. fat), 67 mg chol., 271 mg sodium, 4 g carbo., 2 g fiber, 26 g pro.
Daily values: 51% vit. A, 36% vit. C, 12% calcium, 19% iron

super suppers

181

chicken WITH FRUIT SALSA

Juicy chicken breasts go Southwestern with a salsa bursting with flavor. The chipotle chiles—smoked jalapeño peppers—are not for the faint of heart. Use the lower range for a milder salsa.

Prep: 20 minutes
Stand: 30 minutes
Broil: 12 minutes
Makes: 4 servings

1½ cups finely chopped pineapple

1 to 2 canned chipotle peppers in adobo sauce, drained, seeded, and finely chopped

2 tablespoons snipped chives

1 tablespoon honey

1 teaspoon finely shredded lime peel or lemon peel

2 teaspoons lime juice or lemon juice

4 skinless, boneless chicken breast halves (about 1 pound total)

1 teaspoon cooking oil

1 teaspoon dried thyme, crushed

¼ teaspoon salt

¼ teaspoon black pepper

1 For salsa, in a medium bowl stir together pineapple, chipotle peppers, chives, honey, lime or lemon peel, and lime or lemon juice. Let stand at room temperature for 30 minutes.

2 Meanwhile, rinse chicken; pat dry. Lightly brush chicken with cooking oil. In a small bowl stir together thyme, salt, and black pepper; rub onto both sides of chicken. Place chicken on the unheated rack of broiler pan. Broil 4 to 5 inches from heat for 12 to 15 minutes or until chicken is tender and no longer pink, turning once. (Or, grill chicken on the lightly greased rack of an uncovered grill directly over medium coals for 12 to 15 minutes or until chicken is tender and no longer pink, turning once.) Serve chicken with salsa.

Nutrition facts per serving: 182 cal., 5 g total fat (1 g sat. fat), 59 mg chol., 227 mg sodium, 13 g carbo., 1 g fiber, 22 g pro.
Daily values: 6% vit. A, 19% vit. C, 2% calcium, 8% iron

super suppers

chicken WITH POBLANO SALSA

Dark green poblano peppers are very mild, sweet chile peppers with just a whisper of heat. The poblano often is used for classic chiles rellenos. If you can't find poblanos, use Anaheim peppers instead.

Prep: 50 minutes
Bake: 15 minutes
Makes: 4 servings

1 large fresh poblano pepper
1 large clove garlic
  Nonstick spray coating
⅓ cup fine dry bread crumbs
1 tablespoon chili powder
1 teaspoon ground cumin
4 skinless, boneless chicken breast halves (about 1 pound total)
3 tablespoons refrigerated or frozen egg product, thawed
½ cup chopped tomatillo or tomato
1 medium tomato, chopped
¼ cup finely chopped onion
2 tablespoons snipped cilantro

❶ To roast poblano pepper and garlic, quarter the pepper, removing seeds and membranes. Place pepper pieces and unpeeled garlic clove on a foil-lined baking sheet. Bake, uncovered, in a 450° oven for 20 to 25 minutes or until the pepper skins are charred. Remove garlic; set aside to cool. Bring up the edges of foil and seal around the pepper pieces. Let pepper stand for 20 minutes to steam. Peel pepper pieces and garlic. Chop pepper; mash garlic.

❷ Meanwhile, spray a 2-quart rectangular baking dish with nonstick coating; set aside. In a shallow dish combine the bread crumbs, chili powder, and cumin. Rinse chicken; pat dry. Dip chicken in egg product; coat with bread crumb mixture. Arrange chicken in prepared baking dish. Bake, uncovered, in a 375° oven for 15 to 20 minutes or until chicken is tender and no longer pink.

❸ For salsa, in a medium bowl combine the poblano pepper, garlic, tomatillo or tomato, tomato, onion, and cilantro. Serve sauce over chicken.

Nutrition facts per serving: 195 cal., 5 g total fat (1 g sat. fat), 60 mg chol., 161 mg sodium, 12 g carbo., 2 g fiber, 25 g pro.
Daily values: 13% vit. A, 66% vit. C, 4% calcium, 17% iron

super suppers

sesame CHICKEN

There's no reason to think of fried chicken as permanently off-limits. For our sesame "fried" chicken recipe, we traded the frying pan for the oven and ended up with a crispy, juicy chicken that only tastes taboo.

Prep: 15 minutes
Bake: 45 minutes
Makes: 4 servings

Nonstick spray coating

3 **tablespoons sesame seeds**

3 **tablespoons all-purpose flour**

¼ **teaspoon salt**

¼ **teaspoon ground red pepper**

4 **skinless chicken breast halves (about 2 pounds total)**

3 **tablespoons reduced-sodium teriyaki sauce**

1 **tablespoon margarine or butter, melted**

1 Spray a large baking sheet with nonstick coating; set aside. In a large plastic bag combine sesame seeds, flour, salt, and red pepper. Rinse the chicken; pat dry. Dip chicken in teriyaki sauce. Add chicken to the mixture in the plastic bag; close bag. Shake bag to coat chicken.

2 Place chicken, bone side down, on prepared baking sheet. Drizzle melted margarine or butter over chicken.

3 Bake in a 400° oven about 45 minutes or until chicken is tender and no longer pink.

Nutrition facts per serving: 275 cal., 11 g total fat (2 g sat. fat), 89 mg chol., 490 mg sodium, 7 g carbo., 1 g fiber, 35 g pro.
Daily values: 4% vit. A, 0% vit. C, 2% calcium, 12% iron

Butter vs. Margarine

For years, people spread the wrong word about butter—that it's "bad" for you. But when comparing butter and stick margarine, the major difference is taste. Both products have 11 to 12 grams of fat and 100 to 108 calories per tablespoon. Either should be used in small amounts. Many brands of spreads and tub margarine are slightly lower in fat, which makes them lower in calories. These products have been whipped with water to lower the calories and make them easy to spread. Water in the product means water on your toast, causing it to be soggy. Whipped spreads are not recommended for baking. Even stick margarines may not give you the best results, depending on the oil content. Too much oil can wreak havoc with certain baked things, such as pastry or streusel. When in doubt, use butter.

chicken BURRITOS

Say "Con mucho gusto!" to these mango salsa-topped chicken burritos. And, if the heat index starts to climb too high, just dab them with a little palate-soothing light sour cream.

Start to Finish: 1 hour
Makes: 8 burritos

- ½ **cup finely chopped plum tomato**
- ½ **cup finely chopped, peeled mango**
- ¼ **cup finely chopped red onion**
- 4 **tablespoons lime juice**
- 3 **tablespoons snipped cilantro**
- 2 **to 3 teaspoons finely chopped, seeded jalapeño pepper**
- 12 **ounces skinless, boneless chicken breast halves**
- ½ **cup water**
- ¼ **teaspoon salt**
- ⅛ **to ¼ teaspoon ground red pepper**
- 8 **6-inch corn tortillas**
- 1½ **cups shredded romaine or leaf lettuce**
- ¼ **cup light dairy sour cream**

1 For salsa, in a medium bowl combine the tomato, mango, red onion, 2 tablespoons of the lime juice, the cilantro, and jalapeño pepper. Cover and chill for 30 minutes.

2 In a large heavy skillet place the chicken and the water. Bring to boiling; reduce heat. Simmer, covered, for 12 to 14 minutes or until chicken is tender and no longer pink. Drain well; let cool until easy to handle. Using two forks, shred the chicken. Toss shredded chicken with the remaining lime juice, the salt, and ground red pepper.

3 Meanwhile, wrap the tortillas in foil. Bake in a 350° oven for 10 minutes or until warm.

4 To serve, spoon shredded chicken down centers of warm tortillas. Top each with salsa, romaine or leaf lettuce, and sour cream. Roll up.

Nutrition facts per burrito: 129 cal., 2 g total fat (1 g sat. fat), 23 mg chol., 138 mg sodium, 17 g carbo., 1 g fiber, 10 g pro.
Daily values: 9% vit. A, 22% vit. C, 5% calcium, 5% iron

super suppers

rosemary CHICKEN

You may have to fend off the neighbors once they get a whiff of this aromatic grilled chicken. Better yet, invite them to join your family for a backyard picnic.

Prep: 15 minutes
Grill: 35 minutes
Marinate: 6 hours
Makes: 6 servings

2 to 2½ pounds meaty chicken pieces (breasts, thighs, and drumsticks)

½ cup dry white wine or chicken broth

2 tablespoons olive oil

4 cloves garlic, minced

4 teaspoons snipped fresh rosemary

1 tablespoon finely shredded lemon peel

¼ teaspoon salt (optional)

¼ teaspoon black pepper (optional)

1 If desired, skin chicken. Place chicken in a self-sealing plastic bag set in a shallow dish.

2 For marinade, in a blender container or food processor bowl combine wine, oil, garlic, snipped rosemary, lemon peel, and, if desired, salt and pepper. Cover and blend or process about 15 seconds or until well combined. Pour over chicken. Close bag. Marinate in the refrigerator for 6 hours or overnight, turning bag occasionally.

3 Drain chicken, reserving marinade. For a charcoal grill, place chicken bone side up on the rack of an uncovered grill directly over medium coals. Grill for 35 to 45 minutes or until no longer pink (170°F for breasts, 180°F for thighs and drumsticks), turning and brushing once with marinade halfway through grilling. (For a gas grill, preheat grill. Reduce heat to medium. Place chicken on grill rack; cover and grill as above.) Discard any remaining marinade.

Nutrition Facts per serving: 227 cal., 13 g total fat (3 g sat. fat), 69 mg chol., 62 mg sodium, 1 g carbo., 0 g fiber, 22 g pro.
Daily Values: 3% vit. C, 2% calcium, 6% iron

chicken WITH ROQUEFORT

French Roquefort cheese lends a touch of old-world elegance to this creamy chicken dish.

Prep: 15 minutes
Grill: 12 minutes
Makes: 4 servings

½ **cup fat-free plain yogurt**

¼ **cup chopped red onion**

2 **tablespoons crumbled Roquefort or other blue cheese**

1 **tablespoon snipped fresh chives**

⅛ **teaspoon white pepper**

2 **small pears, halved lengthwise, cored, and stemmed**

Lemon juice

4 **medium skinless, boneless chicken breast halves (1 pound)**

Salt

Black pepper

1 For sauce, in a small bowl combine yogurt, onion, Roquefort cheese, chives, and white pepper. Cover and chill until ready to serve. Brush cut sides of pears with lemon juice. Set aside.

2 Sprinkle chicken with salt and pepper. For a charcoal grill, place chicken on the rack of an uncovered grill directly over medium coals. Grill for 5 minutes. Turn chicken. Place pears on grill, cut side down. Grill chicken and pears for 7 to 10 minutes or until chicken is no longer pink (170°F). (For a gas grill, preheat grill. Reduce heat to medium. Place chicken, then pears on grill rack over heat. Cover and grill as above.) Serve chicken and pears with sauce.

Nutrition Facts per serving: 199 cal., 5 g total fat (2 g sat. fat), 63 mg chol., 168 mg sodium, 14 g carbo., 2 g fiber, 25 g pro.
Daily Values: 2% vit. A, 9% vit. C, 8% calcium, 6% iron

plum chicken KABOBS

Lean chicken breasts, fresh pineapple, sugar snap peas, and sweet pepper form the lineup for these meal-in-one kabobs. Serve with a simply seasoned rice pilaf.

Prep: 20 minutes
Grill: 8 minutes
Makes: 4 servings

1 **pound skinless, boneless chicken breast halves, cut into 1-inch pieces**

1½ **teaspoons Jamaican jerk seasoning**

1 **cup sugar snap peas or pea pods, strings and tips removed**

1 **cup pineapple cubes**

1 **medium red sweet pepper, cut into 1-inch pieces**

¼ **cup plum preserves or jam**

1 Sprinkle chicken with about half of the jerk seasoning; toss gently to coat. Cut any large snap peas in half crosswise.

2 On 4 long or 8 short skewers, alternately thread chicken, sugar snap peas, pineapple, and sweet pepper, leaving a ¼-inch space between pieces. For sauce, in a small saucepan stir remaining jerk seasoning into plum preserves. Cook and stir just until preserves are melted; set aside.

3 For a charcoal grill, place kabobs on the rack of an uncovered grill directly over medium coals. Grill for 8 to 12 minutes or until chicken is no longer pink and vegetables are tender, turning once and brushing occasionally with sauce during the last 5 minutes of grilling. (For a gas grill, preheat grill. Reduce heat to medium. Place kabobs on grill rack directly over heat. Cover and grill as above.)

Nutrition Facts per serving: 221 cal., 2 g total fat (1 g sat. fat), 66 mg chol., 185 mg sodium, 23 g carbo., 2 g fiber, 27 g pro.
Daily Values: 43% vit. A, 111% vit. C, 4% calcium, 8% iron

super suppers

easy marinated CHICKEN

Widely used in Chinese cooking, hoisin sauce is thick, dark, and spicy-sweet. Stir it into marinades or pass as a table condiment.

Prep: 10 minutes
Grill: 12 minutes
Marinate: 2 hours
Makes: 8 servings

8 skinless, boneless chicken breast halves (2 pounds)

½ cup bottled oil and vinegar salad dressing

3 tablespoons soy sauce

2 tablespoons bottled hoisin sauce

½ teaspoon ground ginger

Bottled hoisin sauce

❶ Place chicken breasts in a self-sealing plastic bag set in a deep bowl. For marinade, in a small bowl combine salad dressing, soy sauce, the 2 tablespoons hoisin sauce, and ginger. Pour marinade over chicken; seal bag. Marinate in the refrigerator for 2 to 24 hours, turning bag occasionally. Drain chicken, discarding marinade.

❷ For a charcoal grill, place chicken on the rack of an uncovered grill directly over medium coals. Grill for 12 to 15 minutes or until no longer pink (170°F). (For a gas grill, preheat grill. Reduce heat to medium. Place chicken on grill rack over heat. Cover and grill as above.) Pass additional hoisin sauce for dipping.

Nutrition Facts per serving: 189 cal., 5 g total fat (1 g sat. fat), 82 mg chol., 286 mg sodium, 1 g carbo., 0 g fiber, 33 g pro.
Daily Values: 1% vit. A, 2% vit. C, 2% calcium, 5% iron

super suppers

Marinating Dos and Don'ts

Marinating meats adds both flavor and tenderness. For the best results follow these guidelines: Always marinate in the refrigerator to keep the food at the proper temperature. Never save and reuse a marinade. If you plan to baste or make a sauce with the marinade, set some aside before adding the meat. Or, if the marinade has been in contact with the meat, bring it to a rolling boil for 1 to 2 minutes before using as a sauce. To make cleanup easy, marinate in a self-sealing plastic bag instead of a dish.

turkey with cilantro PESTO

Cilantro pesto is the southwestern answer to Italy's basil pesto. Savor it with chicken, fish, or shrimp.

Prep: 15 minutes
Grill: 12 minutes
Makes: 8 servings

2 **pounds turkey breast tenderloins**

Salt

Black pepper

1½ **cups lightly packed fresh cilantro sprigs and/or fresh basil leaves**

⅓ **cup walnuts**

3 **tablespoons olive oil**

2 **tablespoons lime juice**

2 **cloves garlic, minced**

¼ **teaspoon salt**

Lime wedges or lemon wedges (optional)

1. Split each turkey breast tenderloin in half horizontally. Sprinkle turkey with salt and pepper; set aside.

2. For cilantro pesto, in a blender container or food processor bowl combine cilantro, walnuts, oil, lime juice, garlic, and the ¼ teaspoon salt. Cover and blend or process until nearly smooth. Divide pesto in half. Chill half of the pesto to serve with turkey.

3. For a charcoal grill, place turkey on the rack of an uncovered grill directly over medium coals. Grill for 7 minutes; turn. Brush lightly with the unchilled half of the cilantro pesto. Grill for 5 to 8 minutes more or until turkey is no longer pink (170°F). (For a gas grill, preheat grill. Reduce heat to medium. Place turkey on grill rack over heat. Cover and grill as above.) Discard remainder of cilantro pesto used as a brush-on.

4. Serve turkey with remaining chilled pesto. If desired, serve with lime wedges to squeeze over turkey.

Nutrition Facts per serving: 209 cal., 9 g total fat (1 g sat. fat), 70 mg chol., 195 mg sodium, 2 g carbo., 1 g fiber, 29 g pro.
Daily Values: 18% vit. A, 11% vit. C, 3% calcium, 9% iron

super suppers

turkey and wild rice PILAF

Another time chill the cooked mixture—it's delicious served as a main-dish salad.

Prep: 20 minutes
Cook: 43 minutes
Makes: 4 servings

1 cup sliced celery

¼ cup chopped onion

1 tablespoon butter or margarine

⅓ cup wild rice, rinsed and drained

1 14-ounce can reduced-sodium chicken broth

⅓ cup long grain rice

12 ounces cooked smoked turkey, cubed

2 medium red apples, coarsely chopped

1 large carrot, peeled and cut into thin, bite-size strips

2 tablespoons snipped fresh parsley

❶ In a large skillet cook celery and onion in hot butter over medium heat about 10 minutes or until tender. Add uncooked wild rice; cook and stir for 3 minutes. Add broth. Bring to boiling; reduce heat. Cover and simmer for 20 minutes. Stir in uncooked long grain rice. Return to boiling; reduce heat. Cover and simmer about 20 minutes more or until wild rice and long grain rice are tender and most of the liquid is absorbed.

❷ Stir in turkey, apples, and carrot. Cook, uncovered, for 3 to 4 minutes more or until heated through and liquid is absorbed. Stir in parsley.

Nutrition Facts per serving: 289 cal., 7 g total fat (2 g sat. fat), 44 mg chol., 1,231 mg sodium, 37 g carbo., 3 g fiber, 21 g pro.
Daily Values: 65% vit. A, 14% vit. C, 3% calcium, 12% iron

crunchy parmesan TURKEY

Wheat germ adds crunch to the cheesy coating on these turkey steaks.

Start to Finish: 25 minutes
Makes: 4 servings

¼ **cup seasoned fine dry bread crumbs**

¼ **cup toasted wheat germ**

¼ **cup grated Parmesan cheese**

2 **teaspoons sesame seeds or ¼ teaspoon dried Italian seasoning, crushed**

1 **egg**

¼ **teaspoon seasoned salt or ¼ teaspoon each salt and black pepper**

4 **turkey breast slices, cut ½ inch thick (about 1 pound)**

1 **tablespoon olive oil or cooking oil**

1 For coating, in a plastic bag combine bread crumbs, wheat germ, Parmesan cheese, and sesame seeds. Seal bag; shake to combine. In a small shallow bowl beat egg with a fork. Stir in the seasoned salt.

2 Dip turkey breast slices into the egg mixture, allowing excess to drain off. Coat with bread crumb mixture.

3 In a large nonstick skillet cook turkey in hot oil over medium heat for 6 to 8 minutes or until no longer pink (170°F), turning once. Transfer turkey to serving platter.

Nutrition Facts per serving: 258 cal., 9 g total fat (2 g sat. fat), 127 mg chol., 432 mg sodium, 9 g carbo., 1 g fiber, 35 g pro.
Daily Values: 2% vit. A, 1% vit. C, 10% calcium, 13% iron

super suppers

grilled TURKEY MOLE

Mole (MOH-lay), a Mexican specialty, is a rich, reddish-brown sauce that contains an unexpected ingredient—chocolate. Chili powder, garlic, and tomatoes also flavor this sauce, a common accompaniment to poultry.

Prep: 25 minutes
Marinate: 2 to 4 hours
Grill: 8 minutes
Makes: 6 servings

- 6 **4-ounce turkey breast tenderloin steaks**
- ¼ **cup lime juice**
- 1 **tablespoon chili powder**
- 2 **teaspoons bottled hot pepper sauce**
- 1 **tablespoon margarine or butter**
- ½ **cup chopped onion**
- 2 **teaspoons sugar**
- 1 **clove garlic, minced**
- 1 **7½-ounce can tomatoes, undrained and cut up**
- ¼ **cup canned diced green chile peppers**
- 1½ **teaspoons unsweetened cocoa powder**
- 1½ **teaspoons chili powder**
- ⅛ **teaspoon salt**
- **Fat-free dairy sour cream (optional)**

1 Rinse turkey; pat dry. Place the turkey in a plastic bag set in a shallow dish. For marinade, in a small bowl stir together the lime juice, the 1 tablespoon chili powder, and the hot pepper sauce. Pour over turkey. Close bag. Marinate in the refrigerator for 2 to 4 hours, turning bag occasionally.

2 Meanwhile, for the mole sauce, in a medium saucepan heat margarine or butter over medium-high heat until melted. Cook and stir the onion, sugar, and garlic in hot margarine or butter about 7 minutes or until onion is tender. Stir in the undrained tomatoes, chile peppers, cocoa powder, the 1½ teaspoons chili powder, and the salt. Bring to boiling; reduce heat. Simmer, covered, for 10 minutes. Remove from heat; set aside.

3 Drain the turkey, discarding the marinade. Grill turkey on the lightly greased rack of an uncovered grill directly over medium coals for 8 to 10 minutes or until turkey is tender and no longer pink, turning once. Serve with mole sauce and, if desired, sour cream.

Nutrition facts per serving: 156 cal., 5 g total fat (1 g sat. fat), 50 mg chol., 213 mg sodium, 6 g carbo., 1 g fiber, 22 g pro.
Daily values: 9% vit. A, 19% vit. C, 4% calcium, 10% iron

Turkey Talk

Turkey white meat is naturally low in fat. It has a slightly heartier taste than chicken and is versatile enough to be used as a substitute in place of higher fat meats. Like all meats, turkey is a good source of vital iron, zinc, and vitamin B-12.

If you only think of turkey at Thanksgiving, think again—whether you broil it, bake it, or grill it, turkey is a versatile meat for any time of year.

turkey PAPRIKASH

Paprikash (PAH-pree-kash) is the quintessential comfort food of Hungary. It usually is stewed with bacon drippings. We've updated the traditional method to lower the fat—but kept the rich flavor.

Prep: 25 minutes
Cook: 16 minutes
Makes: 4 servings

12 **ounces turkey breast tenderloins**

Nonstick spray coating

2 **teaspoons cooking oil**

2 **cups sliced fresh mushrooms**

1 **medium green sweet pepper, cut into thin bite-size strips**

1 **medium onion, cut into thin wedges**

2 **cloves garlic, minced**

2 **tablespoons low-sodium tomato paste**

1 **tablespoon paprika**

½ **teaspoon dried marjoram, crushed**

¼ **teaspoon salt**

¼ **teaspoon black pepper**

1 **cup reduced-sodium chicken broth**

1 **8-ounce carton fat-free dairy sour cream**

2 **tablespoons all-purpose flour**

2 **cups hot cooked noodles**

1 **tablespoon snipped parsley**

❶ Rinse turkey; pat dry. Cut the turkey crosswise into ½-inch slices. Spray a large nonstick skillet with the nonstick coating. Preheat skillet over medium-high heat. Brown turkey slices on both sides in skillet. Remove turkey from skillet.

❷ Carefully add the oil to hot skillet; add the mushrooms, sweet pepper, onion, and garlic to skillet. Cook and stir the vegetables until crisp-tender. In a bowl combine tomato paste, paprika, marjoram, salt, and black pepper. Gradually stir in about ½ cup of the chicken broth; add mixture to skillet. Add turkey to skillet. Bring to boiling; reduce heat. Simmer, covered, about 15 minutes or until turkey is tender.

❸ Meanwhile, stir together sour cream and flour. Stir in remaining chicken broth; add to skillet. Cook and stir until thickened and bubbly. Cook and stir for 1 minute more.

❹ To serve, spoon the turkey and sauce mixture over the cooked noodles and sprinkle with parsley.

Nutrition facts per serving: 319 cal., 5 g total fat (1 g sat. fat), 37 mg chol., 386 mg sodium, 40 g carbo., 3 g fiber, 27 g pro.
Daily values: 20% vit. A, 37% vit. C, 9% calcium, 21% iron

super suppers

salmon WITH MANGO SALSA

The mango is more than just another pretty fruit. It's a nutrition powerhouse that contains generous amounts of vitamins A, C, and E plus lots of fiber.

Prep: 15 minutes
Grill: 20 minutes
Marinate: 4 hours
Makes: 4 servings

- 4   6- to 8-ounce fresh or frozen salmon fillets (with skin), 1 inch thick
- 2   tablespoons sugar
- 1½ teaspoons finely shredded lime peel
- ¾   teaspoon salt
- ¼   teaspoon cayenne pepper
- 1   large ripe mango, peeled, seeded, and cut into thin bite-size strips
- ½   of a medium cucumber, seeded and cut into thin bite-size strips
- 2   green onions, sliced
- 3   tablespoons lime juice
- 1   tablespoon snipped fresh cilantro or 2 teaspoons snipped fresh mint
- 1   small jalapeño pepper, seeded and chopped*
- 1   clove garlic, minced

❶ Thaw fish, if frozen. Rinse fish; pat dry. Place fish skin side down in a shallow dish.

❷ For rub, in a small bowl stir together sugar, lime peel, ½ teaspoon of the salt, and the cayenne pepper. Sprinkle rub evenly over fish; rub in with your fingers. Cover and marinate in the refrigerator for 4 to 24 hours.

❸ Meanwhile, for salsa, in a medium bowl combine mango, cucumber, green onions, lime juice, cilantro, jalapeño pepper, garlic, and remaining ¼ teaspoon salt. Cover and chill until ready to serve.

❹ In a grill with a cover arrange medium-hot coals around a drip pan. Test for medium heat above the pan. Place fish skin side down on the greased grill rack directly over drip pan, tucking under any thin edges. Cover and grill for 20 to 25 minutes or until fish flakes easily when tested with a fork. If desired, remove skin from fish. Serve fish with salsa.

*Note: Because chile peppers, such as jalapeños, contain volatile oils that can burn your skin and eyes, avoid direct contact with them as much as possible. When working with chile peppers, wear plastic or rubber gloves. If your bare hands do touch the chile peppers, wash your hands and nails well with soap and warm water.

Nutrition Facts per serving: 352 cal., 15 g total fat (3 g sat. fat), 105 mg chol., 520 mg sodium, 18 g carbo., 2 g fiber, 37 g pro.
Daily Values: 50% vit. A, 38% vit. C, 3% calcium, 6% iron

super suppers

rosemary tuna KABOBS

Seafood has a reputation for being delicate. Not so with swordfish and tuna. These varieties are sturdy enough to marinate, skewer, and grill. Don't marinate for longer than 2 hours or the fish will toughen.

Prep: 25 minutes
Marinate: 2 hours
Broil: 8 minutes
Makes: 4 servings

¾ **pound fresh or frozen tuna steaks, 1 inch thick**

1 **teaspoon finely shredded lemon peel**

¼ **cup lemon juice**

1 **tablespoon cooking oil**

1 **tablespoon snipped fresh rosemary or 1 teaspoon dried rosemary, crushed**

2 **cloves garlic, minced**

¼ **teaspoon salt**

⅛ **teaspoon pepper**

8 **to 10 whole tiny new potatoes (about ¾ pound)**

4 **baby pattypan squash, halved lengthwise, or 1 medium zucchini, halved lengthwise and cut into 1-inch pieces**

Nonstick spray coating

4 **cherry tomatoes**

Hot cooked rice (optional)

1 Thaw tuna, if frozen. Rinse tuna; pat dry. Cut into 1-inch pieces. Place tuna in a plastic bag set in a shallow dish. For the marinade, in a small bowl stir together the lemon peel, lemon juice, cooking oil, rosemary, garlic, salt, and pepper. Pour over tuna. Close bag. Marinate in refrigerator for 2 hours, turning bag occasionally.

2 Meanwhile, scrub potatoes; cut any large potatoes in half. In a medium saucepan cook potatoes in a small amount of boiling water for 15 to 20 minutes or just until tender; drain. Rinse with cold water. Set aside.

3 Drain tuna, reserving marinade. On 4 long metal skewers, alternately thread the tuna, potatoes, and squash or zucchini, leaving about ¼-inch space between pieces. Spray the unheated rack of a broiler pan with nonstick coating. Place kabobs on rack. Brush with marinade. Broil 4 inches from heat for 5 minutes. Turn kabobs; brush with some of the marinade. Discard remaining marinade. Broil kabobs for 3 to 4 minutes more or until tuna flakes easily when tested with a fork and squash is tender. To serve, place a tomato on the end of each kabob. If desired, serve with rice.

Nutrition facts per serving: 235 cal., 7 g total fat (1 g sat. fat), 34 mg chol., 220 mg sodium, 23 g carbo., 2 g fiber, 19 g pro.
Daily values: 5% vit. A, 45% vit. C, 2% calcium, 16% iron

super suppers

apricot-sauced SALMON

Salmon is one of the richest sources for the omega-3 fatty acids that help protect against heart disease. Apricots are rich in cancer-fighting antioxidants. Teamed together, the result is a delicious and dynamite health duo.

Prep: 20 minutes
Broil: 8 minutes
Makes: 4 servings

4 **fresh or frozen salmon steaks, ¾ inch thick (about 1¼ pounds total)**
  Nonstick spray coating
2 **teaspoons cornstarch**
¼ **teaspoon salt**
  Dash ground red pepper
1 **5½-ounce can apricot nectar**
1 **tablespoon honey**
1 **tablespoon white wine vinegar**
2 **cups watercress leaves or shredded spinach or romaine**
½ **of a medium cucumber, thinly sliced**
1 **tablespoon white wine vinegar**
2 **green onions, sliced (¼ cup)**

① Thaw the salmon, if frozen. Rinse salmon; pat dry. Spray the unheated rack of a broiler pan with nonstick coating. Place salmon on rack. Broil 4 to 5 inches from heat for 8 to 12 minutes or until the salmon flakes easily when tested with a fork. (Or, spray a grill basket with nonstick coating. Place salmon in basket. Grill salmon on the grill rack of an uncovered grill directly over medium coals for 8 to 12 minutes or until salmon flakes easily with a fork, turning once.)

② Meanwhile, for sauce, in a small saucepan combine the cornstarch, salt, and ground red pepper. Gradually stir in the nectar; add honey and 1 tablespoon vinegar. Cook and stir over medium heat until thickened and bubbly. Cook and stir for 2 minutes more. Remove from heat. Cover; keep warm.

③ In a large bowl toss together the watercress, spinach, or romaine; cucumber; and 1 tablespoon vinegar. Divide among 4 serving plates. To serve, place salmon on watercress mixture and spoon sauce over each serving. Sprinkle with green onions.

Nutrition facts per serving: 181 cal., 5 g total fat (1 g sat. fat), 25 mg chol., 228 mg sodium, 13 g carbo., 1 g fiber, 21 g pro.
Daily values: 18% vit. A, 39% vit. C, 3% calcium, 8% iron

super suppers

201

salmon-vegetable PACKETS

The packets go straight from the oven to the dinner plate. It's easy enough for any day of the week.

Prep: 25 minutes
Bake: 30 minutes
Oven: 350°F
Makes: 4 servings

- 4 **4-ounce fresh or frozen skinless salmon fillets, ¾ inch thick**
- 2 **cups thinly bias-sliced carrots**
- 2 **cups sliced fresh mushrooms**
- 4 **green onions, sliced**
- 2 **teaspoons finely shredded orange peel**
- 2 **teaspoons snipped fresh oregano or ½ teaspoon dried oregano, crushed**
- 4 **cloves garlic, halved**
- ¼ **teaspoon salt**
- ¼ **teaspoon black pepper**
- 4 **teaspoons olive oil**
- 2 **medium oranges, thinly sliced**
- 4 **sprigs fresh oregano (optional)**

1 Thaw fish, if frozen. Rinse fish; pat dry with paper towels. Set aside. In a small saucepan cook carrots, covered, in a small amount of boiling water for 2 minutes. Drain and set aside. Tear off four 24-inch pieces of heavy foil. Fold each in half to make an 18×12-inch rectangle.

2 In a large bowl combine carrots, mushrooms, green onions, orange peel, oregano, garlic, salt, and pepper. Divide vegetable mixture among foil rectangles.

3 Place fish on top of the vegetable mixture. Drizzle fish with oil; sprinkle lightly with additional salt and pepper. Top with orange slices and, if desired, oregano sprigs. For each packet, bring up 2 opposite edges of foil and seal with a double fold. Fold remaining ends to completely enclose the food, allowing space for steam to build. Place the foil packets in a single layer in a large baking pan.

4 Bake in a 350° oven about 30 minutes or until fish flakes easily when tested with a fork and carrots are tender. Transfer the packets to dinner plates. Open slowly to allow steam to escape.

Nutrition Facts per serving: 226 cal., 9 g total fat (1 g sat. fat), 20 mg chol., 288 mg sodium, 19 g carbo., 5 g fiber, 19 g pro.
Daily Values: 198% vit. A, 71% vit. C, 6% calcium, 14% iron

super suppers

salmon with TROPICAL RICE

The key here is the complex flavor of coriander seeds—a cross between caraway and sage, with a lemon bite. Because it takes so little time to snip, shred, and crush the ingredients, put the rice on to cook first.

Start to Finish: 30 minutes
Oven: 450°F
Makes: 4 servings

- 1 1½-pound fresh or frozen salmon fillet
- 2 tablespoons coriander seeds, coarsely crushed
- 1 tablespoon packed brown sugar
- 1 teaspoon lemon-pepper seasoning
- 1 tablespoon butter or margarine, melted
- 2 cups cooked rice
- 1 medium mango, seeded, peeled, and chopped
- 1 tablespoon snipped fresh cilantro
- 1 teaspoon finely shredded lemon peel

1 Thaw salmon, if frozen. Rinse fish; pat dry with paper towels. Measure thickness of fish. Place fish skin side down in a greased shallow baking pan.

2 In a small bowl stir together coriander seeds, brown sugar, and lemon-pepper seasoning. Brush top and sides of fish with melted butter. Sprinkle fish with coriander mixture, pressing in slightly.

3 Stir together rice, mango, cilantro, and lemon peel. Spoon rice mixture around fish. Bake, uncovered, in a 450° oven for 4 to 6 minutes per ½-inch thickness of fish or until fish flakes easily when tested with a fork.

4 To serve, cut fish into 4 serving-size pieces. Serve fish on top of rice mixture.

Nutrition Facts per serving: 384 cal., 10 g total fat (3 g sat. fat), 96 mg chol., 421 mg sodium, 36 g carbo., 3 g fiber, 37 g pro.
Daily Values: 47% vit. A, 28% vit. C, 6% calcium, 17% iron

super suppers

vegetable-topped FISH

Salsa and summer squash make a tasty but amazingly easy sauce for baked fillets.

Start to Finish: 15 minutes
Oven: 450°F
Makes: 4 servings

1 **pound fresh or frozen fish fillets**

2 **teaspoons butter or margarine, melted**

⅛ **teaspoon salt**

⅛ **teaspoon black pepper**

1 **8-ounce jar (about 1 cup) salsa**

1 **small yellow summer squash or zucchini, halved lengthwise and cut into ¼-inch slices**

1 Thaw fish, if frozen. Rinse fish and pat dry. Measure thickness of fish. Place fish in a greased shallow baking pan, tucking under any thin edges. Brush fish with melted butter. Sprinkle with salt and pepper. Bake, uncovered, in a 450° oven until fish flakes easily when tested with a fork (allow 4 to 6 minutes per ½-inch thickness).

2 Meanwhile, in a small saucepan stir together salsa and summer squash. Bring to boiling; reduce heat. Cover and simmer for 5 to 6 minutes or until squash is crisp-tender. Serve squash mixture over fish.

Nutrition Facts per serving: 131 cal., 3 g total fat (0 g sat. fat), 48 mg chol., 403 mg sodium, 5 g carbo., 1 g fiber, 22 g pro.
Daily Values: 10% vit. A, 21% vit. C, 4% calcium, 6% iron

fish WITH CHERRY RELISH

By making the relish a day ahead, you save time and allow the flavors to blend. If swordfish is unavailable, or if you prefer a different fish, try halibut, tuna, or any other firm-fleshed fish.

Prep: 20 minutes
Grill: 6 minutes
Makes: 4 servings

4 **fresh or frozen swordfish steaks, ¾ inch thick (about 1¼ pounds total)**

½ **cup dried tart cherries, snipped**

2 **tablespoons raspberry vinegar, balsamic vinegar, or white wine vinegar**

1 **tablespoon water**

⅓ **cup chopped red onion**

1 **teaspoon olive oil**

1½ **teaspoons sugar**

Dash bottled hot pepper sauce

½ **teaspoon dried thyme, crushed**

¼ **teaspoon paprika**

¼ **teaspoon black pepper**

⅛ **teaspoon onion powder**

⅛ **teaspoon ground red pepper**

1 **teaspoon olive oil**

1 **teaspoon raspberry vinegar, balsamic vinegar, or white wine vinegar**

Nonstick spray coating

① Thaw swordfish, if frozen. Rinse swordfish; pat dry. Set aside.

② For the relish, in a small bowl stir together the cherries, the 2 tablespoons vinegar, and water; set aside. In a small saucepan cook the onion in 1 teaspoon olive oil until tender. Stir in cherry mixture, sugar, and hot pepper sauce. Keep warm over low heat until serving time, stirring occasionally.

③ In a small bowl stir together thyme, paprika, black pepper, onion powder, and ground red pepper. Combine 1 teaspoon olive oil and the 1 teaspoon vinegar. Lightly brush both sides of swordfish with the oil mixture. Rub the herb mixture onto both sides of the swordfish.

④ Spray a cold grill rack with nonstick coating. Grill swordfish on the sprayed rack of an uncovered grill directly over medium coals for 6 to 9 minutes or until swordfish flakes easily when tested with a fork, turning once. (Or, spray the unheated rack of a broiler pan with nonstick spray coating. Place the swordfish on the rack. Broil 4 inches from the heat for 6 to 9 minutes or until swordfish flakes easily when tested with a fork). Serve with relish.

Nutrition facts per serving with about 2 tablespoons relish: 254 cal.,
8 g total fat (2 g sat. fat), 56 mg chol., 128 mg sodium, 16 g carbo., 1 g fiber,
29 g pro.
Daily values: 14% vit. A, 3% vit. C, 1% calcium, 9% iron

orange SHRIMP KABOBS

With shrimp, turkey bacon, and a special orange-flavored sauce and sweet pepper combo, this dish is definitely company fare.

Prep: 30 minutes
Grill: 8 minutes
Makes: 4 servings

16 fresh or frozen jumbo shrimp in shells (about 1 pound total)

8 slices turkey bacon, halved crosswise

2 red and/or yellow sweet peppers, cut into 1-inch pieces

2 teaspoons finely shredded orange peel

2 tablespoons orange juice

2 teaspoons snipped fresh rosemary

2 cups hot cooked rice

1 cup cooked or canned black beans, rinsed and drained

1 Thaw shrimp, if frozen. Peel and devein shrimp, leaving tails intact. Rinse shrimp; pat dry with paper towels.

2 Wrap each shrimp in a half slice of the bacon. On long metal skewers, alternately thread bacon-wrapped shrimp and sweet pepper pieces, leaving a ¼-inch space between pieces. In a small bowl combine 1 teaspoon of the orange peel, the orange juice, and rosemary. Brush over kabobs.

3 For a charcoal grill, place kabobs on the greased rack of an uncovered grill directly over medium coals. Grill for 8 to 10 minutes or until shrimp are opaque and bacon is crisp, turning once halfway through grilling. (For a gas grill, preheat grill. Reduce heat to medium. Place kabobs on greased grill rack over heat. Cover and grill as above.)

4 Meanwhile, in a medium saucepan stir together remaining orange peel, cooked rice, and black beans; heat through. Serve with shrimp and peppers.

Nutrition Facts per serving: 340 cal., 7 g total fat (1 g sat. fat), 149 mg chol., 509 mg sodium, 40 g carbo., 5 g fiber, 28 g pro.
Daily Values: 8% vit. A, 253% vit. C, 8% calcium, 23% iron

super suppers

herb-pecan CRUSTED SNAPPER

Butter, chopped pecans, fresh herbs, and a touch of lemon and garlic make a toasty crust for meaty red snapper. This combination is terrific on fresh walleye too.

Prep: 15 minutes
Grill: 4 to 6 minutes per
    ½-inch thickness
Makes: 4 servings

- **4 5- or 6-ounce fresh or frozen red snapper fillets with skin, ½ to 1 inch thick**
- **⅓ cup finely chopped pecans**
- **2 tablespoons fine dry bread crumbs**
- **2 tablespoons butter or margarine, softened**
- **1 teaspoon finely shredded lemon peel**
- **1 teaspoon bottled minced garlic (2 cloves)**
- **1 tablespoon snipped fresh flat-leaf parsley**
- **¼ teaspoon salt**
- **⅛ teaspoon black pepper**
- **Dash cayenne pepper**
- **Snipped fresh flat-leaf parsley (optional)**
- **Lemon wedges (optional)**

1 Thaw fish, if frozen; rinse and pat dry with paper towels. Measure thickness of fish. In a small bowl combine pecans, bread crumbs, butter, lemon peel, garlic, the 1 tablespoon parsley, salt, black pepper, and cayenne pepper.

2 For a charcoal grill, place fish skin side down on the greased rack of an uncovered grill directly over medium coals. Spoon pecan mixture on top of fillets; spread slightly. Grill until fish flakes easily when tested with a fork. Allow 4 to 6 minutes per ½-inch thickness of fish. (For a gas grill, preheat grill. Reduce heat to medium. Place fish on greased grill rack over heat. Spoon pecan mixture on top of fillets; spread slightly. Cover and grill as above.) If desired, sprinkle fish with additional snipped parsley and serve with lemon wedges.

Nutrition Facts per serving: 276 cal., 16 g total fat (5 g sat. fat), 68 mg chol., 395 mg sodium, 4 g carbo., 1 g fiber, 31 g pro.
Daily Values: 9% vit. A, 4% vit. C, 5% calcium, 7% iron

super suppers

snapper VERACRUZ

Snapper Veracruz, one of Mexico's best-known fish recipes, is a melding of flavors. The recipe includes Spanish green olives and capers with jalapeño peppers from Jalapa, the capital of the state of Veracruz.

Start to Finish: 30 minutes
Makes: 6 servings

1½ **pounds fresh or frozen skinless red snapper or other fish fillets, ½ to ¾ inch thick**

⅛ **teaspoon salt**

⅛ **teaspoon black pepper**

1 **large onion, sliced and separated into rings**

2 **cloves garlic, minced**

1 **tablespoon cooking oil**

2 **large tomatoes, chopped (2 cups)**

¼ **cup sliced pimiento-stuffed green olives**

¼ **cup dry white wine**

2 **tablespoons capers, drained**

1 **to 2 fresh jalapeño or serrano chile peppers, seeded and chopped,* or 1 to 2 canned jalapeño chile peppers, rinsed, drained, seeded, and chopped**

½ **teaspoon sugar**

1 **bay leaf**

① Thaw fish, if frozen. Rinse fish; pat dry with paper towels. Cut fish into 6 serving-size pieces. Sprinkle fish with salt and black pepper.

② For sauce, in a large skillet cook onion and garlic in hot oil until onion is tender. Stir in tomatoes, olives, wine, capers, jalapeño peppers, sugar, and bay leaf. Bring to boiling. Add fish to skillet. Return to boiling; reduce heat. Cover and simmer for 6 to 10 minutes or until fish flakes easily when tested with a fork. Use a slotted spatula to carefully transfer fish from skillet to a serving platter. Cover and keep warm.

③ Gently boil sauce in skillet for 5 to 6 minutes or until reduced to about 2 cups, stirring occasionally. Discard bay leaf. Spoon sauce over fish.

*Note: Because chile peppers, such as jalapeños, contain volatile oils that can burn your skin and eyes, avoid direct contact with them as much as possible. When working with chile peppers, wear plastic or rubber gloves. If your bare hands do touch the chile peppers, wash your hands and nails well with soap and warm water.

Nutrition Facts per serving: 178 cal., 6 g total fat (1 g sat. fat), 41 mg chol., 384 mg sodium, 6 g carbo., 1 g fiber, 25 g pro.
Daily Values: 12% vit. A, 26% vit. C, 4% calcium, 7% iron

super suppers

sesame-teriyaki SEA BASS

Golden teriyaki glaze and toasty sesame seeds make a tantalizing coat for these lightly panfried sea bass fillets. Complete the meal with braised mixed cabbage and couscous pilaf.

Start to Finish: 30 minutes
Makes: 4 servings

- 4　4-ounce fresh or frozen sea bass fillets, 1 inch thick
- ¼　teaspoon black pepper
- 3　tablespoons soy sauce
- 3　tablespoons sweet rice wine (mirin)
- 2　tablespoons dry white wine
- 1½　teaspoons sugar
- 1½　teaspoons honey
- 2　teaspoons cooking oil
- 1　tablespoon white or black sesame seeds, toasted*

① Thaw fish, if frozen. Rinse fish; pat dry with paper towels. Sprinkle the fish with pepper; set aside.

② For glaze, in a small saucepan combine soy sauce, rice wine, dry white wine, sugar, and honey. Bring to boiling; reduce heat. Simmer, uncovered, about 10 minutes or until glaze is reduced to about ¼ cup.

③ Meanwhile, in a large nonstick skillet cook the fish in hot oil over medium heat for 8 to 12 minutes or until fish flakes easily when tested with a fork, gently turning once.

④ To serve, arrange the fish on a serving platter. Drizzle the glaze over the fish; sprinkle with sesame seeds.

*Note: To toast sesame seeds, in a nonstick skillet cook and stir sesame seeds over medium heat about 1 minute or just until golden brown. Watch closely so the seeds don't burn. Remove from heat and transfer to a bowl to cool completely.

Nutrition Facts per serving: 185 cal., 6 g total fat (1 g sat. fat), 47 mg chol., 851 mg sodium, 6 g carbo., 0 g fiber, 22 g pro.
Daily Values: 5% vit. A, 4% vit. C, 1% calcium, 5% iron

super suppers

Something's Fishy

Sea bass is a saltwater fish sometimes referred to as sea perch. A 3-ounce serving contains about 100 calories and only 2 grams of fat. Incorporating more fish into one's diet is often recommended to people trying to eat healthier, but buying fresh fish can be intimidating.

Follow these simple tips to ensure you're buying fresh, healthy fish: Choose fish with firm, shiny flesh and a mild salty scent. Avoid fish with a very strong fishy odor. Select fish that's moist, not dry.

couscous cakes WITH SALSA

Couscous is made with ground semolina, as are some pastas, but it acts like a grain in this recipe and often substitutes for barley or bulgur.

Start to Finish: 20 minutes
Makes: 4 servings

- ½ of a 15-ounce can (about ¾ cup) black beans, rinsed and drained
- ⅔ cup purchased corn relish
- 2 small roma tomatoes, chopped
- 1½ teaspoons lime juice
- ¼ teaspoon ground cumin
- ½ cup quick-cooking couscous
- 2 tablespoons whole wheat flour
- ½ teaspoon sugar
- ¼ teaspoon baking soda
- ⅛ teaspoon salt
- ¾ cup buttermilk or sour milk*
- 1 slightly beaten egg
- 1 tablespoon cooking oil

① For salsa, in a medium bowl combine beans, corn relish, tomatoes, lime juice, and cumin. Set aside.

② In another medium bowl combine uncooked couscous, whole wheat flour, sugar, baking soda, and salt. In a small bowl combine buttermilk, egg, and oil. Stir buttermilk mixture into flour mixture. Lightly grease a griddle or skillet; heat over medium heat. For each cake, spoon about 2 tablespoons of batter onto the hot griddle or skillet. Cook for 4 to 6 minutes or until browned, turning to other sides when bottoms are lightly browned and edges are slightly dry.

③ To serve, spoon salsa mixture over cakes.

*Note: To make ¾ cup sour milk, place 2 teaspoons lemon juice or vinegar in a glass measuring cup. Add enough fat-free milk to make ¾ cup total liquid; stir. Let stand for 5 minutes before using.

Nutrition Facts per serving: 262 cal., 6 g total fat (1 g sat. fat), 55 mg chol., 453 mg sodium, 46 g carbo., 5 g fiber, 10 g pro.
Daily Values: 7% vit. A, 15% vit. C, 8% calcium, 7% iron

super suppers

spicy black BEAN PATTIES

These vegetarian burgers infused with cilantro, chipotle pepper, and cumin are a great source of protein with little fat.

Prep: 20 minutes
Grill: 8 minutes
Makes: 4 servings

- ½ of a medium avocado, seeded and peeled
- 1 tablespoon lime juice
  Salt
  Black pepper
- 2 slices whole wheat bread, torn
- 3 tablespoons fresh cilantro leaves
- 2 cloves garlic
- 1 15-ounce can black beans, rinsed and drained
- 1 canned chipotle pepper in adobo sauce
- 1 to 2 teaspoons adobo sauce
- 1 teaspoon ground cumin
- 1 beaten egg
- 1 small roma tomato, chopped

1. For guacamole, in a small bowl mash the avocado. Stir in lime juice; season to taste with salt and black pepper. Cover surface with plastic wrap and chill until ready to serve.

2. Place the torn bread in a food processor bowl. Cover and process or blend until bread resembles coarse crumbs. Transfer to a large bowl; set aside.

3. Place cilantro and garlic in the food processor bowl. Cover and process until finely chopped. Add beans, chipotle pepper, adobo sauce, and cumin. Cover and process until beans are coarsely chopped and mixture begins to pull away from the side of the bowl or container. Add mixture to bread crumbs. Add egg; mix well. Shape into four ½-inch-thick patties.

4. For a charcoal grill, place patties on the lightly greased rack of an uncovered grill directly over medium coals. Grill for 8 to 10 minutes or until patties are heated through, turning once halfway through grilling. (For a gas grill, lightly grease grill rack; preheat grill. Reduce heat to medium. Place patties on grill rack over heat. Cover and grill as above.)

5. To serve, top with guacamole and chopped tomato.

Nutrition Facts per serving: 178 cal., 7 g total fat (1 g sat. fat), 53 mg chol., 487 mg sodium, 25 g carbo., 9 g fiber, 11 g pro.
Daily Values: 9% vit. A, 12% vit. C, 7% calcium, 16% iron

Spicing It Up

Adding extra zip to low-fat cooking makes healthy eating a lot more enjoyable. This is even more true for such meatless dishes as vegetables, pastas, and beans, which tend to have milder flavors than meat, poultry, and fish. Spices are the perfect addition. They come from plants native to tropical areas and are known for their strong flavors and aromas. In addition to traditional combinations, more unique mixtures, such as cinnamon and chili powder or cumin and curry, will get you good results.

super suppers

214

veggie-filled BURGERS

To keep these turkey burgers juicy, be careful not to overcook them. Use an instant-read thermometer to check the temperature at the center of the patties.

Prep: 25 minutes
Grill: 12 minutes
Makes: 4 servings

- 2 **tablespoons milk**
- ½ **cup finely shredded carrot**
- ¼ **cup thinly sliced green onion**
- ¼ **cup soft whole wheat bread crumbs**
- ¼ **teaspoon dried Italian seasoning, crushed**
- ¼ **teaspoon garlic salt**
- ⅛ **teaspoon black pepper**
- ¾ **pound lean ground turkey or chicken**
- ¼ **cup Dijon-style mustard**
- ½ **teaspoon curry powder**
- 4 **whole wheat hamburger buns, toasted**
- 4 **lettuce leaves (optional)**
- ½ **cup shredded zucchini (optional)**
- 1 **medium sliced tomato (optional)**

1 In a medium bowl stir together milk, carrot, green onion, bread crumbs, Italian seasoning, garlic salt, and pepper. Add ground turkey; mix well. Shape the mixture into four ½-inch-thick patties.

2 For a charcoal grill, place patties on the greased rack of an uncovered grill directly over medium-hot coals. Grill, uncovered, about 12 minutes or until an instant-read thermometer inserted into the side of a patty registers 165°F, turning once. (For a gas grill, grease rack; preheat grill. Reduce heat to medium-hot. Place patties on grill rack; cover and grill patties as directed above.)

3 Meanwhile, stir together mustard and curry powder. Serve patties on buns. If desired, top with lettuce leaves, shredded zucchini, sliced tomato, and mustard mixture.

Nutrition Facts per serving: 257 cal., 9 g total fat (4 g sat. fat), 54 mg chol., 409 mg sodium, 24 g carbo., 3 g fiber, 20 g pro.
Daily Values: 71% vit. A, 4% vit. C, 17% iron

super suppers

vegetable STRUDEL

Calzone lovers will appreciate this flaky phyllo dough strudel studded with vegetables, tomatoes, and cheese. Remember to place the frozen phyllo in the fridge the day before using to allow for thawing.

Prep: 40 minutes
Bake: 25 minutes
Stand: 10 minutes
Makes: 4 servings

5 cups fresh spinach leaves

2 medium red sweet peppers, cut into 1-inch strips

1 medium yellow summer squash, cut into 1-inch strips

2 carrots, shredded

½ cup sliced fresh mushrooms

4 green onions, sliced (½ cup)

¼ cup oil-packed dried tomatoes, drained and chopped

3 tablespoons grated Parmesan cheese

1 tablespoon snipped fresh oregano or ½ teaspoon dried oregano, crushed

⅛ teaspoon salt

⅛ teaspoon black pepper

Dash ground red pepper

Butter-flavor nonstick spray coating

6 sheets frozen phyllo dough, thawed

2 tablespoons fine dry bread crumbs

1 For filling, place the spinach in large colander; set aside. In a large saucepan cook sweet peppers, summer squash, carrots, mushrooms, and green onions in 4 cups boiling water for 2 to 3 minutes. Pour over spinach to drain; rinse immediately with cold water. Drain well, pressing out excess moisture. Transfer vegetables to a large bowl. Stir in the dried tomatoes, 2 tablespoons of the Parmesan cheese, the oregano, salt, black pepper, and ground red pepper. Set filling aside.

2 Spray a large baking sheet with nonstick coating. Place 1 sheet of phyllo on a dry kitchen towel. (Keep remaining sheets covered with plastic wrap to prevent drying out.) Spray with nonstick coating. Place another sheet on top; spray with nonstick coating. Sprinkle with half of the bread crumbs. Place 2 more sheets of phyllo on top, spraying each with nonstick coating. Sprinkle with remaining crumbs. Add remaining 2 sheets of phyllo, spraying each with nonstick coating.

3 Spoon filling along 1 long side of phyllo stack about 1½ inches from edges. Fold in the short sides over the filling. Starting from the long side with filling, roll up jelly-roll style.

4 Place strudel, seam side down, on the prepared baking sheet. Spray top with nonstick coating. Using a sharp knife, score into 8 slices, cutting through the top layer only. Sprinkle with remaining Parmesan cheese.

5 Bake in a 375° oven for 25 to 30 minutes or until the strudel is golden. Let stand for 10 minutes before serving. To serve, cut along scored lines into slices.

Nutrition facts per serving: 182 cal., 5 g total fat (1 g sat. fat), 4 mg chol., 466 mg sodium, 29 g carbo., 4 g fiber, 8 g pro.
Daily values: 156% vit. A, 158% vit. C, 14% calcium, 24% iron

ravioli with SWEET PEPPERS

This pretty vegetable and pasta main dish scores high in flavor and nutrients. Each serving provides more than 100 percent of your daily vitamin A and C needs.

Start to Finish: 20 minutes
Makes: 4 servings

- 1 **9-ounce package refrigerated light cheese ravioli**
- ⅔ **cup chopped red sweet pepper**
- ⅔ **cup chopped green sweet pepper**
- 1 **medium carrot, cut into thin bite-size strips**
- ⅓ **cup chopped onion**
- 2 **cloves garlic, minced**
- 1 **tablespoon olive oil**
- 1 **cup chopped tomato**
- ¼ **cup reduced-sodium chicken broth or vegetable broth**
- 3 **tablespoons snipped fresh basil or 2 teaspoons dried basil, crushed**

1 Cook pasta according to package directions, except omit any oil or salt. Drain. Return pasta to saucepan; cover and keep warm.

2 Meanwhile, in a large nonstick skillet cook sweet pepper, carrot, onion, and garlic in hot oil over medium-high heat about 5 minutes or until vegetables are tender. Stir in tomato, broth, and basil. Cook and stir about 2 minutes more or until heated through.

3 Add vegetable mixture to the cooked pasta; toss gently to combine.

Nutrition Facts per serving: 280 cal., 9 g total fat (4 g sat. fat), 26 mg chol., 381 mg sodium, 39 g carbo., 2 g fiber, 14 g pro.
Daily Values: 137% vit. A, 115% vit. C, 32% calcium, 13% iron

super suppers

grilled brie SANDWICHES

Another time try this sophisticated grilled cheese with watercress in place of half of the spinach.

Start to Finish: 20 minutes
Makes: 4 servings

- 2 **cloves garlic, minced**
- 1 **tablespoon olive oil or cooking oil**
- 8 **ounces torn fresh spinach (6 cups)**
- 8 **ounces cold Brie, cut into ⅛-inch slices**
- 8 **slices firm-texture whole grain bread**
- **Butter or margarine**

1 In a large skillet cook garlic in hot oil for 30 seconds. Add spinach. Cook over medium heat, tossing until spinach begins to wilt; remove from heat. Set aside.

2 Divide cheese among 4 slices of the bread. Top with spinach-garlic mixture. Cover with remaining bread slices. Lightly spread the outside of each sandwich with butter.

3 In a large skillet cook 2 sandwiches over medium-low heat for 5 to 7 minutes or until golden. Turn sandwiches and cook for 2 minutes more or until sandwiches are golden and cheese melts. Transfer to a warm oven. Repeat with remaining sandwiches.

Nutrition Facts per serving: 427 cal., 29 g total fat (16 g sat. fat), 79 mg chol., 762 mg sodium, 24 g carbo., 6 g fiber, 18 g pro.
Daily Values: 64% vit. A, 20% vit. C, 20% calcium, 29% iron

super suppers

corn and tomato PUDDING

The classic bread pudding dessert is reinvented as a luscious meatless main course. If using the French bread option, choose only firm, dry bread—fresh bread is too soft to soak up the milk and eggs and hold its shape.

Prep: 20 minutes
Bake: 30 minutes
Oven: 375°F
Makes: 6 servings

3 **tablespoons snipped dried tomatoes (not oil-packed)**

4 **eggs**

1½ **cups milk**

1 **tablespoon snipped fresh basil or 1 teaspoon dried basil, crushed**

4 **cups torn whole wheat English muffins or dry French bread**

1½ **cups fresh or frozen whole kernel corn**

1 **cup shredded reduced-fat cheddar cheese or Monterey Jack cheese with jalapeño pepper (4 ounces)**

Thin tomato wedges (optional)

1 In a small bowl soak the dried tomatoes in enough hot water to cover for 10 minutes; drain.

2 Meanwhile, in a medium bowl beat together eggs, milk, and basil; set aside. In a 2-quart square baking dish toss together drained tomatoes, torn English muffins, corn, and cheese.

3 Carefully pour egg mixture evenly over the muffin mixture. Bake in a 375° oven about 30 minutes or until a knife inserted near center comes out clean. Cool slightly. If desired, serve on top of tomato wedges.

Note: You'll need about 5 cups fresh bread cubes to make 4 cups dry cubes. Cut bread into ½-inch slices; cut into cubes. Spread in a single layer in a shallow baking pan. Bake in a 300°F oven for 10 to 15 minutes or until dry, stirring twice; cool. (Bread will continue to dry and crisp as it cools.) Or let bread cubes stand, loosely covered, at room temperature for 8 to 12 hours.

Nutrition Facts per serving: 268 cal., 9 g total fat (4 g sat. fat), 160 mg chol., 393 mg sodium, 31 g carbo., 3 g fiber, 17 g pro.
Daily Values: 10% vit. A, 7% vit. C, 30% calcium, 11% iron

Dairy Differences

While different dairy liquids cause slight texture changes in foods, the biggest differences are the fat and calories they'll contribute to your recipe. One cup of whole milk has 150 calories and 8 grams of fat. The same amount of 2 percent milk contains 120 calories and 5 grams of fat; 1 percent has 100 calories, 2.5 grams of fat; and skim or fat-free milk has just 80 calories and no fat. An equal amount of half-and-half has 320 calories and 32 grams of fat, and light cream has a whopping 480 calories and 48 grams of fat in 1 cup.

super suppers

crustless cheese QUICHE

By omitting the pastry crust from this healthful quiche recipe, you can cut 9 grams of fat and 141 calories per serving. The feta and cheddar cheeses lend tangy flavor and smooth texture.

Prep: 20 minutes
Bake: 40 minutes
Stand: 5 minutes
Oven: 350°F
Makes: 8 servings

Nonstick cooking spray

1 **cup refrigerated or frozen egg product, thawed**

⅓ **cup whole wheat pastry flour**

¼ **teaspoon black pepper**

⅛ **teaspoon salt**

1½ **cups low-fat cottage cheese (12 ounces), drained**

1 **10-ounce package frozen chopped broccoli, cooked and drained**

1 **cup crumbled feta cheese (4 ounces)**

1 **cup shredded reduced-fat cheddar cheese (4 ounces)**

① Lightly coat a 9-inch pie plate with nonstick cooking spray; set aside.

② In a medium bowl combine egg product, flour, pepper, and salt. Stir in cottage cheese, broccoli, feta cheese, and cheddar cheese. Spoon into prepared pie plate.

③ Bake in a 350° oven for 40 to 45 minutes or until a knife inserted near center comes out clean. Cool on a wire rack for 5 to 10 minutes before serving.

Nutrition Facts per serving: 158 cal., 6 g total fat (4 g sat. fat), 26 mg chol., 531 mg sodium, 8 g carbo., 1 g fiber, 16 g pro.
Daily Values: 23% vit. A, 24% vit. C, 23% calcium, 6% iron

slow cooker
FAVORITES

It's such a good feeling to come home and have dinner ready when you walk in the door. That's the appeal of the slow cooker. But don't limit yourself to soups and roasts when there are so many fantastic slow cooker recipes, like Easy Beef Burgundy and Hot Pepper Pork Sandwiches.

Spicy Steak and Beans, *recipe page 224*

spicy steak AND BEANS

Queso fresco (KAY-so FRESK-o) means "fresh cheese" in Spanish, and you can find it in large supermarkets and Mexican food stores.

slow cooker

Prep: 25 minutes
Cook: 7 to 9 hours (low) or
3½ to 4½ hours (high);
plus 30 minutes (high)
Makes: 6 servings

1½ pounds beef flank steak

1 10-ounce can chopped tomatoes with green chile peppers, undrained

½ cup chopped onion

2 cloves garlic, minced

1 tablespoon snipped fresh oregano or 1 teaspoon dried oregano, crushed

1 teaspoon chili powder

1 teaspoon ground cumin

¼ teaspoon salt

¼ teaspoon black pepper

2 small green, red, and/or yellow sweet peppers, cut into strips

1 15-ounce can pinto beans, rinsed and drained

Hot cooked brown rice (optional)

Crumbled queso fresco or feta cheese (optional)

① Trim fat from meat. Place meat in a 3½- or 4-quart slow cooker. In a bowl stir together undrained tomatoes, onion, garlic, dried oregano (if using), chili powder, cumin, salt, and black pepper. Pour over meat.

② Cover and cook on low-heat setting for 7 to 9 hours or on high-heat setting for 3½ to 4½ hours.

③ If using low-heat setting, turn to high-heat setting. Stir in sweet pepper strips and pinto beans. Cover and cook for 30 minutes more. Remove meat; cool slightly. Shred or thinly slice meat across the grain. Stir fresh oregano (if using) into bean mixture.

④ If desired, spoon rice into soup bowls. Arrange meat on top of rice. Spoon bean mixture over meat. If desired, sprinkle with cheese.

Nutrition Facts per serving: 262 cal., 8 g total fat (3 g sat. fat), 45 mg chol., 452 mg sodium, 17 g carbo., 4 g fiber, 29 g pro.
Daily Values: 9% vit. A, 37% vit. C, 8% calcium, 18% iron

jerk beef ROAST

Jamaican jerk seasoning is the must-have ingredient for this roast. You'll enjoy its spicy-sweet combination of chiles, thyme, cinnamon, ginger, allspice, and cloves.

Prep: 30 minutes
Cook: 8 to 10 hours (low) or
4 to 5 hours (high)
Makes: 6 servings

1 2- to 2½-pound boneless
   beef chuck pot roast

¾ cup water

¼ cup raisins

¼ cup steak sauce

3 tablespoons balsamic vinegar

2 tablespoons sugar (optional)

2 tablespoons quick-cooking
   tapioca

1 teaspoon cracked black
   pepper

1 teaspoon Jamaican jerk
   seasoning

2 cloves garlic, minced
   Hot cooked brown rice
   (optional)

① Trim fat from meat. If necessary, cut roast to fit into a 3½- or 4-quart slow cooker. Place meat in the cooker. In a bowl combine the water, raisins, steak sauce, balsamic vinegar, sugar (if desired), tapioca, pepper, Jamaican jerk seasoning, and garlic. Pour mixture over roast.

② Cover and cook on low-heat setting for 8 to 10 hours or on high-heat setting for 4 to 5 hours. Skim fat from the cooking liquid. Serve beef with the cooking liquid and, if desired, hot cooked rice.

Nutrition Facts per serving: 237 cal., 6 g total fat (2 g sat. fat), 89 mg chol., 310 mg sodium, 12 g carbo., 1 g fiber, 33 g pro.
Daily Values: 2% vit. A, 4% vit. C, 2% calcium, 23% iron

Picking the Right Roast

Selecting a roast may be more difficult than it seems. At the meat counter you're faced with many types of roasts from rib to chuck arm pot to round tip. In addition to looking for a lean roast, you must consider how you're going to cook it. The leanest roasts are round roasts, a category that includes eye round, top round, bottom round, and tenderloin roast. All of these—except the bottom round—are excellent for roasting or cooking at a high heat. For bottom round, you're better off with moist cooking, such as in a covered pot with liquid.

sloppy joes WITH A KICK

There's nothing ho-hum about this familiar favorite! Sassy ingredients give it a lively twist.

Prep: 20 minutes
Cook: 6 to 8 hours (low) or
3 to 4 hours (high)
Makes: 8 servings

1½ pounds lean ground beef

1 cup chopped onion

1 clove garlic, minced

1 6-ounce can vegetable juice

½ cup catsup

½ cup water

2 tablespoons no-calorie,
heat-stable granular sugar
substitute

2 tablespoons chopped, canned
jalapeño peppers (optional)

1 tablespoon prepared mustard

2 teaspoons chili powder

1 teaspoon Worcestershire
sauce

8 whole wheat hamburger
buns, split and toasted

Shredded reduced-fat
cheddar cheese (optional)

Sweet pepper strips
(optional)

1 In a large skillet cook ground beef, onion, and garlic until meat is brown and onion is tender. Drain off fat.

2 Meanwhile, in a 3½- or 4-quart slow cooker combine vegetable juice, catsup, water, sugar substitute, jalapeño peppers (if desired), mustard, chili powder, and Worcestershire sauce. Stir in meat mixture.

3 Cover and cook on low-heat setting for 6 to 8 hours or on high-heat setting for 3 to 4 hours. Spoon meat mixture onto bun halves. If desired, sprinkle with cheese and serve with sweet pepper strips.

Nutrition Facts per serving: 310 cal., 13 g total fat (5 g sat. fat), 53 mg chol., 522 mg sodium, 27 g carbo., 3 g fiber, 21 g pro.
Daily Values: 12% vit. A, 13% vit. C, 7% calcium, 21% iron

slow cooker

227

round steak WITH HERBS

Cream of celery soup is the flavor base in this beef recipe. If you like, try other soup varieties such as cream of mushroom or onion.

slow cooker

Prep: 10 minutes
Cook: 10 to 12 hours (low) or
5 to 6 hours (high)
Makes: 6 servings

2 pounds beef round steak, cut
¾ inch thick

1 medium onion, sliced

1 10¾-ounce can condensed
cream of celery soup

½ teaspoon dried oregano,
crushed

¼ teaspoon dried thyme,
crushed

¼ teaspoon black pepper

Hot cooked whole wheat
pasta (optional)

1 Trim fat from meat. Cut steak into serving-size portions. Place onion in a 3½- or 4-quart slow cooker; place meat on top of onion. In a small bowl combine soup, oregano, thyme, and pepper; pour over meat.

2 Cover and cook on low-heat setting for 10 to 12 hours or on high-heat setting for 5 to 6 hours. If desired, serve steak with hot cooked pasta.

Nutrition Facts per serving: 249 cal., 9 g total fat (3 g sat. fat), 78 mg chol., 475 mg sodium, 5 g carbo., 1 g fiber, 34 g pro.
Daily Values: 3% vit. A, 1% vit. C, 3% calcium, 17% iron

easy BEEF BURGUNDY

The canned soups and onion soup mix do most of the work—all you have to do is cut up the meat and mushrooms.

Prep: 20 minutes
Cook: 8 to 10 hours (low) or
4 to 5 hours (high)
Makes: 6 servings

1½ **pounds beef stew meat, trimmed and cut into 1-inch pieces**

2 **tablespoons cooking oil**

1 **10¾-ounce can reduced-fat and reduced-sodium condensed cream of celery soup**

1 **10¾-ounce can reduced-fat and reduced-sodium condensed cream of mushroom soup** .

¾ **cup Burgundy**

1 **envelope (½ of a 2-ounce package) onion soup mix**

3 **cups sliced fresh mushrooms (8 ounces)**

Hot cooked whole wheat pasta or brown rice (optional)

① In a large skillet brown meat, half at a time, in hot oil. Drain off fat. In a 3½- to 5-quart slow cooker combine celery soup, mushroom soup, Burgundy, and onion soup mix. Stir in meat and mushrooms.

② Cover and cook on low-heat setting for 8 to 10 hours or on high-heat setting for 4 to 5 hours. If desired, serve over hot cooked pasta.

Nutrition Facts per serving: 301 cal., 13 g total fat (3 g sat. fat), 58 mg chol., 628 mg sodium, 12 g carbo., 0 g fiber, 27 g pro.
Daily Values: 1% calcium, 16% iron

Wine for Flavor

Cooking with wine is a great way to boost flavor without adding fat and with few extra calories. Common knowledge dictates the use of cheap, not necessarily great tasting, wine in cooking, but you might want to rethink this advice. When you cook with wine, the liquid evaporates, leaving a more concentrated flavor. Of course you don't need to break the bank, but you should at least use wine that you like to be sure you'll enjoy the stronger flavor brought out by the cooking.

so-easy PEPPER STEAK

In the mood for Mexican, Cajun, or Italian? Choose the appropriately seasoned tomatoes for robust flavor that usually comes only from a long list of seasonings.

Prep: 15 minutes
Cook: 10 to 12 hours (low) or
 5 to 6 hours (high)
Makes: 8 servings

2 pounds boneless beef round
 steak, cut ¾ to 1 inch thick

 Salt and black pepper

1 14½-ounce can Cajun-,
 Mexican-, or Italian-style
 stewed tomatoes, undrained

⅓ cup Italian-style tomato paste

½ teaspoon bottled hot pepper
 sauce

1 16-ounce package frozen
 sweet pepper stir-fry
 vegetables (yellow, green,
 and red peppers and onion)

 Hot cooked noodles or hot
 mashed potatoes

❶ Trim fat from meat. Cut meat into 8 serving-size pieces. Lightly sprinkle with salt and black pepper. Place meat in a 3½- or 4-quart slow cooker. In a medium bowl combine tomatoes, tomato paste, and hot pepper sauce. Pour over meat in cooker. Add frozen vegetables.

❷ Cover and cook on low-heat setting for 10 to 12 hours or on high-heat setting for 5 to 6 hours. Serve over hot cooked noodles.

Nutrition Facts per serving: 303 cal., 6 g total fat (2 g sat. fat), 80 mg chol., 416 mg sodium, 29 g carbo., 2 g fiber, 30 g pro.
Daily Values: 7% vit. A, 47% vit. C, 2% calcium, 22% iron

beef WITH MUSHROOMS

Cook a package of frozen mashed potatoes to serve with this saucy round steak. If you like, stir snipped fresh basil or grated Parmesan cheese into the cooked potatoes.

slow cooker

Prep: 10 minutes
Cook: 8 to 10 hours (low) or
4 to 5 hours (high)
Makes: 4 servings

1 **pound boneless beef round steak, cut 1 inch thick**

1 **medium onion, sliced**

1 **4-ounce jar whole mushrooms, drained**

1 **12-ounce jar beef gravy**

¼ **cup water**

1 Trim fat from meat. Cut meat into 4 serving-size pieces. Place onion slices in a 3½- or 4-quart slow cooker. Arrange mushrooms over onions; add beef. In a small bowl stir together gravy and water. Pour over beef.

2 Cover and cook on low-heat setting for 8 to 10 hours or on high-heat setting for 4 to 5 hours.

Nutrition Facts per serving: 193 cal., 4 g total fat (2 g sat. fat), 47 mg chol., 744 mg sodium, 9 g carbo., 2 g fiber, 29 g pro.
Daily Values: 3% vit. A, 2% calcium, 16% iron

brisket IN ALE

The flavorful gravy—made from the beer-spiked cooking liquid—is the finishing touch to this tender meat dish.

Prep: 25 minutes
Cook: 10 to 12 hours (low) or
5 to 6 hours (high); plus
10 minutes
Makes: 10 servings

- 1 **3- to 4-pound fresh beef brisket**
- 2 **medium onions, thinly sliced and separated into rings**
- 1 **bay leaf**
- 1 **12-ounce can beer**
- ¼ **cup chili sauce**
- 2 **tablespoons no-calorie, heat-stable granular sugar substitute**
- ½ **teaspoon dried thyme, crushed**
- ¼ **teaspoon salt**
- ¼ **teaspoon black pepper**
- 1 **clove garlic, minced**
- 2 **tablespoons cornstarch**
- 2 **tablespoons cold water**

1 Trim fat from meat. If necessary, cut brisket to fit into a 3½- to 6-quart slow cooker. Place the onions, bay leaf, and brisket in the cooker. In a medium bowl combine beer, chili sauce, sugar substitute, thyme, salt, pepper, and garlic; pour over meat.

2 Cover and cook on low-heat setting for 10 to 12 hours or on high-heat setting for 5 to 6 hours.

3 Using a slotted spoon, transfer brisket and onions to a serving platter; cover with foil to keep warm. Discard bay leaf.

4 For gravy, pour juices into a large measuring cup; skim fat. Measure 2½ cups liquid; discard remaining liquid. In a medium saucepan stir together cornstarch and water; stir in the cooking liquid. Cook and stir until thickened and bubbly; cook and stir for 2 minutes more. Pass gravy with meat.

Nutrition Facts per serving: 170 cal., 6 g total fat (2 g sat. fat), 46 mg chol., 216 mg sodium, 6 g carbo., 1 g fiber, 20 g pro.

super-simple BEEF STEW

Super-simple is right. It's hard to believe so few ingredients add up to such a satisfying one-dish winner.

Prep: 15 minutes
Cook: 8 to 9 hours (low) or
4 to 4½ hours (high);
plus 10 minutes (high)
Makes: 4 servings

12 ounces small red potatoes, quartered (about 2 cups)

4 medium carrots, cut into ½-inch pieces

1 small red onion, cut into wedges

1 pound beef stew meat

1 10¾-ounce can condensed cream of mushroom or cream of celery soup

1 cup beef broth

½ teaspoon dried marjoram or dried thyme, crushed

1 9-ounce package frozen cut green beans, thawed

1 In a 3½- or 4-quart slow cooker place potatoes, carrots, onion, stew meat, soup, beef broth, and marjoram. Stir to combine.

2 Cover and cook on low-heat setting for 8 to 9 hours or on high-heat setting for 4 to 4½ hours.

3 If using low-heat setting, turn to high-heat setting. Stir in thawed green beans. Cover and cook for 10 to 15 minutes more or just until green beans are tender.

Nutrition Facts per serving: 365 cal., 13 g total fat (4 g sat. fat), 54 mg chol., 830 mg sodium, 32 g carbo., 6 g fiber, 31 g pro.
Daily Values: 315% vit. A, 44% vit. C, 9% calcium, 27% iron

slow cooker

seeded PORK ROAST

A savory blend of anise, fennel, caraway, dill, and celery seeds creates a crustlike coating for this ultratender pork roast. The cooking liquid contains apple juice, which lends a subtle sweetness.

Prep: 25 minutes
Cook: 9 to 11 hours (low) or
4½ to 5½ hours (high);
plus 10 minutes (high)
Makes: 8 servings

1 2½- to 3-pound boneless pork
shoulder roast

1 tablespoon soy sauce

2 teaspoons anise seeds,
crushed

2 teaspoons fennel seeds,
crushed

2 teaspoons caraway seeds,
crushed

2 teaspoons dillseeds, crushed

2 teaspoons celery seeds,
crushed

½ cup beef broth

⅔ cup apple juice

1 tablespoon cornstarch

① Remove netting from roast, if present. If necessary, cut roast to fit into a 3½- to 5-quart slow cooker. Trim fat from meat. Brush soy sauce over surface of roast. On a large piece of foil combine the anise seeds, fennel seeds, caraway seeds, dillseeds, and celery seeds. Roll roast in seeds to coat evenly.

② Place roast in cooker. Pour broth and ⅓ cup of the apple juice around roast.

③ Cover and cook on low-heat setting for 9 to 11 hours or on high-heat setting for 4½ to 5½ hours.

④ Transfer roast to a serving platter. For gravy, strain cooking juices and skim fat; transfer juices to small saucepan. Combine remaining apple juice and cornstarch; add to juices in saucepan. Cook and stir until thickened and bubbly. Cook and stir 2 minutes more. Pass gravy with roast.

Nutrition Facts per serving: 220 cal., 9 g total fat (3 g sat. fat), 92 mg chol., 285 mg sodium, 5 g carbo., 0 g fiber, 29 g pro.
Daily Values: 3% vit. C, 4% calcium, 14% iron

brunswick STEW

Early Virginia settlers made this hearty stew with squirrel meat. Our updated version simmers all day in your slow cooker and features chicken and ham.

Prep: 20 minutes
Cook: 8 to 10 hours (low) or 4 to 5 hours (high); plus 45 minutes (high)
Makes: 6 servings

- 3 **medium onions, cut into thin wedges**
- 2 **pounds meaty chicken pieces (breasts, thighs, drumsticks), skinned**
- 1½ **cups diced cooked ham (8 ounces)**
- 1 **14½-ounce can diced tomatoes, undrained**
- 1 **14-ounce can chicken broth**
- 4 **cloves garlic, minced**
- 1 **tablespoon Worcestershire sauce**
- 1 **teaspoon dry mustard**
- 1 **teaspoon dried thyme, crushed**
- ¼ **teaspoon black pepper**
- ¼ **teaspoon bottled hot pepper sauce**
- 1 **10-ounce package frozen sliced okra**
- 1 **cup frozen baby lima beans**
- 1 **cup frozen whole kernel corn**

1 Place onion in a 3½- to 4-quart slow cooker. Top with chicken and ham. In a small bowl combine undrained tomatoes, broth, garlic, Worcestershire sauce, mustard, thyme, pepper, and hot pepper sauce; pour over chicken and ham.

2 Cover and cook on low-heat setting for 8 to 10 hours or on high-heat setting for 4 to 5 hours.

3 If desired, remove chicken; cool slightly. (Keep lid on the slow cooker.) Remove meat from chicken bones; cut meat into bite-size pieces. Return chicken to cooker; discard bones.

4 Add okra, lima beans, and corn to slow cooker. If using low-heat setting turn to high-heat setting. Cover and cook 45 minutes more or until vegetables are tender.

Nutrition Facts per serving: 417 cal., 11 g total fat (3 g sat. fat), 124 mg chol., 1,252 mg sodium, 36 g carbo., 7 g fiber, 43 g pro.
Daily Values: 17% vit. A, 65% vit. C, 15% calcium, 26% iron

hot pepper pork SANDWICHES

You can adjust the heat level by varying the number of jalapeños you use. Want to turn up the heat even more? Leave the pepper seeds intact.

Prep: 20 minutes
Cook: 11 to 12 hours (low) or
5½ to 6 hours (high)
Makes: 8 servings

1 **2½- to 3-pound boneless pork shoulder roast**

2 **teaspoons fajita seasoning**

1 **or 2 fresh jalapeño peppers, seeded, if desired, and finely chopped,* or 1 large green or red sweet pepper, seeded and cut into bite-size strips**

2 **10-ounce cans enchilada sauce**

8 **whole grain hamburger buns or kaiser rolls, split and, if desired, toasted**

1 Trim fat from meat. If necessary, cut roast to fit into a 3½- or 4-quart slow cooker. Place meat in the cooker. Sprinkle with fajita seasoning. Add peppers and enchilada sauce.

2 Cover and cook on low-heat setting for 11 to 12 hours or on high-heat setting for 5½ to 6 hours. Transfer roast to a cutting board. Using 2 forks, shred meat. Stir shredded meat into juices in slow cooker. Using a slotted spoon, spoon shredded meat mixture into toasted buns.

*Note: Because chile peppers, such as jalapeños, contain volatile oils that can burn your skin and eyes, avoid direct contact with them as much as possible. When working with chile peppers, wear plastic or rubber gloves. If your bare hands do touch the chile peppers, wash your hands and nails well with soap and warm water.

Nutrition Facts per serving: 262 cal., 9 g total fat (3 g sat. fat), 58 mg chol., 778 mg sodium, 23 g carbo., 3 g fiber, 22 g pro.
Daily Values: 4% vit. A, 6% vit. C, 7% calcium, 18% iron

slow cooker

thyme and garlic CHICKEN

Thyme, garlic, a little orange juice, and a splash of balsamic vinegar flavor these moist, fork-tender chicken breasts.

Prep: 15 minutes
Cook: 5 to 6 hours (low) or
2½ to 3 hours (high);
plus 10 minutes
Makes: 6 to 8 servings

6 **cloves garlic, minced**

1½ **teaspoons dried thyme, crushed**

3 **to 4 pounds whole chicken breasts (with bone), halved and skinned**

¼ **cup orange juice**

1 **tablespoon balsamic vinegar**

① Sprinkle garlic and thyme over chicken pieces. Place chicken in a 3½- or 4-quart slow cooker. Pour orange juice and vinegar over chicken.

② Cover and cook on low-heat setting for 5 to 6 hours or on high-heat setting for 2½ to 3 hours.

③ Remove chicken from cooker; cover with foil to keep warm. Skim fat from cooking juices. Strain juices into a saucepan. Bring to boiling; reduce heat. Boil gently, uncovered, about 10 minutes or until reduced to 1 cup. Pass juices with chicken.

Nutrition Facts per serving: 178 cal., 2 g total fat (0 g sat. fat), 85 mg chol., 78 mg sodium, 3 g carbo., 0 g fiber, 34 g pro.
Daily Values: 2% vit. A, 13% vit. C, 3% calcium, 7% iron

mediterranean CHICKEN

If you think you've served chicken in every way imaginable, you'll love this dish. The flavors of artichokes, olives, and thyme lend a Mediterranean accent.

Prep: 20 minutes
Cook: 7 to 8 hours (low) or
       3½ to 4 hours (high)
Makes: 6 servings

2 **cups sliced fresh mushrooms**

1 **14½-ounce can diced tomatoes, undrained**

1 **8- or 9-ounce package frozen artichoke hearts**

1 **cup chicken broth**

½ **cup chopped onion**

½ **cup sliced, pitted ripe olives or ¼ cup capers, drained**

¼ **cup dry white wine or chicken broth**

3 **tablespoons quick-cooking tapioca**

2 **to 3 teaspoons curry powder**

¾ **teaspoon dried thyme, crushed**

¼ **teaspoon salt**

¼ **teaspoon black pepper**

1½ **pounds skinless, boneless chicken breast halves and/or thighs**

   Hot cooked brown rice (optional)

1 In a 3½- or 4-quart slow cooker place mushrooms, undrained tomatoes, frozen artichoke hearts, broth, onion, olives, and wine. Stir in tapioca, curry powder, thyme, salt, and pepper. Add chicken; spoon some of the tomato mixture over the chicken.

2 Cover and cook on low-heat setting for 7 to 8 hours or on high-heat setting for 3½ to 4 hours. If desired, serve with hot cooked rice.

Nutrition Facts per serving: 227 cal., 4 g total fat (1 g sat. fat), 66 mg chol., 578 mg sodium, 15 g carbo., 4 g fiber, 29 g pro.
Daily Values: 3% vit. A, 22% vit. C, 8% calcium, 13% iron

slow cooker

Oh, Tomato!

Canned tomatoes are a terrific pantry staple. They're available whole, pureed, diced, and seasoned. With few calories, tomatoes boost both the flavor and the nutritional impact of a recipe. They're loaded with the antioxidant lycopene, which may prevent prostate cancer as well as other cancers and heart disease. Canned tomatoes, because they are cooked, have a much higher level of lycopene.

chicken IN WINE SAUCE

Chicken and hearty vegetables are simmered in a delicate wine-flavored sauce. Choose dark meat chicken—thighs or drumsticks—for this dish.

Prep: 20 minutes
Cook: 8 to 9 hours (low) or
      4 to 4½ hours (high);
      plus 10 minutes
Makes: 6 servings

4 **medium red-skin potatoes, quartered**

4 **medium carrots, cut into ½-inch pieces**

2 **stalks celery, cut into 1-inch pieces**

1 **small onion, sliced**

3 **pounds chicken thighs or drumsticks, skinned**

1 **tablespoon snipped fresh parsley**

½ **teaspoon salt**

½ **teaspoon dried rosemary, crushed**

½ **teaspoon dried thyme, crushed**

¼ **teaspoon black pepper**

1 **clove garlic, minced**

1 **cup chicken broth**

½ **cup dry white wine**

3 **tablespoons butter or margarine**

3 **tablespoons all-purpose flour**

   Snipped fresh thyme (optional)

❶ In a 5- or 6-quart slow cooker place potatoes, carrots, celery, and onion. Place chicken pieces on top of vegetables. Sprinkle with parsley, salt, rosemary, dried thyme, pepper, and garlic; add broth and wine.

❷ Cover and cook on low-heat setting for 8 to 9 hours or on high-heat setting for 4 to 4½ hours. Using a slotted spoon, transfer chicken and vegetables to a serving platter; cover with foil to keep warm.

❸ For gravy, skim fat from cooking juices; strain juices. In a large saucepan melt butter. Stir in flour and cook for 1 minute. Add cooking juices. Cook and stir until thickened and bubbly. Cook and stir 2 minutes more. If desired, sprinkle chicken and vegetables with snipped fresh thyme. Pass gravy with the chicken and vegetables.

Nutrition Facts per serving: 328 cal., 11 g total fat (5 g sat. fat), 124 mg chol., 544 mg sodium, 24 g carbo., 3 g fiber, 29 g pro.
Daily Values: 213% vit. A, 33% vit. C, 5% calcium, 14% iron

ginger-tomato CHICKEN

Chicken drumsticks and thighs are great for the slow cooker. They stay moist and tender during the long cooking time.

Prep: 20 minutes
Cook: 6 to 7 hours (low) or
3 to 3½ hours (high)
Makes: 6 servings

12 **chicken drumsticks and/or thighs, skinned (2½ to 3 pounds)**

2 **14½-ounce cans tomatoes**

2 **tablespoons quick-cooking tapioca**

1 **tablespoon grated fresh ginger**

1 **tablespoon snipped fresh cilantro or parsley**

4 **cloves garlic, minced**

2 **teaspoons brown sugar (optional)**

½ **teaspoon crushed red pepper**

½ **teaspoon salt**

Hot cooked brown rice (optional)

1 Place chicken pieces in a 3½- or 4-quart slow cooker.

2 Drain 1 can of tomatoes; chop tomatoes from both cans. For sauce, in a medium bowl combine chopped tomatoes and the juice from 1 can, the tapioca, ginger, cilantro, garlic, brown sugar (if using), crushed red pepper, and salt. Pour sauce over chicken.

3 Cover and cook on low-heat setting for 6 to 7 hours or on high-heat setting for 3 to 3½ hours. Skim fat from sauce. Serve chicken with sauce in shallow bowls. If desired, serve with brown rice.

Nutrition Facts per serving: 168 cal., 4 g total fat (1 g sat. fat), 81 mg chol., 472 mg sodium, 10 g carbo., 1 g fiber, 23 g pro.
Daily Values: 18% vit. A, 40% vit. C, 6% calcium, 10% iron

slow cooker

italian chicken AND PASTA

For a colorful variation, try spinach or red pepper fettuccine.

Prep: 15 minutes
Cook: 5 to 6 hours (low) or
2½ to 3 hours (high)
Makes: 4 servings

12 ounces skinless, boneless chicken thighs

1 9-ounce package frozen Italian-style green beans

1 cup fresh mushrooms, quartered

1 small onion, sliced ¼ inch thick

1 14½-ounce can Italian-style stewed tomatoes, undrained

1 6-ounce can Italian-style tomato paste

1 teaspoon dried Italian seasoning, crushed

2 cloves garlic, minced

6 ounces fettuccine, cooked and drained

3 tablespoons finely shredded Parmesan cheese

① Cut chicken into 1-inch pieces; set aside. In a 3½- or 4-quart slow cooker place green beans, mushrooms, and onion. Place chicken on vegetables.

② In a small bowl combine undrained tomatoes, tomato paste, Italian seasoning, and garlic. Pour over chicken.

③ Cover and cook on low-heat setting for 5 to 6 hours or on high-heat setting for 2½ to 3 hours. Serve over hot cooked fettuccine. Sprinkle with Parmesan cheese.

Nutrition Facts per serving: 405 cal., 7 g total fat (2 g sat. fat), 75 mg chol., 728 mg sodium, 55 g carbo., 4 g fiber, 28 g pro.
Daily Values: 7% vit. A, 46% vit. C, 15% calcium, 26% iron

slow cooker

teriyaki and orange CHICKEN

Here's a sauce that's sweet and full of flavor. Use orange sections or slices to garnish the meal.

Prep: 15 minutes
Cook: 4 to 5 hours (low) or
    2 to 2½ hours (high)
Makes: 4 servings

1 **16-ounce package frozen loose-pack broccoli, carrots, and water chestnuts**

2 **tablespoons quick-cooking tapioca**

1 **pound skinless, boneless chicken breast halves or thighs, cut into 1-inch pieces**

¾ **cup chicken broth**

3 **tablespoons orange marmalade**

2 **tablespoons bottled teriyaki sauce**

1 **teaspoon dry mustard**

½ **teaspoon ground ginger**

2 **cups hot cooked brown rice**

1 In a 3½- or 4-quart slow cooker combine frozen vegetables and tapioca. Add chicken.

2 In a small bowl combine chicken broth, orange marmalade, teriyaki sauce, dry mustard, and ginger. Pour over mixture in cooker.

3 Cover and cook on low-heat setting for 4 to 5 hours or on high-heat setting for 2 to 2½ hours. Serve with hot cooked rice.

Nutrition Facts per serving: 375 cal., 4 g total fat (1 g sat. fat), 79 mg chol., 790 mg sodium, 52 g carbo., 4 g fiber, 30 g pro.
Daily Values: 40% vit. A, 16% vit. C, 3% calcium, 17% iron

barbecued TURKEY THIGHS

Who needs a grill for barbecue? These shapely, saucy thighs keep their form nicely during slow heat cooking and can hold their own among other grilled turkey dishes.

Prep: 15 minutes
Cook: 10 to 12 hours (low) or
 5 to 6 hours (high)
Makes: 4 to 6 servings

½ **cup catsup**

2 **tablespoons no-calorie, heat-stable granular sugar substitute**

1 **tablespoon quick-cooking tapioca**

1 **tablespoon vinegar**

1 **teaspoon Worcestershire sauce**

¼ **teaspoon ground cinnamon**

¼ **teaspoon crushed red pepper**

2 **to 2½ pounds turkey thighs (about 2 thighs) or meaty chicken pieces (breasts, thighs, and drumsticks), skinned**

Hot cooked brown rice or whole wheat pasta (optional)

1 In a 3½- or 4-quart slow cooker combine catsup, sugar substitute, tapioca, vinegar, Worcestershire sauce, cinnamon, and red pepper. Place turkey thighs meaty side down on catsup mixture.

2 Cover and cook on low-heat setting for 10 to 12 hours or high-heat setting for 5 to 6 hours. Transfer turkey to a serving dish. Pour cooking juices into a small bowl; skim off fat. Serve turkey with cooking juices and, if desired, hot cooked rice.

Nutrition Facts per serving: 225 cal., 6 g total fat (2 g sat. fat), 100 mg chol., 444 mg sodium, 12 g carbo., 1 g fiber, 30 g pro.
Daily Values: 8% vit. A, 9% vit. C, 5% calcium, 17% iron

Slow Cooker Tips

After a long day there's nothing like coming home to the aroma of a hot meal cooking in a slow cooker. While the time saved at night is terrific, putting the meal together in the morning is a bit more challenging. To eliminate this problem, simply prepare the meal the night before. Brown meats, if necessary, cut and chop veggies, and measure liquids. If your slow cooker has a removable cook well, place all the ingredients in it and refrigerate overnight. If not, place everything in a plastic bag to refrigerate overnight and put into the slow cooker in the morning.

turkey CHABLIS

Only wines grown in the village of Chablis, France, are truly Chablis wines. But did you know that the grape used in these wines is Chardonnay? You can use a Chardonnay in this recipe or your favorite dry white wine.

Prep: 15 minutes
Cook: 9 to 10 hours (low) or
4½ to 5 hours (high)
Makes: 6 to 8 servings

¾ cup dry white wine

½ cup chopped onion

1 bay leaf

1 clove garlic, minced

1 3½- to 4-pound frozen boneless turkey, thawed

1 teaspoon dried rosemary, crushed

¼ teaspoon black pepper

⅓ cup half-and-half, light cream, or milk

2 tablespoons cornstarch

1 In a 3½- to 6-quart slow cooker combine wine, onion, bay leaf, and garlic. Remove netting from turkey, if present. Remove gravy packet, if present, and chill for another use. In a small bowl combine rosemary and pepper. Sprinkle rosemary mixture evenly over turkey; rub in with your fingers. Place turkey in cooker.

2 Cover and cook on low-heat setting for 9 to 10 hours or on high-heat setting for 4½ to 5 hours. Remove turkey from cooker, reserving juices. Cover turkey and keep warm.

3 For gravy, strain juices into a glass measuring cup; skim off fat. Measure 1⅓ cups juices. Pour juices into a small saucepan. Combine half-and-half and cornstarch; stir into juices in saucepan. Cook and stir over medium heat until thickened and bubbly. Cook and stir for 2 minutes more.

4 Slice turkey; arrange on a serving platter. Spoon some of the gravy over turkey. Pass remaining gravy.

Nutrition Facts per serving: 365 cal., 9 g total fat (3 g sat. fat), 176 mg chol., 193 mg sodium, 5 g carbo., 0 g fiber, 58 g pro.
Daily Values: 1% vit. A, 2% vit. C, 6% calcium, 23% iron

slow cooker

bean-and-rice-stuffed PEPPERS

Five easy ingredients make a delicious, healthy meatless meal.

Prep: 15 minutes
Cook: 6 to 6½ hours (low) or
3 to 3½ hours (high)
Makes: 4 servings

4 medium green, red, or yellow sweet peppers

1 cup cooked converted rice

1 15-ounce can chili beans with chili gravy

4 ounces Monterey Jack cheese, shredded (1 cup)

1 15-ounce can chunky tomato sauce with onion, celery, and green pepper

1 Halve the sweet peppers lengthwise, removing tops, membranes, and seeds. Stir together rice, beans, and ½ cup of the cheese; spoon into peppers. Pour tomato sauce into the bottom of a 5- or 6-quart slow cooker. Place peppers filled side up in cooker.

2 Cover and cook on low-heat setting for 6 to 6½ hours or on high heat setting for 3 to 3½ hours. Transfer peppers to a serving plate. Spoon tomato sauce over peppers; sprinkle with remaining cheese.

Nutrition Facts per serving: 323 cal., 11 g total fat (5 g sat. fat), 25 mg chol., 918 mg sodium, 41 g carbo., 9 g fiber, 16 g pro.
Daily Values: 86% vit. A, 206% vit. C, 34% calcium, 16% iron

slow cooker

pasta WITH EGGPLANT SAUCE

Chunks of eggplant cook in a traditional spaghetti sauce, making a tasty low-calorie alternative to ground beef or sausage.

Prep: 20 minutes
Cook: 7 to 8 hours (low) or
      3½ to 4 hours (high)
Makes: 6 servings

1 medium eggplant

½ cup chopped onion

1 28-ounce can Italian-style tomatoes, undrained and cut up

1 6-ounce can Italian-style tomato paste

1 4-ounce can sliced mushrooms, drained

2 cloves garlic, minced

¼ cup dry red wine

¼ cup water

1½ teaspoons dried oregano, crushed

½ cup pitted kalamata olives or pitted ripe olives, sliced

2 tablespoons snipped fresh parsley

Salt

Black pepper

4 cups hot cooked penne pasta

⅓ cup grated or shredded Parmesan cheese

2 tablespoons toasted pine nuts (optional)

1 Peel eggplant, if desired; cut eggplant into 1-inch cubes. In a 3½- to 5-quart slow cooker combine eggplant, onion, undrained tomatoes, tomato paste, mushrooms, garlic, wine, water, and oregano.

2 Cover and cook on low-heat setting for 7 to 8 hours or on high-heat setting for 3½ to 4 hours. Stir in olives and parsley. Season to taste with salt and pepper. Serve over pasta. Top with Parmesan cheese and, if desired, toasted pine nuts.

Nutrition Facts per serving: 259 cal., 6 g total fat (1 g sat. fat), 4 mg chol., 804 mg sodium, 42 g carbo., 7 g fiber, 10 g pro.
Daily Values: 18% vit. A, 37% vit. C, 13% calcium, 20% iron

meatless BURRITOS

Everyone likes burritos, and this recipe makes enough to serve a crowd. For easy accompaniments pick up a fruit salad from the deli and a package or two of Mexican-style rice mix.

Prep: 20 minutes
Cook: 6 to 8 hours (low) or
3 to 4 hours (high)
Makes: 16 servings

- 3 15-ounce cans red kidney and/or black beans, rinsed and drained
- 1 14½-ounce can diced tomatoes, undrained
- 1½ cups bottled salsa or picante sauce
- 1 11-ounce can whole kernel corn with sweet peppers, drained
- 1 fresh jalapeño chile pepper, seeded and finely chopped (optional)
- 2 teaspoons chili powder
- 2 cloves garlic, minced
- 16 8- to 10-inch flour tortillas, warmed
- 2 cups shredded lettuce
- 1 cup shredded taco cheese or cheddar cheese (4 ounces)
  Sliced green onions and/or dairy sour cream (optional)

1 In a 3½- or 4-quart slow cooker combine beans, undrained tomatoes, salsa, corn, jalapeño pepper (if desired), chili powder, and garlic.

2 Cover and cook on low-heat setting for 6 to 8 hours or on high-heat setting for 3 to 4 hours.

3 To serve, spoon some bean mixture just below center of each tortilla. Top with lettuce and cheese. If desired, top with green onions and/or sour cream. Fold bottom edge of each tortilla up and over filling. Fold in opposite sides; roll up from bottom.

Nutrition Facts per serving: 205 cal., 3 g total fat (2 g sat. fat), 7 mg chol., 471 mg sodium, 34 g carbo., 6 g fiber, 8 g pro.
Daily Values: 10% vit. A, 14% vit. C, 12% calcium, 13% iron

slow cooker

253

vegetable chili WITH PASTA

Finely chop the onion to ensure that it's fully cooked. When you're ready to serve this family-style supper, sprinkle each serving with cheese.

Prep: 20 minutes
Cook: 4 to 5 hours (low) or
2 to 2½ hours (high)
Makes: 5 servings

1 **15-ounce can garbanzo beans, rinsed and drained**

1 **15-ounce can red kidney beans, rinsed and drained**

2 **14½-ounce cans diced tomatoes, undrained**

1 **8-ounce can tomato sauce**

1 **cup finely chopped onion**

½ **cup chopped green or yellow sweet pepper**

2 **cloves garlic, minced**

2 **to 3 teaspoons chili powder**

½ **teaspoon dried oregano, crushed**

⅛ **teaspoon ground red pepper (optional)**

1 **cup wagon wheel pasta or elbow macaroni**

   Shredded cheddar cheese (optional)

❶ In a 3½- or 4-quart slow cooker combine beans, undrained tomatoes, tomato sauce, onion, sweet pepper, garlic, chili powder, oregano, and, if desired, red pepper.

❷ Cover; cook on low-heat setting for 4 to 5 hours or on high-heat setting for 2 to 2½ hours.

❸ Cook pasta according to package directions; drain. Stir cooked pasta into bean mixture. Serve in bowls and, if desired, sprinkle with cheddar cheese.

Nutrition Facts per serving: 273 cal., 2 g total fat (0 g sat. fat), 0 mg chol., 868 mg sodium, 53 g carbo., 10 g fiber, 14 g pro.
Daily Values: 13% vit. A, 57% vit. C, 13% calcium, 22% iron

sloppy veggie SANDWICHES

Instead of making sandwiches, try serving the vegetable mixture on tostada shells with shredded lettuce, chopped tomato, and shredded cheese for a taco-style salad.

Prep: 20 minutes
Cook: 3 to 3½ hours (high),
plus 30 minutes (high)
Makes: 8 sandwiches

1 **cup chopped carrots**

1 **cup chopped celery**

⅔ **cup brown lentils, rinsed and drained**

⅔ **cup uncooked regular brown rice**

½ **cup chopped onion**

2 **tablespoons brown sugar**

2 **tablespoons prepared mustard**

½ **teaspoon salt**

⅛ **to ¼ teaspoon cayenne pepper**

1 **clove garlic, minced**

2 **14-ounce cans vegetable or chicken broth**

1 **15-ounce can tomato sauce**

2 **tablespoons cider vinegar**

8 **whole wheat hamburger buns or French-style rolls, split and toasted**

❶ In a 3½- or 4-quart slow cooker combine carrots, celery, lentils, brown rice, onion, brown sugar, mustard, salt, cayenne pepper, and garlic. Stir in vegetable broth.

❷ Cover and cook on high-heat setting for 3 to 3½ hours. Stir in tomato sauce and vinegar. Cover and cook for 30 minutes more. Serve mixture on toasted buns.

Nutrition Facts per sandwich: 261 cal., 4 g total fat (1 g sat. fat), 0 mg chol., 1,036 mg sodium, 50 g carbo., 8 g fiber, 11 g pro.
Daily Values: 78% vit. A, 5% vit. C, 7% calcium, 21% iron

slow cooker

squash AND LENTIL SOUP

The magic of this soup is garam masala, found in the spice aisle of most supermarkets. This blend of ground spices can include cinnamon, nutmeg, cloves, coriander, cumin, cardamom, pepper, chiles, fennel, and mace.

Prep: 25 minutes
Cook: 8 to 9 hours (low) or
     4 to 4½ hours (high)
Makes: 5 to 6 servings

- 1 **cup dry lentils**
- 2½ **cups peeled butternut squash, cut into ¾-inch pieces**
- ½ **cup chopped onion**
- ½ **cup chopped carrot**
- ½ **cup chopped celery**
- 2 **cloves garlic, minced**
- 1 **teaspoon garam masala**
- 4 **cups chicken broth or vegetable broth**

① Rinse and drain lentils. In a 3½- or 4-quart slow cooker combine lentils, squash, onion, carrot, and celery. Sprinkle garlic and garam masala over vegetables. Pour broth over all.

② Cover and cook on low-heat setting for 8 to 9 hours or on high-heat setting for 4 to 4½ hours. Ladle into bowls.

Nutrition Facts per serving: 199 cal., 2 g total fat (0 g sat. fat), 0 mg chol., 639 mg sodium, 31 g carbo., 13 g fiber, 16 g pro.
Daily Values: 107% vit. A, 17% vit. C, 6% calcium, 22% iron

indian VEGETABLE SOUP

Chock-full of nutty garbanzo beans, red-skin potatoes, and chunks of eggplant, this curried soup makes a hearty meal.

Prep: 30 minutes
Cook: 8 to 10 hours (low) or
      4 to 5 hours (high)
Makes: 6 to 8 servings

1 medium eggplant, cut into ½-inch cubes (5 to 6 cups)

1 pound red-skin potatoes, cut into 1-inch pieces (3 cups)

2 cups chopped tomatoes or one 14½-ounce can low-sodium tomatoes, undrained and cut up

1 15-ounce can garbanzo beans (chickpeas), rinsed and drained

1 tablespoon grated fresh ginger

1½ teaspoons mustard seeds

1½ teaspoons ground coriander

1 teaspoon curry powder

¼ teaspoon black pepper

4 cups vegetable broth or chicken broth

2 tablespoons snipped fresh cilantro

① In a 4- to 6-quart slow cooker combine eggplant, potatoes, undrained tomatoes, and garbanzo beans. Sprinkle vegetables with ginger, mustard seeds, coriander, curry powder, and pepper. Pour broth over all.

② Cover and cook on low-heat setting for 8 to 10 hours or on high-heat setting for 4 to 5 hours. Ladle into bowls and sprinkle with cilantro.

Nutrition Facts per serving: 162 cal., 2 g total fat (0 g sat. fat), 0 mg chol., 889 mg sodium, 30 g carbo., 7 g fiber, 8 g pro.
Daily Values: 7% vit. A, 33% vit. C, 4% calcium, 10% iron

slow cooker

soups
& STEWS

A hearty soup paired with salad or bread is a satisfying meal. Generally, soups are chock-full of vegetables, making them a nutritious choice. From hot to cold to meatless to meat-brimmed, this chapter includes a variety of soups and stews to enjoy for lunch or dinner.

Shrimp Gazpacho, *recipe page 290*

mulligatawny SOUP

Nourishing and delicious are the best words to describe this hearty chicken soup. To reap all the rewards of this Indian-inspired dish, sop up the rich, curried broth with chunks of warm bread.

soups and stews

Prep: 25 minutes
Cook: 35 minutes
Makes: 6 (1⅓-cup) servings

1	**tablespoon cooking oil**
1	**cup chopped onion**
1	**cup coarsely chopped carrots**
1	**cup sliced celery**
1⅓	**cups chopped, peeled, tart apples**
2 to 3	**teaspoons curry powder**
¼	**teaspoon salt**
3	**cups reduced-sodium chicken broth**
3	**cups water**
1	**14½-ounce can low-sodium stewed tomatoes**
2	**cups chopped cooked chicken or turkey**

① In a Dutch oven heat cooking oil over medium heat. Cook and stir onion, carrots, and celery in hot oil about 10 minutes or until crisp-tender. Reduce heat to medium-low; add apples, curry powder, and salt. Cook, covered, for 5 minutes. Stir in the chicken broth, water, and undrained tomatoes. Bring to boiling; reduce heat. Simmer, covered, for 10 minutes. Stir in the chicken or turkey; simmer for 10 minutes more.

Nutrition facts per serving: 197 cal., 7 g total fat (1 g sat. fat), 45 mg chol., 517 mg sodium, 17 g carbo., 4 g fiber, 17 g pro.
Daily values: 62% vit. A, 16% vit. C, 3% calcium, 8% iron

chicken chili MONTEREY

This "white" chili packs all the punch of the traditional "bowl of red," and then some. For a distinctive look, use blue corn tortillas instead of the more traditional yellow ones.

Prep: 20 minutes
Cook: 10 minutes
Makes: 4 (1½-cup) servings

- **1 tablespoon cooking oil**
- **½ cup chopped onion**
- **2 cloves garlic, minced**
- **2 to 3 teaspoons chili powder**
- **½ teaspoon ground cumin**
- **1 15-ounce can reduced-sodium navy beans, great Northern beans, or white kidney beans, rinsed and drained**
- **1 14½-ounce can reduced-sodium chicken broth**
- **1¾ cups water**
- **½ of a 4½-ounce can (about ¼ cup) diced green chile peppers**
- **1½ cups chopped cooked chicken**
- **1 to 2 tablespoons snipped fresh cilantro or parsley**
- **2 6-inch corn tortillas, cut into thin, bite-size strips**
- **¼ cup shredded reduced-fat Monterey Jack cheese**

❶ In a large saucepan heat oil over medium heat. Cook and stir the onion and garlic in hot oil about 4 minutes or until onion is tender; stir in the chili powder and cumin. Cook and stir for 1 minute more. Stir in beans, chicken broth, water, and chile peppers. Bring to boiling; reduce heat. Simmer, covered, for 10 minutes, stirring occasionally. Stir in the chicken and cilantro or parsley. Heat through. Top each serving with tortilla strips and cheese.

Nutrition facts per serving: 301 cal., 11 g total fat (2 g sat. fat), 56 mg chol., 472 mg sodium, 26 g carbo., 6 g fiber, 27 g pro.
Daily values: 6% vit. A, 11% vit. C, 13% calcium, 22% iron

soups and stews

5-spice CHICKEN NOODLE SOUP

Asian dishes abound with flavor-packed ingredients. This soup is no exception, with its highlights of soy, five-spice powder, and ginger. All add a flavor punch without adding lots of calories or fat.

Start to Finish: 20 minutes
Makes: 4 (1½-cup) servings

- 2½ **cups water**
- 1¼ **cups reduced-sodium chicken broth**
- 2 **green onions, thinly bias-sliced**
- 2 **teaspoons reduced-sodium soy sauce**
- 2 **cloves garlic, minced**
- ¼ **teaspoon five-spice powder**
- ⅛ **teaspoon ground ginger**
- 2 **cups chopped bok choy**
- 1 **medium red sweet pepper, thinly sliced into strips**
- 2 **ounces dried somen noodles, broken into 2-inch lengths, or 2 ounces dried fine noodles**
- 1½ **cups chopped cooked chicken**

1 In a large saucepan combine water, chicken broth, green onions, soy sauce, garlic, five-spice powder, and ginger. Bring to boiling. Stir in bok choy, sweet pepper strips, and noodles. Return to boiling; reduce heat. Boil gently, uncovered, for 3 to 5 minutes or until noodles are just tender. Stir in the cooked chicken. Heat through.

Nutrition facts per serving: 181 cal., 4 g total fat (1 g sat. fat), 51 mg chol., 556 mg sodium, 14 g carbo., 1 g fiber, 20 g pro.
Daily values: 27% vit. A, 83% vit. C, 4% calcium, 8% iron

soups and stews

wild rice CHICKEN SOUP

The flavors of Mediterranean cuisine shine through in this recipe with zucchini, garlic, fresh herbs, and Madeira. It's a sunny twist on old-fashioned chicken and rice soup.

Start to Finish: 25 minutes
Makes: 6 (1⅔-cup) servings

- 1 6.2-ounce package quick-cooking long-grain and wild rice mix
- 2 14½-ounce cans reduced-sodium chicken broth
- 4 cloves garlic, minced
- 1 tablespoon snipped fresh thyme or 1 teaspoon dried thyme, crushed
- 4 cups chopped tomatoes
- 1 9-ounce package frozen chopped cooked chicken
- 1 cup finely chopped zucchini
- ¼ teaspoon freshly ground pepper
- 1 tablespoon Madeira or dry sherry (optional)

① Prepare rice mix according to package directions, except omit the seasoning packet and the margarine.

② Meanwhile, in a Dutch oven combine chicken broth, garlic, and dried thyme (if using); bring to boiling. Stir in the tomatoes, chicken, zucchini, fresh thyme (if using), and pepper. Return to boiling; reduce heat. Simmer, covered, for 5 minutes. Stir in cooked rice and, if desired, Madeira or dry sherry. Heat through.

Nutrition facts per serving: 236 cal., 5 g total fat (1 g sat. fat), 38 mg chol., 440 mg sodium, 31 g carbo., 2 g fiber, 18 g pro.
Daily values: 10% vit. A, 48% vit. C, 2% calcium, 16% iron

Living Wild

Wild rice is known for its chewy texture and nutlike flavor. But its name is a misnomer—it isn't rice at all. It's a long-grain marsh grass. Wild rice takes longer to cook than other rices (up to an hour) and costs more, too. Fortunately, wild rice is available in timesaving rice mixes (such as the one called for above) that allow you to enjoy it more conveniently and less expensively.

moroccan CHICKEN SOUP

Spices were a big commodity along the ancient trade routes that ran through the North African countries between Asia and Europe. That legacy is still apparent in modern Moroccan cuisine.

Prep: 30 minutes
Cook: 12 minutes
Makes: 6 (1½-cup) servings

1 teaspoon paprika
1 teaspoon ground cumin
¼ teaspoon ground coriander
¼ teaspoon ground turmeric
Dash ground red pepper
12 ounces skinless, boneless chicken breast halves
2 teaspoons olive oil
¾ cup chopped onion
2 cloves garlic, minced
1 14½-ounce can reduced-sodium chicken broth
1¾ cups water
1 cup cubed, peeled acorn squash or butternut squash
1 cup cubed, peeled turnip
½ cup bias-sliced carrot
⅛ teaspoon salt
1 tablespoon lemon juice

1 In a small bowl stir together paprika, cumin, coriander, turmeric, and red pepper; set aside. Rinse chicken; pat dry. Cut chicken into bite-size strips. Toss chicken with 2 teaspoons of the spice mixture, reserving remaining spice mixture.

2 In a large saucepan heat olive oil over medium-high heat. Cook and stir chicken in hot oil for 3 to 4 minutes or until chicken is no longer pink. Use a slotted spoon to remove chicken from pan; keep warm.

3 Add onion and garlic to drippings in pan. (If necessary, add an additional 1 teaspoon olive oil to the pan.) Cook and stir until onion is tender. Stir in chicken broth, water, squash, turnip, carrot, salt, and reserved spice mixture. Bring to boiling; reduce heat. Simmer, covered, for 12 to 15 minutes or until vegetables are tender. Stir in chicken and lemon juice. Heat through.

Nutrition facts per serving: 166 cal., 6 g total fat (1 g sat. fat), 45 mg chol., 431 mg sodium, 11 g carbo., 3 g fiber, 19 g pro.
Daily values: 64% vit. A, 21% vit. C, 4% calcium, 12% iron

soups and stews

chicken TORTELLINI SOUP

This soup is no ordinary chicken soup. Chunks of chicken and vegetables share the bowl with lightly cooked,
iron-rich leafy greens and plump, cheesy tortellini.

soups and stews

Start to Finish: 40 minutes

Makes: 6 (1⅓-cup) servings

- 12 ounces skinless, boneless chicken breast halves
- 2 teaspoons olive oil
- 3 cloves garlic, minced
- 2 14½-ounce cans reduced-sodium chicken broth
- 3 cups sliced fresh mushrooms
- 1¾ cups water
- 2 medium carrots, cut into matchstick strips (1 cup)
- 2 cups packed torn fresh purple kale or spinach
- 1 teaspoon dried tarragon, crushed
- 1 9-ounce package refrigerated cheese-filled tortellini

1 Rinse chicken; pat dry. Cut the chicken into ¾-inch pieces. In a Dutch oven heat olive oil over medium-high heat. Cook and stir chicken and garlic in hot oil for 5 to 6 minutes or until chicken is no longer pink. Stir in chicken broth, mushrooms, water, carrots, kale (if using), and tarragon.

2 Bring mixture to boiling; reduce heat. Simmer, covered, for 2 minutes. Add tortellini. Simmer, covered, for 5 to 6 minutes more or until tortellini is tender. Stir in the spinach (if using).

Nutrition facts per serving: 254 cal., 7 g total fat (2 g sat. fat), 50 mg chol., 596 mg sodium, 27 g carbo., 3 g fiber, 21 g pro.
Daily values: 90% vit. A, 33% vit. C, 10% calcium, 16% iron

mexican-style TURKEY SOUP

This spicy soup provides health-protective phytochemicals in every bite. For maximum benefits choose the most vividly colored fruits and veggies.

soups and stews

Start to Finish: 40 minutes
Makes: 5 or 6 servings

- 1 cup chopped onion
- 1 large red sweet pepper, chopped
- 1 tablespoon cooking oil
- 1 teaspoon ground cumin
- 1 teaspoon chili powder
- ½ teaspoon paprika
- 5 cups reduced-sodium chicken broth
- 1½ cups peeled, cubed winter squash
- 1 large tomato, chopped
- ¼ teaspoon salt
- ¼ teaspoon black pepper
- 2 cups chopped cooked turkey or chicken
- 1 cup frozen whole kernel corn
- 2 tablespoons snipped fresh cilantro

1 In a Dutch oven cook onion and sweet pepper in hot oil over medium heat about 5 minutes or until tender, stirring occasionally. Stir in cumin, chili powder, and paprika; cook and stir for 30 seconds.

2 Add broth, squash, tomato, salt, and black pepper. Bring to boiling; reduce heat. Simmer, covered, about 20 minutes or until squash is tender, stirring occasionally. Stir in turkey, corn, and cilantro; heat through.

Nutrition Facts per serving: 205 cal., 6 g total fat (1 g sat. fat), 43 mg chol., 790 mg sodium, 17 g carbo., 3 g fiber, 22 g pro.
Daily Values: 73% vit. A, 102% vit. C, 4% calcium, 10% iron

Phytochemicals

Fruits and vegetables contain vitamins, minerals, and fiber. They also contain unique substances called phytochemicals. These compounds, of which more than 4,000 have been identified, can help promote good health and ward off diseases. They have been shown to play roles in preventing some cancers and maintaining eye health. Phytochemicals are also often responsible for the colors of fruits and vegetables, such as the red in tomatoes, the blue in blueberries, and the green in broccoli. To maximize your phytochemical intake, be sure to choose a variety of colors in the produce department.

curried CHICKEN SOUP

You can use leftover cooked chicken in this quick soup or buy a roasted chicken from your supermarket's deli.

Start to Finish: 20 minutes
Makes: 5 servings

5 **cups water**

1 **3-ounce package chicken-flavor ramen noodles**

2 **to 3 teaspoons curry powder**

1 **cup sliced fresh mushrooms**

2 **cups cubed cooked chicken**

1 **medium apple, cored and coarsely chopped**

½ **cup canned sliced water chestnuts**

1 In a large saucepan combine the water, the flavoring packet from noodles, and curry powder. Bring to boiling.

2 Break up noodles. Add the noodles and mushrooms to mixture in saucepan; reduce heat. Simmer, uncovered, for 3 minutes. Stir in chicken, apple, and water chestnuts; heat through.

Nutrition Facts per serving: 221 cal., 8 g total fat (1 g sat. fat), 54 mg chol., 362 mg sodium, 17 g carbo., 1 g fiber, 20 g pro.
Daily Values: 1% vit. A, 4% vit. C, 2% calcium, 10% iron

chicken MINESTRONE SOUP

The Italian word minestrone means "big soup," and countless variations of the bean-and-vegetable soup are big in American kitchens. This version calls for broth as well as chicken breasts for extra flavor.

Start to Finish: 45 minutes
Makes: 8 servings

- 1 **cup sliced carrot**
- ½ **cup chopped celery**
- ½ **cup chopped onion**
- 1 **tablespoon olive oil**
- 3 **14-ounce cans chicken broth**
- 2 **15- to 19-ounce cans white kidney beans (cannellini beans), rinsed and drained**
- 8 **to 10 ounces skinless, boneless chicken breasts, cut into bite-size pieces**
- 1 **cup fresh green beans, cut into ½-inch pieces (4 ounces)**
- ¼ **teaspoon black pepper**
- 1 **cup dried bow tie pasta**
- 1 **medium zucchini, quartered lengthwise and cut into ½-inch slices**
- 1 **14½-ounce can diced tomatoes with basil, garlic, and oregano, undrained**
  Crackers (optional)

❶ In a 5- to 6-quart Dutch oven cook carrots, celery, and onion in hot oil over medium heat for 5 minutes, stirring frequently. Add broth, white kidney beans, chicken, green beans, and pepper. Bring to boiling; add pasta. Reduce heat and simmer, uncovered, for 5 minutes.

❷ Stir in zucchini. Return to boiling; reduce heat. Simmer, uncovered, for 8 to 10 minutes more or until pasta is tender and green beans are crisp-tender. Stir in undrained tomatoes; heat through. If desired, serve with crackers.

Nutrition Facts per serving: 181 cal., 4 g total fat (1 g sat. fat), 16 mg chol., 1,079 mg sodium, 27 g carbo., 7 g fiber, 16 g pro.
Daily Values: 86% vit. A, 15% vit. C, 8% calcium, 14% iron

soups and stews

turkey NOODLE SOUP

The tangy flavor of lemon lends a delightfully brisk lift to a classic turkey noodle soup. The tangy addition is a refreshing variation on a timeless favorite.

soups and stews

Prep: 20 minutes
Cook: 26 minutes
Makes: 5 (1½-cup) servings

- **3 cups reduced-sodium chicken broth**
- **2¼ cups water**
- **1½ cups chopped cooked turkey or chicken**
- **1 cup thinly sliced carrots**
- **1 medium onion, cut into thin wedges**
- **½ cup thinly sliced celery**
- **2 teaspoons snipped fresh thyme or 1 teaspoon dried thyme, crushed**
- **2 cups dried wide noodles**
- **1 medium yellow summer squash, quartered lengthwise and sliced (1⅓ cups)**
- **2 tablespoons lemon juice**

1 In a large saucepan combine the chicken broth, water, turkey or chicken, carrots, onion, celery, and dried thyme (if using). Bring mixture to boiling; reduce heat. Simmer, covered, for 15 minutes.

2 Stir in the noodles and squash. Cook, uncovered, for 10 to 12 minutes more or until the noodles are tender. Stir in the lemon juice and fresh thyme (if using). Cook, uncovered, for 1 minute more.

Nutrition facts per serving: 192 cal., 4 g total fat (1 g sat. fat), 41 mg chol., 459 mg sodium, 20 g carbo., 3 g fiber, 18 g pro.
Daily values: 66% vit. A, 10% vit. C, 2% calcium, 9% iron

cajun BEAN SOUP

True Cajun cooks will tell you that it isn't the spices that make a dish authentic, it's the trio of onion, sweet peppers, and celery. The hot sauce in this recipe is optional, but it adds a spirited touch.

Start to Finish: 35 minutes
Makes: 8 (1½-cup) servings

- 2 teaspoons cooking oil
- 1¼ cups chopped onion
- 1¼ cups chopped green sweet pepper
- ¾ cup finely chopped celery
- 3 cloves garlic, minced
- 2½ cups reduced-sodium chicken broth
- 2½ cups water
- 1 14½-ounce can low-sodium stewed tomatoes
- 2 cups sliced fresh or frozen okra
- 1 15-ounce can reduced-sodium navy beans, rinsed and drained
- 1 15-ounce can reduced-sodium red kidney beans, rinsed and drained
- 4 ounces cooked smoked turkey sausage, halved lengthwise and sliced
- 1 bay leaf
- 1 teaspoon dried thyme, crushed
- ¼ teaspoon black pepper
- ⅛ teaspoon salt
- Bottled hot pepper sauce (optional)
- 4 cups hot cooked rice

① In a Dutch oven heat oil over medium-high heat. Cook and stir the onion, sweet pepper, celery, and garlic in the hot oil for 8 to 10 minutes or until vegetables are tender, stirring occasionally.

② Stir in the broth, water, undrained tomatoes, okra, beans, sausage, bay leaf, thyme, black pepper, salt, and, if desired, hot pepper sauce. Bring to boiling; reduce heat. Simmer, covered, about 10 minutes or until okra is tender. Discard the bay leaf. Serve over hot rice.

Nutrition facts per serving: 274 cal., 4 g total fat (0 g sat. fat), 7 mg chol., 430 mg sodium, 50 g carbo., 7 g fiber, 13 g pro.
Daily values: 6% vit. A, 44% vit. C, 8% calcium, 21% iron

soups and stews

sausage & PEPPERS SOUP

Serve this soup on a cold and wintry day. It's hearty, it's healthy, it's spicy—and best of all, it's Italian. Did we mention that it can be made in under 30 minutes?

soups and stews

Prep: 10 minutes
Cook: 15 minutes
Makes: 4 (1½-cup) servings

¼ **pound bulk hot Italian turkey sausage**

1 **small green sweet pepper, thinly sliced**

1 **small yellow sweet pepper, thinly sliced**

1 **medium onion, cut into thin wedges**

2 **cloves garlic, minced**

1 **14½-ounce can reduced-sodium chicken broth**

1¾ **cups water**

1 **14½-ounce can low-sodium tomatoes, undrained and cut up**

1½ **cups cubed potatoes**

1 **tablespoon snipped fresh basil or 1 teaspoon dried basil, crushed**

¼ **teaspoon crushed red pepper (optional)**

1 In a large saucepan cook and stir sausage, sweet peppers, onion, and garlic over medium heat about 5 minutes or until sausage is browned. Drain off fat.

2 Stir in broth, water, undrained tomatoes, potatoes, and dried basil (if using). Bring to boiling; reduce heat. Simmer, covered, for 10 to 15 minutes or until potatoes are just tender. Stir in the fresh basil (if using), and, if desired, the crushed red pepper.

Nutrition facts per serving: 146 cal., 4 g total fat (1 g sat. fat), 21 mg chol., 472 mg sodium, 21 g carbo., 2 g fiber, 8 g pro.
Daily values: 21% vit. A, 94% vit. C, 4% calcium, 13% iron

Broth Basics

Although there is no Recommended Daily Allowance set for sodium, a daily limit of 2,400 mg of sodium is commonly suggested. A comparison of three chicken broth products illustrates the difference in the sodium content of each (note: brands will vary). All are based on 1 cup chicken broth:

Low sodium: 54 mg	
Reduced sodium: 620 mg*	
Regular: 985 mg	
1 bouillon cube: 900 to 1,000 mg	

*Due to better flavor, reduced-sodium broth rather than low-sodium broth is generally used in recipes in this book.

vegetable BEEF SOUP

Here's a home and hearth recipe that's great for cold evenings. Huge chunks of beef, a lot of fall vegetables, and hearty noodles turn a brimming bowl of soup into a bona fide, stick-to-your ribs meal.

Prep: 25 minutes
Cook: 65 minutes
Makes: 6 (1½-cup) servings

- 1 pound boneless beef top round steak
- 2 teaspoons olive oil
- 1½ cups chopped onion
- 2½ cups water
- 1 14½-ounce can beef broth
- 1 14½-ounce can low-sodium stewed tomatoes
- 2 teaspoons Italian seasoning, crushed
- ½ teaspoon pepper
- 1 bay leaf
- 3 medium turnips, peeled and cut into ½-inch pieces (3 cups)
- 1½ cups cubed red potatoes
- 1 cup sliced carrots
- 1½ cups dried wide noodles
- 2 tablespoons snipped fresh oregano or thyme (optional)

1 Trim fat from beef. Cut beef into 1-inch cubes. In a Dutch oven heat olive oil over medium-high heat. Cook and stir beef and onion in hot oil until beef is browned. Stir in the water, beef broth, undrained tomatoes, Italian seasoning, pepper, and bay leaf. Bring to boiling; reduce heat. Simmer, covered, for 40 minutes.

2 Stir in the turnips, potatoes, and carrots. Simmer, covered, for 15 minutes. Stir in the noodles. Simmer, uncovered, about 10 minutes more or until noodles and vegetables are tender. Remove bay leaf. If desired, stir in oregano or thyme.

Nutrition facts per serving: 272 cal., 6 g total fat (2 g sat. fat), 60 mg chol., 345 mg sodium, 32 g carbo., 6 g fiber, 23 g pro.
Daily values: 62% vit. A, 34% vit. C, 5% calcium, 25% iron

soups and stews

275

italian MEATBALL SOUP

Go Italian with this family-pleasing soup, as easy to make as it is hearty. Another day, partner the second half of the bag of frozen meatballs with prepared pasta sauce for a classic spaghetti-and-meatballs dinner.

Start to Finish: 25 minutes
Makes: 4 servings

1 **14½-ounce can diced tomatoes with onion and garlic, undrained**

1 **14-ounce can reduced-sodium beef broth**

1½ **cups water**

½ **teaspoon dried Italian seasoning, crushed**

½ **of a 16-ounce package frozen Italian-style cooked meatballs**

½ **cup small dried pasta (such as ditalini or orzo)**

1 **cup frozen loose-pack mixed vegetables**

1 **tablespoon shredded or grated Parmesan cheese (optional)**

1 In a large saucepan stir together undrained tomatoes, beef broth, water, and Italian seasoning. Bring to boiling. Add meatballs, pasta, and frozen vegetables. Return to boiling; reduce heat. Cover and simmer about 10 minutes or until pasta and vegetables are tender. If desired, sprinkle individual servings with cheese.

Nutrition Facts per serving: 275 cal., 13 g total fat (6 g sat. fat), 37 mg chol., 1,113 mg sodium, 25 g carbo., 4 g fiber, 15 g pro.
Daily Values: 37% vit. A, 19% vit. C, 6% calcium, 18% iron

soups and stews

sausage and greens RAGOÛT

Look in your supermarket's produce section for washed, packaged escarole, Swiss chard, kale, or spinach.

Start to Finish: 35 minutes
Makes: 4 servings

- 1 **8-ounce package cooked chicken andouille sausage links or cooked smoked turkey sausage links, cut into ½-inch slices**
- 1 **medium yellow crookneck squash, cut into ½-inch pieces**
- 1 **14-ounce can reduced-sodium chicken broth**
- 1 **tablespoon snipped fresh rosemary or 1 teaspoon dried rosemary, crushed**
- 2 **cups coarsely chopped fresh escarole, Swiss chard, baby kale, and/or spinach leaves**
- 1 **15-ounce can white kidney beans (cannellini beans), rinsed and drained**
- 1 **cup carrots cut into thin, bite-size sticks**
  Freshly ground black pepper
  Purchased garlic croutons (optional)

1 In a large saucepan combine sausage, squash, broth, and rosemary. Bring to boiling; reduce heat. Simmer, uncovered, for 5 minutes. Stir in escarole, beans, and carrots. Return to boiling; reduce heat. Cover and simmer about 5 minutes more or until vegetables are tender. Season to taste with pepper. If desired, top each serving with croutons.

Nutrition Facts per serving: 156 cal., 8 g total fat (2 g sat. fat), 20 mg chol., 785 mg sodium, 20 g carbo., 7 g fiber, 16 g pro.
Daily Values: 87% vit. A, 6% vit. C, 4% calcium, 13% iron

hamburger-vegetable SOUP

Looking for a new way to serve always easy, always satisfying ground beef? Try this family favorite—it's quick, abundant with colorful vegetables, and low-fat to boot.

Start to Finish: 35 minutes
Makes: 6 servings

- **1 pound lean ground beef or pork**
- **½ cup chopped onion**
- **½ cup chopped green sweet pepper**
- **4 cups beef broth**
- **1 cup frozen whole kernel corn**
- **1 7½-ounce can tomatoes, undrained and cut up**
- **½ of a 10-ounce package frozen lima beans**
- **½ cup chopped peeled potato or frozen loose-pack hash brown potatoes**
- **1 medium carrot, cut into thin bite-size strips**
- **1 tablespoon snipped fresh basil or 1 teaspoon dried basil, crushed**
- **1 teaspoon Worcestershire sauce**
- **1 bay leaf**
- **⅛ teaspoon black pepper**

1 In a large saucepan cook ground beef, onion, and sweet pepper until meat is brown and onion is tender. Drain off fat. Stir in beef broth, corn, undrained tomatoes, lima beans, potato, carrot, basil, Worcestershire sauce, bay leaf, and black pepper.

2 Bring mixture to boiling; reduce heat. Cover and simmer for 15 to 20 minutes or until vegetables are tender. Discard bay leaf.

Nutrition Facts per serving: 215 cal., 8 g total fat (3 g sat. fat), 48 mg chol., 652 mg sodium, 18 g carbo., 3 g fiber, 18 g pro.
Daily Values: 64% vit. A, 38% vit. C, 3% calcium, 15% iron

soups and stews

teriyaki beef SOUP

For an even faster stove top-to-table time, cut up the beef and vegetables for this "on-the-fly" soup the evening before. The next day, you'll be able to toss the whole meal together in the time it takes to cook the rice.

Prep: 20 minutes
Cook: 18 minutes
Makes: 5 (1½-cup) servings

8 ounces boneless beef sirloin steak

2 teaspoons olive oil

1 large shallot, cut into thin rings

4 cups water

1 cup unsweetened apple juice

2 carrots, cut into matchstick strips (1 cup)

⅓ cup long-grain rice

1 tablespoon grated fresh ginger

1 teaspoon instant beef bouillon granules

3 cloves garlic, minced

2 cups coarsely chopped broccoli

1 to 2 tablespoons reduced-sodium teriyaki sauce

1 tablespoon dry sherry (optional)

1 Trim fat from beef. Cut beef into bite-size strips. In a large saucepan heat olive oil over medium-high heat. Cook and stir beef and shallot in hot oil for 2 to 3 minutes or until beef is brown. Remove beef mixture with a slotted spoon; set aside.

2 In the same saucepan combine water, apple juice, carrots, uncooked rice, ginger, bouillon granules, and garlic. Bring to boiling; reduce heat. Simmer, covered, about 15 minutes or until the carrots are tender.

3 Stir in the broccoli and beef mixture. Simmer, covered, for 3 minutes. Stir in the teriyaki sauce and, if desired, the dry sherry.

Nutrition facts per serving: 197 cal., 6 g total fat (2 g sat. fat), 30 mg chol., 382 mg sodium, 22 g carbo., 2 g fiber, 13 g pro.
Daily values: 76% vit. A, 58% vit. C, 3% calcium, 16% iron

soups and stews

chipotle BEEF CHILI

Smoked jalapeños are called "chipotles." They have all the heat of jalapeño peppers, plus a mellow smoky flavor. Look for chipotles en adobo in Mexican or Latin American groceries or large supermarkets.

soups and stews

Prep: 15 minutes
Cook: 20 minutes
Makes: 3 (1½-cup) servings

- 8 **ounces beef top sirloin steak**
- **Nonstick spray coating**
- 1 **teaspoon olive oil**
- 1 **cup chopped onion**
- 2 **cloves garlic, minced**
- 1 **14½-ounce can low-sodium tomatoes, undrained and cut up**
- 1 **8-ounce can low-sodium tomato sauce**
- 1 **cup water**
- 2 **to 3 teaspoons chopped, canned chipotle peppers in adobo sauce**
- 1 **teaspoon dried basil, crushed**
- 1 **teaspoon dried oregano, crushed**
- 1 **teaspoon chili powder**
- ¼ **teaspoon salt (optional)**
- ¼ **teaspoon ground cumin**
- 1½ **cups frozen whole kernel corn**

1 Trim fat from beef. Cut beef into bite-size strips. Spray a large saucepan with nonstick coating. Preheat on medium-high heat. Cook and stir beef in saucepan over medium-high heat for 2 to 3 minutes or until beef is browned. Remove beef from saucepan; set aside.

2 Carefully add oil to hot saucepan. Cook onion and garlic in hot oil until tender. Stir in undrained tomatoes, tomato sauce, water, chipotle peppers, basil, oregano, chili powder, salt (if desired), and cumin. Bring to boiling; reduce heat. Simmer, covered, for 15 minutes, stirring occasionally.

3 Add the frozen corn. Return to simmering. Simmer, covered, for 5 minutes more, stirring occasionally. Return beef to saucepan. Heat through.

Nutrition facts per serving: 355 cal., 12 g total fat (3 g sat. fat), 50 mg chol., 598 mg sodium, 43 g carbo., 4 g fiber, 23 g pro.
Daily values: 84% vit. A, 65% vit. C, 9% calcium, 33% iron

beef goulash SOUP

A single teaspoon of unsweetened cocoa powder contributes a hint of New World uniqueness to an Old World Hungarian goulash. Don't be surprised if your family asks for this soup time and time again.

Prep: 25 minutes
Cook: 30 minutes
Makes: 4 (1½-cup) servings

- **6 ounces boneless beef sirloin steak**
- **1 teaspoon olive oil**
- **1 medium onion, cut into thin wedges**
- **2 cups water**
- **1 14½-ounce can beef broth**
- **1 14½-ounce can low-sodium tomatoes, undrained and cut up**
- **½ cup thinly sliced carrot**
- **1 teaspoon unsweetened cocoa powder**
- **1 clove garlic, minced**
- **1 cup thinly sliced cabbage**
- **1 ounce dried wide noodles (about ¾ cup)**
- **2 teaspoons paprika**
- **¼ cup fat-free dairy sour cream**

1 Trim fat from beef. Cut beef into ½-inch cubes. In a large saucepan heat olive oil over medium-high heat. Cook and stir beef in hot oil over medium-high heat about 6 minutes or until beef is browned. Add onion wedges; cook and stir about 3 minutes or until tender.

2 Stir in the water, beef broth, undrained tomatoes, carrot, cocoa powder, and garlic. Bring to boiling; reduce heat. Simmer about 15 minutes or until beef is tender. Stir in the cabbage, noodles, and paprika. Simmer for 5 to 7 minutes more or until noodles are tender but firm. Remove from heat; stir in sour cream until combined.

Nutrition facts per serving: 178 cal., 6 g total fat (2 g sat. fat), 34 mg chol., 400 mg sodium, 17 g carbo., 2 g fiber, 15 g pro.
Daily values: 55% vit. A, 47% vit. C, 7% calcium, 18% iron

soups and stews

Red Meat Facts

Including beef in a healthful diet is fine—just choose lean cuts most often. Also, remove all visible fat. Select the following for the leanest cuts: arm pot roast, bottom round roast, eye round roast, round tip roast, top round roast or steak, sirloin steak, T-bone steak, or top loin steak.

beef-vegetable RAGOÛT

This recipe fits the bill for a casual get-together and it's ready in only 30 minutes.

Start to Finish: 30 minutes
Makes: 4 servings

- 8 **ounces dried wide noodles**
- 12 **ounces beef tenderloin, cut into ¾-inch cubes**
- 2 **tablespoons olive oil or cooking oil**
- 1½ **cups packaged sliced fresh crimini or button mushrooms**
- ½ **cup chopped onion**
- 2 **cloves garlic, minced**
- 3 **tablespoons all-purpose flour**
- ½ **teaspoon salt**
- ¼ **teaspoon black pepper**
- 1 **14-ounce can beef broth**
- ¼ **cup port wine or dry sherry**
- 2 **cups sugar snap peas**
- 1 **cup cherry tomatoes, halved**

1 In a large saucepan, cook the noodles according to the package directions.

2 Meanwhile, in a large skillet cook and stir the beef in hot oil over medium heat for 2 to 3 minutes or until meat is done as desired. Remove meat, reserving drippings in skillet. Set meat aside.

3 Cook mushrooms, onion, and garlic in reserved drippings for 4 to 5 minutes or until tender. Sprinkle flour, salt, and pepper over mushroom mixture; stir in. Carefully add broth and wine. Cook and stir until thickened and bubbly.

4 Stir sugar snap peas into the mushroom mixture. Cook for 2 to 3 minutes more or until peas are tender. Stir in meat and tomatoes; heat through.

5 Drain noodles; transfer to a serving platter. Spoon the meat and vegetable mixture over noodles.

Nutrition Facts per serving: 535 cal., 16 g total fat (4 g sat. fat), 97 mg chol., 694 mg sodium, 61 g carbo., 5 g fiber, 31 g pro.
Daily Values: 6% vit. A, 48% vit. C, 7% calcium, 36% iron

oven-baked CASSOULET

A French cassoulet traditionally is simmered for hours. Baking this version in the oven slashes the cooking time to about 40 minutes. For a touch of freshness, top with snipped parsley just before serving.

soups and stews

Prep: 20 minutes
Bake: 40 minutes
Makes: 5 (1⅓-cup) servings

Nonstick spray coating

12 **ounces lean boneless pork, cut into ½-inch cubes**

1 **teaspoon cooking oil**

1 **cup chopped onion**

1 **cup chopped carrots**

3 **cloves garlic, minced**

2 **15-ounce cans white kidney beans, rinsed and drained**

4 **plum tomatoes, chopped**

⅔ **cup reduced-sodium chicken broth**

⅔ **cup water**

2 **ounces cooked turkey kielbasa, halved lengthwise and cut into ¼-inch-thick slices**

1 **teaspoon dried thyme, crushed**

¼ **teaspoon dried rosemary, crushed**

¼ **teaspoon pepper**

2 **tablespoons snipped fresh parsley**

① Spray a Dutch oven with nonstick coating. Preheat over medium-high heat. Cook and stir pork in Dutch oven until pork is browned. Remove pork from pan. Reduce heat. Carefully add cooking oil to hot Dutch oven. Cook the onion, carrots, and garlic in hot oil until onion is tender.

② Stir pork, beans, tomatoes, chicken broth, water, kielbasa, thyme, rosemary, and pepper into Dutch oven. Bake, covered, in a 325° oven for 40 to 45 minutes or until pork and carrots are tender. To serve, sprinkle each serving with parsley.

Range-top method: Prepare as directed above, except instead of baking, cover and simmer about 15 minutes or until the pork and carrots are tender.

Nutrition facts per serving: 243 cal., 7 g total fat (2 g sat. fat), 38 mg chol., 497 mg sodium, 32 g carbo., 10 g fiber, 23 g pro.
Daily values: 68% vit. A, 26% vit. C, 5% calcium, 21% iron

pork & CABBAGE SOUP

Good old-fashioned pork and beans are treated to a new-fashioned, upscale makeover. For convenience, use coleslaw mix, found in the produce section, in place of the chopped cabbage.

Start to Finish: 35 minutes
Makes: 6 (1½-cup) servings

- 2 **teaspoons olive oil**
- 12 **ounces pork tenderloin, cut into ¾-inch cubes**
- 1 **cup chopped onion**
- 3 **cloves garlic, minced**
- 2 **14½-ounce cans reduced-sodium chicken broth**
- 3 **cups chopped cabbage**
- 1 **14½-ounce can low-sodium stewed tomatoes**
- 1 **teaspoon dried sage, crushed**
- ½ **teaspoon dried rosemary, crushed**
- ¼ **teaspoon ground nutmeg**
- ⅛ **teaspoon ground red pepper**
- 2 **15-ounce cans reduced-sodium navy beans or great Northern beans, rinsed and drained**
- ½ **cup finely shredded Parmesan cheese (optional)**

① In a Dutch oven heat olive oil over medium-high heat. Cook and stir the pork, onion, and garlic in hot oil until pork is no longer pink. Stir in chicken broth, cabbage, undrained tomatoes, sage, rosemary, nutmeg, and red pepper.

② Bring mixture to boiling; reduce heat. Simmer, covered, about 10 minutes or until cabbage is tender. Stir in beans. Heat through. If desired, sprinkle each serving with shredded Parmesan cheese.

Nutrition facts per serving: 260 cal., 5 g total fat (1 g sat. fat), 40 mg chol., 466 mg sodium, 32 g carbo., 10 g fiber, 23 g pro.
Daily values: 6% vit. A, 49% vit. C, 9% calcium, 24% iron

soups and stews

salmon CHOWDER

Rosy-pink salmon is a popular fish because of its great taste. But it also is a rich source of omega-3 oils that help protect the cardiovascular system.

Start to Finish: 45 minutes
Makes: 8(1¼-cup) servings

- 1 **pound fresh skinless salmon fillets or one 15-ounce can salmon, rinsed, drained, flaked, and skin and bones removed**
- 1 **tablespoon cooking oil**
- 2 **cups shredded carrots**
- 1 **cup finely chopped onion**
- ½ **cup thinly sliced celery**
- 1½ **cups water**
- 4 **cups reduced-sodium chicken broth**
- 2½ **cups cubed red-skinned potatoes (3 medium)**
- 1 **10-ounce package frozen whole kernel corn**
- 1 **teaspoon snipped fresh dill or ½ teaspoon dried dillweed**
- ¼ **teaspoon salt**
- 2 **cups fat-free milk**
- 2 **tablespoons cornstarch**

1 Rinse fresh salmon; pat dry. Set aside. In a large saucepan heat oil over medium-high heat. Cook and stir carrots, onion, and celery in hot oil about 10 minutes or until the vegetables are tender, stirring occasionally.

2 Meanwhile, to poach fresh salmon, in a large skillet bring water to boiling. Add salmon. Return to boiling; reduce heat. Simmer, covered, for 6 to 8 minutes or until the salmon flakes easily with a fork. Remove salmon from skillet, discarding poaching liquid. Flake salmon into ½-inch pieces; set aside.

3 Stir the broth, potatoes, corn, dill, and salt into vegetables in saucepan. Bring to boiling; reduce heat. Cook, covered, over medium-low heat about 15 minutes or until the potatoes are tender, stirring occasionally.

4 Stir together ½ cup of the milk and cornstarch. Add milk mixture to saucepan. Stir in remaining milk. Cook and stir over medium heat until thickened and bubbly. Cook and stir for 2 minutes more. Gently stir in poached salmon or canned salmon. Heat through.

Nutrition facts per serving: 211 cal., 5 g total fat (1 g sat. fat), 11 mg chol., 487 mg sodium, 30 g carbo., 3 g fiber, 14 g pro.
Daily values: 91% vit. A, 14% vit. C, 8% calcium, 7% iron

shrimp GAZPACHO

Gazpacho—a Spanish soup with tomatoes and onions—traditionally is served cold. We've made this gazpacho into a complete meal by adding succulent shrimp for a zingy thrill of a chill.

soups and stews

Prep: 35 minutes
Chill: 4 to 24 hours
Makes: 6 (1½-cup) servings

- 8 **medium ripe tomatoes, peeled, if desired, and chopped (2½ pounds)**
- 1 **medium cucumber, chopped**
- 1 **medium green or red sweet pepper, seeded and chopped**
- ¾ **cup low-sodium vegetable juice or low-sodium tomato juice**
- ½ **cup clam juice**
- ¼ **cup chopped onion**
- 3 **tablespoons red wine vinegar**
- 2 **tablespoons snipped fresh cilantro**
- 2 **tablespoons olive oil**
- 1 **clove garlic, minced**
- ¼ **teaspoon ground cumin**
- 1 **8-ounce package frozen, peeled, cooked small shrimp, thawed**

   Fat-free dairy sour cream (optional)

1 In a large mixing bowl combine tomatoes, cucumber, sweet pepper, vegetable juice or tomato juice, clam juice, onion, vinegar, cilantro, olive oil, garlic, and cumin. Gently fold the shrimp into the tomato mixture.

2 Cover and chill 4 to 24 hours to allow flavors to blend. To serve, ladle into serving bowls. If desired, top each with a spoonful of sour cream.

Nutrition facts per serving: 141 cal., 6 g total fat (1 g sat. fat), 74 mg chol., 154 mg sodium, 15 g carbo., 4 g fiber, 11 g pro.
Daily values: 22% vit. A, 121% vit. C, 3% calcium, 37% iron

Shellfish Facts

Cholesterol is something shrimp have a lot of. These denizens of the deep contain 166 mg cholesterol per 3-ounce serving, about half of the recommended daily limit (300 mg). But that doesn't mean you need to go fishing for something else when you have a hankering for shrimp. Shrimp have some great attributes—they are low in fat, saturated fat, and calories. So, go ahead and satisfy your craving—just watch your total cholesterol intake from all foods.

crab & corn CHOWDER

So rich and creamy, you'll be tempted to feel guilty. There's no need! This chowder has only 1 gram of fat. If you like, substitute one 6-ounce package of chunk-style imitation crab meat for the cooked crab.

Start to Finish: 30 minutes
Makes: 4 (1½-cup) servings

1½ **cups reduced-sodium chicken broth**

1⅓ **cups water**

1 **10-ounce package frozen whole kernel corn**

⅔ **cup cubed, peeled potato**

⅓ **cup finely chopped carrot**

2 **teaspoons snipped fresh thyme or ½ teaspoon dried thyme, crushed**

2 **cloves garlic, minced**

¼ **teaspoon salt**

¼ **teaspoon pepper**

1 **cup evaporated fat-free milk**

2 **tablespoons cornstarch**

6 **ounces cooked crabmeat, cut into bite-size pieces (about 1 cup)**

¼ **cup sliced green onions**

1 In a medium saucepan combine the broth, water, corn, potato, carrot, dried thyme (if using), garlic, salt, and pepper. Bring to boiling; reduce heat. Simmer, covered, for 15 to 20 minutes or until potato is tender.

2 Gradually stir the evaporated milk into the cornstarch; stir into the corn mixture. Cook and stir over medium heat until thickened and bubbly. Cook and stir for 2 minutes more. Gently stir in the fresh thyme (if using), crabmeat, and green onions. Heat through.

Nutrition facts per serving: 212 cal., 1 g total fat (0 g sat. fat), 45 mg chol., 520 mg sodium, 34 g carbo., 1 g fiber, 17 g pro.
Daily values: 37% vit. A, 20% vit. C, 20% calcium, 8% iron

soups and stews

spicy SEAFOOD STEW

Health experts recommend eating at least one meal per week that includes fish—let it be this one. Boneless fish fillets and whole shrimp simmer with garlic, herbs, and cajun spices in a bayou blockbuster of a stew.

Prep: 15 minutes
Cook: 25 minutes
Makes: 4 (1⅓-cup) servings

- 8 ounces fresh or frozen skinless fish fillets (halibut, orange roughy, or sea bass)
- 6 ounces fresh or frozen peeled and deveined shrimp
- 2 teaspoons olive oil
- ⅔ cup chopped onion
- ½ cup finely chopped carrot
- ½ cup chopped red or green sweet pepper
- 2 cloves garlic, minced
- 1 14½-ounce can low-sodium tomatoes, undrained and cut up
- 1 8-ounce can low-sodium tomato sauce
- 1 cup reduced-sodium chicken broth
- ¼ cup dry red wine or reduced-sodium chicken broth
- 2 bay leaves
- 1 tablespoon snipped fresh thyme or 1 teaspoon dried thyme, crushed
- ½ teaspoon Cajun seasoning
- ¼ teaspoon ground cumin
- ¼ teaspoon crushed red pepper (optional)

1 Thaw fish and shrimp, if frozen. Rinse fish and shrimp; pat dry. Cut the fish into 1-inch pieces. Cover and chill fish pieces and shrimp until needed.

2 In a large saucepan heat olive oil over medium-high heat. Cook and stir onion, carrot, sweet pepper, and garlic in hot oil until tender. Stir in the undrained tomatoes, tomato sauce, chicken broth, wine or chicken broth, bay leaves, dried thyme (if using), Cajun seasoning, cumin, and, if desired, crushed red pepper. Bring the mixture to boiling; reduce heat. Simmer, covered, for 20 minutes.

3 Gently stir in the fish pieces, shrimp, and fresh thyme (if using). Cover and simmer about 5 minutes more or until the fish flakes easily when tested with a fork and shrimp are opaque. Remove the bay leaves before serving.

Nutrition facts per serving: 199 cal., 5 g total fat (1 g sat. fat), 84 mg chol., 341 mg sodium, 15 g carbo., 3 g fiber, 22 g pro.
Daily values: 69% vit. A, 82% vit. C, 8% calcium, 23% iron

soups and stews

clam-corn CHOWDER

For a healthy lunch at work, make this chowder the night before, then cover and refrigerate it. In the morning heat the soup on the stove and pour it into a preheated insulated vacuum bottle.

soups and stews

Start to Finish: 30 minutes
Makes: 4 servings

- ½ **cup chopped celery**
- ¼ **cup chopped onion**
- 1 **tablespoon butter or margarine**
- ¼ **cup all-purpose flour**
- 1½ **teaspoons snipped fresh marjoram or ½ teaspoon dried marjoram, crushed**
- 1½ **teaspoons snipped fresh thyme or ½ teaspoon dried thyme, crushed**
- ½ **teaspoon dry mustard**
- ¼ **teaspoon black pepper**
- 2⅔ **cups fat-free milk**
- 1 **8-ounce bottle clam juice**
- 1 **teaspoon instant chicken bouillon granules**
- 1 **15-ounce can cream-style corn**
- 1 **6½-ounce can minced clams, drained**
- **Fresh marjoram or thyme (optional)**

1 In a large saucepan cook celery and onion in hot butter until tender. Stir in flour, marjoram, thyme, mustard, and pepper. Add milk, clam juice, and bouillon granules all at once.

2 Cook and stir until thickened and bubbly. Cook and stir for 1 minute more. Stir in corn and clams; heat through. If desired, garnish with additional fresh herbs.

Nutrition Facts per serving: 272 cal., 5 g total fat (1 g sat. fat), 43 mg chol., 870 mg sodium, 36 g carbo., 2 g fiber, 20 g pro.
Daily Values: 18% vit. A, 27% vit. C, 26% calcium, 75% iron

Shellfish for Your Heart

Fish has long been considered a healthy source of protein in the diet. However, shellfish is sometimes given a bad rap because of its high cholesterol content. In actuality, there's no need to avoid shellfish. Foods like lobster, shrimp, scallops, clams, and mussels contain virtually no fat and even less saturated fat, both of which play a greater role in increasing blood cholesterol and one's risk of heart disease than dietary cholesterol alone.

gazpacho TO GO

Keep this easy-to-tote cold soup in mind for summertime picnics or potlucks. Show off gazpacho's mosaic of bright colors by carrying it in a clear plastic storage container.

Prep: 30 minutes
Chill: 2 hours
Makes: 6 servings

- 1 **15-ounce can chunky Italian- or salsa-style tomatoes, undrained**
- 2 **cups quartered yellow pear-shape and/or halved cherry tomatoes**
- 1 **15-ounce can garbanzo beans (chickpeas), rinsed and drained**
- 1¼ **cups vegetable juice**
- 1 **cup beef broth**
- ½ **cup coarsely chopped seeded cucumber**
- ½ **cup coarsely chopped yellow and/or red sweet pepper**
- ¼ **cup coarsely chopped red onion**
- ¼ **cup snipped fresh cilantro**
- 3 **tablespoons lime juice or lemon juice**
- 2 **cloves garlic, minced**
- ¼ **to ½ teaspoon bottled hot pepper sauce**

1 In a large bowl combine undrained canned tomatoes, fresh tomatoes, garbanzo beans, vegetable juice, broth, cucumber, sweet pepper, onion, cilantro, lime juice, garlic, and hot pepper sauce. Cover and chill for 2 to 24 hours.

2 To serve, ladle soup into bowls or mugs.

Nutrition Facts per serving: 136 cal., 3 g total fat (0 g sat. fat), 0 mg chol., 1,145 mg sodium, 23 g carbo., 6 g fiber, 6 g pro.
Daily Values: 21% vit. A, 89% vit. C, 10% calcium, 9% iron

soups and stews

black bean CHILLED SOUP

The Spaniards may have conquered the Southwest, but the Southwest has conquered classical Spanish gazpacho with this recipe. Traditionally served chilled, you can defy tradition and serve it warm.

soups and stews

Prep: 20 minutes
Chill: 4 to 24 hours
Makes: 6 (1-cup) servings

- 4 **cups seeded and quartered tomatoes**
- 1½ **cups hot-style vegetable juice**
- 1 **15-ounce can reduced-sodium black beans, rinsed and drained**
- 1 **cup finely chopped, seeded cucumber**
- 1 **cup finely chopped red or yellow sweet pepper**
- ½ **cup finely chopped red onion**
- 2 **tablespoons balsamic vinegar**
- ¾ **cup plain fat-free yogurt or dairy sour cream**

1 In a food processor bowl or blender container combine half of the tomatoes and ¼ cup of the vegetable juice. Cover and process or blend until tomatoes are coarsely chopped. Pour into a large bowl. Repeat with the remaining tomatoes and ¼ cup more vegetable juice.

2 Stir in the remaining vegetable juice, the beans, cucumber, sweet pepper, onion, and vinegar. Cover and refrigerate for 4 to 24 hours. To serve, ladle soup into bowls. Top each serving with 2 tablespoons of yogurt or sour cream.

Nutrition facts per serving: 122 cal., 1 g total fat (0 g sat. fat), 2 mg chol., 430 mg sodium, 23 g carbo., 5 g fiber, 7 g pro.
Daily values: 31% vit. A, 107% vit. C, 7% calcium, 14% iron

Bean There, Done That

Canned beans are so convenient—after all, you don't always have the time to cook them from the dried stage. But what about the sodium? Don't worry! Many brands of canned beans now come in low-sodium versions. And canned beans are as nutritionally beneficial as those cooked from dried—with protein, minerals, and lots of fiber.

vegetable BARLEY SOUP

Barley has been nourishing folks for thousands of years. This pearl of a grain is so packed with protein that it makes this meatless soup hearty enough to serve as a main dish.

Prep: 15 minutes
Cook: 25 minutes
Makes: 5 (1¾-cup) servings

- 1 14½-ounce can reduced-sodium chicken broth
- 1 14½-ounce can low-sodium tomatoes, undrained and cut up
- 1 cup chopped onion
- ¾ cup vegetable juice
- ½ cup quick-cooking barley
- ½ cup sliced celery
- ½ cup sliced carrot
- 1 tablespoon snipped fresh basil or 1 teaspoon dried basil, crushed
- 1½ teaspoons snipped fresh marjoram or ½ teaspoon dried marjoram, crushed
- 2 cloves garlic, minced
- ¼ teaspoon pepper
- 1 medium yellow summer squash, cut into ¼-inch slices
- 1 9-ounce package frozen cut green beans

1 In a large saucepan stir together the chicken broth, undrained tomatoes, onion, vegetable juice, barley, celery, carrot, dried basil (if using), dried marjoram (if using), garlic, and pepper. Bring to boiling; reduce heat. Simmer, covered, for 20 minutes.

2 Stir in the squash, green beans, fresh basil (if using), and fresh marjoram (if using). Return mixture to boiling. Simmer, covered, 5 to 10 minutes more or until vegetables are tender.

Nutrition facts per serving: 173 cal., 2 g total fat (0 g sat. fat), 0 mg chol., 480 mg sodium, 36 g carbo., 5 g fiber, 7 g pro.
Daily values: 56% vit. A, 55% vit. C, 7% calcium, 13% iron

soups and stews

chunky MINESTRONE

Minestrone is Italian for "big soup," and this one is big indeed—full of zucchini, onion, and carrot. For a vegetarian version, substitute vegetable broth for the chicken broth.

soups and stews

Prep: 15 minutes
Cook: 25 minutes
Makes: 5 (1¾-cup) servings

- 1 **tablespoon olive oil**
- 1½ **cups chopped onion**
- 1 **medium carrot, halved lengthwise and thinly sliced (about ¾ cup)**
- 2 **cloves garlic, minced**
- 3 **cups reduced-sodium chicken broth**
- 2 **14½-ounce cans low-sodium tomatoes, undrained and cut up**
- ¾ **cup water**
- ½ **cup long-grain rice**
- 1 **teaspoon dried Italian seasoning, crushed**
- 4 **cups shredded fresh spinach**
- 1 **15-ounce can reduced-sodium navy beans or white kidney beans, rinsed and drained**
- 1 **medium zucchini, quartered lengthwise and sliced (about 1½ cups)**
- ¼ **teaspoon freshly ground pepper**

  Grated Parmesan cheese (optional)

① In a Dutch oven heat olive oil over medium-high heat. Cook and stir the onion, carrot, and garlic in hot oil about 3 minutes or until onion is tender. Stir in the broth, undrained tomatoes, water, uncooked rice, and Italian seasoning.

② Bring to boiling; reduce heat. Simmer, covered, about 20 minutes or until rice is tender. Stir in the spinach, beans, zucchini, and pepper. Cook, covered, for 5 minutes more. If desired, sprinkle each serving with Parmesan cheese.

Nutrition facts per serving: 246 cal., 4 g total fat (1 g sat. fat), 0 mg chol., 462 mg sodium, 43 g carbo., 9 g fiber, 11 g pro.
Daily values: 72% vit. A, 68% vit. C, 12% calcium, 32% iron

chipotle & CORN CHOWDER

The smoky flavor of the chipotle peppers (dried smoked jalapeño peppers) combines with corn to make a bordertown chowder with substance and sizzle—the Southwest at its best!

Start to Finish: 40 minutes

Makes: 4 (1⅔-cup) servings

- 1 tablespoon olive oil
- 2 cups thinly sliced leeks (6 medium)
- 1 cup chopped red or green sweet pepper
- 3 cups reduced-sodium chicken broth
- 3 cups fresh or frozen whole kernel corn
- 2¼ cups finely chopped red potatoes (3 medium)
- 1 to 3 teaspoons chopped, canned chipotle peppers in adobo sauce
- 1 teaspoon paprika
- 2 tablespoons all-purpose flour

  Salt (optional)

① In a large saucepan heat olive oil over medium heat. Cook and stir leeks and sweet pepper in hot oil about 10 minutes or until tender.

② Add 2¾ cups of the broth to the saucepan. Return to boiling. Stir in corn, potatoes, chipotle peppers, and paprika. Bring to boiling; reduce heat. Simmer, covered, for 10 to 15 minutes or until potatoes are tender.

③ Meanwhile, in a screw-top jar combine the remaining ¼ cup broth and the flour. Cover and shake until smooth; stir into potato mixture. Cook and stir until slightly thickened and bubbly. Cook and stir for 1 minute more. If desired, season with salt.

Nutrition facts per serving: 362 cal., 6 g total fat (1 g sat. fat), 0 mg chol., 535 mg sodium, 74 g carbo., 12 g fiber, 10 g pro.
Daily values: 27% vit. A, 119% vit. C, 6% calcium, 33% iron

ratatouille SOUP

The French word ratatouille means to "beat with a hammer." How this came to be a stew of eggplant, tomatoes, and sweet peppers is not known, but we promise—you won't need a hammer to make this stew.

Start to Finish: 40 minutes
Makes: 6 (1⅔-cup) servings

1 **small eggplant (¾ pound), cubed (4 cups)**

2 **medium zucchini, cut into ½-inch slices (2⅔ cups)**

1 **medium red sweet pepper, cut into 1-inch pieces (1 cup)**

1 **medium onion, thinly sliced**

5 **cloves garlic, sliced**

1 **tablespoon olive oil**

1 **teaspoon dried Italian seasoning, crushed**

2 **14½-ounce cans reduced-sodium chicken broth**

1 **cup dried cavatelli**

1 **15-ounce can reduced-sodium navy beans, rinsed and drained**

2 **medium tomatoes, coarsely chopped**

❶ In a large, shallow roasting pan combine the eggplant, zucchini, sweet pepper, onion, and garlic. In a small bowl combine the olive oil, Italian seasoning, ¼ teaspoon salt, and ¼ teaspoon pepper; drizzle over vegetables, tossing to coat. Bake in a 425° oven about 20 minutes or until vegetables are tender, stirring once.

❷ Meanwhile, in a Dutch oven combine the broth and 3 cups water. Bring to boiling; add cavatelli. Return to boiling. Cook about 12 minutes or until tender. Reduce heat. Stir in the beans, tomatoes, and roasted vegetables. Heat through.

Nutrition facts per serving: 186 cal., 4 g total fat (0 g sat. fat), 0 mg chol., 490 mg sodium, 32 g carbo., 7 g fiber, 8 g pro.
Daily values: 13% vit. A, 54% vit. C, 4% calcium, 16% iron

Bean Business

If you're keeping an eye on sodium, you may substitute low-sodium cooked beans for canned beans by keeping a supply in your freezer. Cook a big batch of dried beans according to package directions (add very little or no salt). Cook them until just tender, as freezing tenderizes them more. Drain, cool, and place in freezer bags or containers in 1¾-cup amounts (1¾ cups cooked beans equal a 15-ounce can of beans). Label and freeze the beans for up to 3 months. To use, place the beans (thawed or frozen) in a saucepan with ½ cup water for each 1¾ cup of beans. Simmer, covered, over low heat until heated through. Drain and use as you would canned beans.

onion & MUSHROOM SOUP

This hearty soup combines the natural sweetness of caramelized onions with the nutlike flavor of wild rice. Plus, it is high in complex carbohydrates and protein—enough to be a meal in itself.

soups and stews

Start to Finish: 40 minutes
Makes: 4 (1¾-cup) servings

1 tablespoon olive oil

4 large onions, cut into ¾-inch chunks (about 4 cups)

1 cup sliced leeks (3 medium)

2 teaspoons brown sugar

3 cups sliced fresh mushrooms, such as shiitake, button, or brown mushrooms

1 cup finely chopped carrots (2 medium)

1 14½-ounce can reduced-sodium chicken broth

1¾ cups water

1½ cups cooked wild rice or brown rice

2 tablespoons dry sherry (optional)

⅛ teaspoon pepper

½ cup cold water

2 tablespoons all-purpose flour

1 In a large saucepan heat olive oil over medium-low heat. Cook onion and leeks in hot oil, covered, for 13 to 15 minutes or until onions and leeks are tender, stirring occasionally. Uncover; stir in brown sugar. Cook and stir over medium-high heat for 4 to 5 minutes more or until onions and leeks are golden brown.

2 Stir mushrooms and carrots into onion mixture. Cook and stir over medium heat about 3 minutes or until mushrooms are tender. Stir in chicken broth, the 1¾ cups water, cooked rice, sherry (if desired), and pepper.

3 In a screw-top jar combine the ½ cup cold water and flour. Cover and shake until smooth; stir into the rice mixture. Cook and stir until slightly thickened and bubbly. Cook and stir for 1 minute more.

Nutrition facts per serving: 234 cal., 5 g total fat (1 g sat. fat), 0 mg chol., 333 mg sodium, 44 g carbo., 8 g fiber, 8 g pro.
Daily values: 81% vit. A, 26% vit. C, 6% calcium, 21% iron

breads
& ROLLS

You'll enjoy these recipes that go beyond a simple slice of bread. Choose from favorites such as scones, focaccia, muffins, and popovers to prepare as a snack or the perfect accompaniment to your meal.

Pear-Almond Muffins, *recipe page 310*

apple-cheddar MUFFINS

Applesauce and dried fruit keep these muffins moist. Spicy and aromatic, they're good for breakfast, brunch, tea, or snacks—especially when served with a cup of tea, cold milk, or hot cider.

Prep: 20 minutes
Bake: 20 minutes
Makes: 12 muffins

Nonstick spray coating

1¼ **cups unprocessed wheat bran (Miller's Bran)**

1 **cup all-purpose flour**

½ **cup shredded reduced-fat sharp cheddar cheese (2 ounces)**

2 **teaspoons baking powder**

½ **teaspoon ground cinnamon**

¼ **teaspoon baking soda**

¼ **teaspoon salt**

¾ **cup unsweetened applesauce**

½ **cup fat-free milk**

3 **tablespoons honey plus 2 packets heat-stable sugar substitute, or ⅓ cup honey**

¼ **cup refrigerated or frozen egg product, thawed**

1 **tablespoon cooking oil**

½ **cup finely snipped dried apples or raisins**

1 Spray twelve 2½-inch muffin cups with nonstick coating; set aside. In a medium bowl combine wheat bran, flour, cheese, baking powder, cinnamon, baking soda, and salt. Make a well in the center of the flour mixture; set aside.

2 In another bowl combine applesauce, milk, honey plus sugar substitute or honey, egg product, and oil. Add applesauce mixture all at once to flour mixture. Stir just until moistened (batter should be lumpy). Fold in dried apples or raisins.

3 Spoon the batter into prepared muffin cups, filling each three-fourths full. Bake in a 400° oven about 20 minutes or until golden. Cool in muffin cups on a wire rack for 5 minutes. Remove from muffin cups; serve warm.

Nutrition facts per muffin: 114 cal., 3 g total fat (1 g sat. fat), 4 mg chol., 184 mg sodium, 21 g carbo., 2 g fiber, 4 g pro.
Daily values: 2% vit. A, 0% vit. C, 9% calcium, 9% iron

Using honey only option: 126 cal. and 24 g carbo.

breads & rolls

apricot-filled MUFFINS

Discover the extraordinary flavor of these muffins bursting with fruit. Tucked inside each muffin is a sweet pocket of your choice of fruit spread.

Prep: 20 minutes
Bake: 18 minutes
Makes: 12 muffins

Nonstick spray coating

1½ **cups all-purpose flour**

3 **tablespoons sugar plus
3 packets heat-stable sugar
substitute, or ⅓ cup sugar**

1 **teaspoon baking powder**

1 **teaspoon ground cinnamon**

¼ **teaspoon baking soda**

⅛ **teaspoon salt**

⅔ **cup buttermilk**

¼ **cup refrigerated or frozen
egg product, thawed**

3 **tablespoons cooking oil**

¼ **cup sugar-free apricot, peach,
or raspberry spread**

1 Spray twelve 2½-inch muffin cups with nonstick coating; set aside. In a medium bowl stir together flour, sugar plus sugar substitute or the sugar, baking powder, cinnamon, baking soda, and salt. Make a well in the center of the flour mixture; set aside.

2 In another bowl stir together buttermilk, egg product, and oil. Add buttermilk mixture all at once to flour mixture. Stir just until moistened (batter should be lumpy).

3 Spoon batter into prepared muffins cups, filling each about one-fourth full. Place about 1 teaspoon of the spreadable fruit in center of each. Top with remaining batter. Bake in a 400° oven for 18 to 20 minutes or until golden. Cool in muffin cups on a wire rack for 5 minutes. Remove from muffin cups; serve warm.

Nutrition facts per muffin: 109 cal., 4 g total fat (1 g sat. fat), 1 mg chol., 103 mg sodium, 18 g carbo., 0 g fiber, 3 g pro.
Daily values: 1% vit. A, 0% vit. C, 4% calcium, 6% iron

Using the ⅓ cup sugar option: 121 cal. and 21 g carbo.

breads & rolls

pumpkin MUFFINS

The secret to these enticing muffins is a combination of moist, rich pumpkin and flavorful buckwheat. Though buckwheat is often thought of as a cereal, it actually is made from the seeds of the buckwheat herb.

Prep: 20 minutes
Bake: 15 minutes
Makes: 12 muffins

Nonstick spray coating

1⅓ **cups all-purpose flour**

¾ **cup buckwheat flour**

¼ **cup sugar plus 2 packets heat-stable sugar substitute, or ⅓ cup sugar**

1½ **teaspoons baking powder**

1 **teaspoon ground cinnamon**

½ **teaspoon baking soda**

½ **teaspoon salt**

2 **slightly beaten eggs**

1 **cup canned pumpkin**

½ **cup fat-free milk**

2 **tablespoons cooking oil**

½ **teaspoon finely shredded orange peel**

¼ **cup orange juice**

① Spray twelve 2½-inch muffin cups with nonstick coating; set pan aside. In a medium bowl combine the all-purpose flour, buckwheat flour, sugar plus sugar substitute or the sugar, baking powder, cinnamon, baking soda, and salt. Make a well in the center of flour mixture; set aside.

② In another bowl combine the eggs, pumpkin, milk, oil, orange peel, and orange juice. Add the egg mixture all at once to the flour mixture. Stir just until moistened (batter should be lumpy).

③ Spoon batter into the prepared muffin cups, dividing the batter evenly. Bake in a 400° oven for 15 to 20 minutes or until the muffins are light brown. Cool in muffin cups on a wire rack for 5 minutes. Remove from muffin cups; serve warm.

Nutrition facts per muffin: 134 cal., 4 g total fat (1 g sat. fat), 36 mg chol., 204 mg sodium, 22 g carbo., 2 g fiber, 4 g pro.
Daily values: 47% vit. A, 6% vit. C, 6% calcium, 9% iron

Using the ⅓ cup sugar option: 141 cal. and 24 g carbo.

breads & rolls

pear-almond MUFFINS

Cream cheese laced with ginger and honey complements these fruit-filled muffins. Store the batter in the refrigerator for up to 3 days and bake a few at a time, if you like.

Prep: 20 minutes
Bake: 15 minutes
Stand: 10 minutes
Oven: 400°F
Makes: 7 muffins

Nonstick cooking spray

⅔ **cup all-purpose flour**

⅓ **cup packed brown sugar**

1½ **teaspoons baking powder**

¼ **teaspoon ground ginger**

⅛ **teaspoon salt**

½ **cup whole bran cereal**

½ **cup fat-free milk**

½ **cup chopped, peeled pear**

2 **tablespoons refrigerated or frozen egg product, thawed**

2 **tablespoons cooking oil**

1 **tablespoon finely chopped**

❶ Lightly coat 7 muffin cups with nonstick cooking spray or line with paper baking cups; set aside. In a medium bowl stir together flour, brown sugar, baking powder, ginger, and salt. Make a well in the center of the flour mixture; set aside.

❷ In another medium bowl stir together cereal and milk; let cereal mixture stand for 5 minutes. Stir in pear, egg product, and oil. Add cereal mixture all at once to flour mixture. Stir just until moistened (batter should be lumpy). (If desired, cover and refrigerate the batter in an airtight container for up to 3 days. Bake muffins as needed.)

❸ Spoon batter into prepared muffin cups, filling each three-fourths full. Sprinkle with nuts.

❹ Bake in a 400° oven for 15 to 18 minutes or until a wooden toothpick inserted near centers comes out clean. Cool in muffin cups on a wire rack for 5 minutes. Remove from muffin cups. Serve warm with Ginger-Cream Spread.

Ginger-Cream Spread: In a small bowl stir together one-third of an 8-ounce tub fat-free cream cheese, 1½ teaspoons honey, and 1½ teaspoons finely chopped crystallized ginger or ⅛ teaspoon ground ginger.

Nutrition Facts per muffin: 165 cal., 5 g total fat (1 g sat. fat), 2 mg chol., 157 mg sodium, 28 g carbo., 2 g fiber, 5 g pro.
Daily Values: 3% vit. A, 5% vit. C, 15% calcium, 9% iron

breads & rolls

caramelized ONION ROLLS

Roll up the flavor of onions! Cooked until caramelized and brown, onions are baked into the simplest of yeast breads—a convenient hot roll mix. Serve these spiral rolls with soup or salad.

Prep: 30 minutes
Rise: 30 minutes
Bake: 20 minutes
Makes: 12 rolls

- **2 large onions, chopped**
- **2 teaspoons oil**
- **1 tablespoon margarine or butter**
- **2 tablespoons brown sugar**
- **Nonstick spray coating**
- **1 16-ounce package hot roll mix**

1 In a large nonstick skillet cook onions in oil and margarine or butter over medium-low heat about 10 minutes, stirring frequently, until tender and golden brown. Stir in brown sugar; continue cooking until sugar melts. Set aside.

2 Spray a 13×9×2-inch baking pan with nonstick coating; set aside. Prepare hot roll mix according to package directions. On a lightly floured surface, roll the dough into a 15×10-inch rectangle. Spread caramelized onions evenly over dough. Roll up dough, jelly-roll style, starting from a long side; seal seam. Cut crosswise into 12 slices. Arrange rolls, cut sides down, in prepared baking pan. Cover and let rise in a warm place until double (about 30 minutes).

3 Bake in a 375° oven for 20 to 30 minutes or until golden brown. Remove from pan; serve warm or cool.

Nutrition facts per roll: 194 cal., 5 g total fat (1 g sat. fat), 18 mg chol., 261 mg sodium, 33 g carbo., 0 g fiber, 6 g pro.
Daily values: 4% vit. A, 1% vit. C, 0% calcium, 7% iron

breads & rolls

easy herb FOCACCIA

Focaccia (foh-KAH-chee-ah) is an Italian yeast bread usually topped with onions, herbs, olive oil, or cheese. Our easy version is made with a hot roll mix. Serve it with pasta or enjoy a slice as a midafternoon snack.

Prep: 20 minutes
Rise: 30 minutes
Bake: 15 minutes
Makes: 24 servings

Nonstick spray coating

1 **16-ounce package hot roll mix**

1 **egg**

2 **tablespoons olive oil**

⅔ **cup finely chopped onion**

1 **teaspoon dried rosemary, crushed**

2 **teaspoons olive oil**

① Spray a 15×10×1-inch baking pan or a 12- to 14-inch pizza pan with nonstick coating; set aside.

② Prepare the hot roll mix according to package directions for the basic dough, using the 1 egg and substituting the 2 tablespoons olive oil for the margarine. Knead dough; allow to rest as directed. If using the large baking pan, roll dough into a 15×10-inch rectangle and carefully transfer to prepared pan. If using the pizza pan, roll dough into a 12-inch circle and carefully transfer to prepared pan.

③ In a skillet cook onion and rosemary in the 2 teaspoons hot olive oil until tender. With fingertips, press indentations every inch or so in dough. Top dough evenly with onion mixture. Cover and let rise in a warm place until nearly double (about 30 minutes).

④ Bake in a 375° oven for 15 to 20 minutes or until golden. Cool 10 minutes on a wire rack. Remove focaccia from pan; cool completely.

Nutrition facts per serving: 88 cal., 2 g total fat (0 g sat. fat), 9 mg chol., 113 mg sodium, 15 g carbo., 0 g fiber, 3 g pro.
Daily values: 0% vit. A, 0% vit. C, 0% calcium, 3% iron

Parmesan and Pine Nut Focaccia: Prepare focaccia as above, except omit the onion, rosemary, and 2 teaspoons olive oil. Make the indentations, then brush the dough with mixture of 1 egg white and 2 tablespoon water. Sprinkle with ¼ cup pine nuts, pressing lightly into dough. Sprinkle with 2 tablespoons fresh grated Parmesan cheese. Bake as directed.

Nutrition facts per serving: 95 cal., 3 g total fat (0 g sat. fat), 9 mg chol., 122 mg sodium, 15 g carbo., 0 g fiber, 4 g pro.
Daily values: 0% vit. A, 0% vit. C, 0% calcium, 4% iron

tomato-basil CORNBREAD

Enjoy old-fashioned cornbread with a new twist! This updated classic has fewer calories and less fat than the original, but the flavor is better than ever due to the addition of basil and zesty dried tomatoes.

Prep: 20 minutes
Bake: 15 minutes
Makes: 12 servings

Nonstick spray coating

1 **cup all-purpose flour**

1 **cup cornmeal**

2 **tablespoons sugar**

2 **tablespoons snipped fresh basil or 1 teaspoon dried basil, crushed**

1 **tablespoon baking powder**

¼ **teaspoon salt**

1 **cup fat-free milk**

½ **cup egg product**

3 **tablespoons cooking oil**

½ **cup dried tomato pieces (not oil-packed)**

① Spray a 9×1½-inch round baking pan with nonstick coating; set aside. In a large bowl combine flour, cornmeal, sugar, basil, baking powder, and salt. In small bowl combine the milk, egg product, and oil. Add the milk mixture all at once to flour mixture. Stir just until moistened (batter should be lumpy). Fold the tomato pieces into the batter. Spoon the batter into prepared pan.

② Bake in a 425° oven for 15 to 20 minutes or until a wooden toothpick inserted into center comes out clean. Cool on a wire rack. Cut into wedges to serve.

Nutrition facts per serving: 138 cal., 4 g total fat (1 g sat. fat), 0 mg chol., 212 mg sodium, 21 g carbo., 1 g fiber, 4 g pro.
Daily values: 4% vit. A, 1% vit. C, 10% calcium, 8% iron

chile & cheese CORNBREAD

Want to be hailed as the hero of the kitchen? Just serve chunks of this pepper-, corn-, and onion-laced cornbread. It's the ideal accompaniment for hot soup, grilled meat, or baked chicken.

Prep: 25 minutes
Bake: 20 minutes
Makes: 18 servings

Nonstick spray coating

1 **tablespoon margarine or butter**

⅓ **cup finely chopped red sweet pepper**

¼ **cup finely chopped red onion**

⅔ **cup whole kernel corn**

3 **tablespoons canned diced green chile peppers, drained**

1⅓ **cups yellow cornmeal**

1¼ **cups all-purpose flour**

2 **teaspoons baking powder**

1 **teaspoon sugar**

½ **teaspoon baking soda**

¼ **teaspoon salt**

1¼ **cups buttermilk**

2 **eggs, slightly beaten**

2 **tablespoons margarine or butter, melted and cooled**

½ **cup shredded, reduced-fat cheddar cheese**

① Spray an 11×7×2-inch baking pan with nonstick coating; set aside. In a medium skillet heat the 1 tablespoon margarine or butter over medium-high heat. Cook and stir sweet pepper and onion for 3 minutes. Add corn and chile peppers; cook and stir for 2 more minutes. Remove from heat; cool slightly.

② Meanwhile, in a large bowl stir together cornmeal, flour, baking powder, sugar, baking soda, and salt. In another bowl stir together the buttermilk, eggs, and the 2 tablespoons melted margarine or butter. Add the buttermilk mixture all at once to flour mixture. Stir just until moistened (batter should be lumpy). Fold in the corn mixture and cheese. Spoon batter into prepared pan. Bake in a 425° oven for 20 to 25 minutes or until golden. Serve warm.

Chile & Cheese Corn Muffins: Prepare as above, except spoon batter into 18 greased or paper-lined 2½-inch muffin cups. Bake in a 425° oven about 20 minutes or until muffins are golden. Cool in muffin cups on a wire rack for 5 minutes. Remove the muffins from the muffin cups; serve warm. If desired, place muffins in an airtight freezer container and freeze for up to 3 months.

Nutrition facts per serving: 119 cal., 4 g total fat (1 g sat. fat), 27 mg chol., 182 mg sodium, 17 g carbo., 1 g fiber, 4 g pro.
Daily values: 6% vit. A, 7% vit. C, 7% calcium, 6% iron

apricot LADDER LOAF

Don't tell! There's no need for everyone to know how easy it is to make this impressive yeast bread. It only takes three main ingredients—frozen bread dough, light preserves, and chopped fruit.

Prep: 30 minutes
Rise: 40 minutes
Bake: 20 minutes
Makes: 2 loaves

Nonstick spray coating

1 **16-ounce loaf frozen white or whole wheat bread dough, thawed***

½ **cup sugar-free apricot, strawberry, or red raspberry spread**

½ **cup chopped apricots; chopped, peeled peaches; blueberries; or raspberries**

① Spray 2 baking sheets with nonstick coating; set aside. Transfer thawed bread dough onto a lightly floured surface. Divide the dough in half. Roll each half of the dough into a 12×7-inch rectangle. Carefully transfer each rectangle to a prepared baking sheet.

② Cut up any large pieces of fruit in the preserves. For each loaf, spoon about ¼ cup of the preserves down the center third of the dough rectangle to within 1 inch of the ends. Sprinkle ¼ cup of the fruit over the preserves. On the long sides, make 2-inch-long cuts from the edges toward the center at 1-inch intervals. Starting at one end, alternately fold opposite strips of dough, at an angle, across filling. Slightly press the ends together in the center to seal. Cover and let rise in a warm place until nearly double (about 40 minutes).

③ Bake in a 350° oven about 20 minutes or until golden brown. Remove from baking sheets. Cool slightly on wire racks; serve warm.

*__Note:__ To quick-thaw frozen bread dough in your microwave oven, remove from wrapper and place dough in a microwave-safe bowl. Cover and cook on 10% power (low) for 15 to 17 minutes or until thawed, rotating dough frequently.

Nutrition facts per serving: 54 cal., 0 g total fat (0 g sat. fat), 0 mg chol., 6 mg sodium, 10 g carbo., 0 g fiber, 1 g pro.
Daily values: 0% vit. A, 1% vit. C, 1% calcium, 0% iron

breads & rolls

wheat & oat BREAD

Even a novice bread baker can succeed with this quick bread. The loaf has a crunchy wheat germ-topped crust and a pleasing nutty flavor. Warm from the oven, this bread is irresistible.

Prep: 20 minutes
Bake: 35 minutes
Makes: 16 servings

Nonstick spray coating

1¾ cups all-purpose flour

¾ cup whole wheat flour

½ cup regular rolled oats, toasted*

3 tablespoons toasted wheat germ

3 tablespoons sugar

2½ teaspoons baking powder

¼ teaspoon salt

1⅓ cups fat-free milk

¼ cup refrigerated or frozen egg product, thawed

2 tablespoons cooking oil

1 tablespoon toasted wheat germ

1 Spray the bottom and sides of an 8×1½-inch round baking pan with nonstick coating; set aside.

2 In a large bowl stir together the all-purpose flour, whole wheat flour, toasted oats, the 3 tablespoons wheat germ, sugar, baking powder, and salt. In another bowl combine milk, egg product, and oil. Add milk mixture all at once to dry mixture. Stir just until moistened (batter should be lumpy). Spread batter in prepared pan. Sprinkle with the 1 tablespoon wheat germ.

3 Bake in a 375° oven for 35 to 40 minutes or until golden brown and a toothpick inserted near the center comes out clean. Cool bread in pan on a wire rack for 10 minutes. Remove from pan; serve warm.

*Note: To toast rolled oats, place in a shallow baking pan. Bake rolled oats in a 350° oven for 5 to 8 minutes or until oats are lightly browned, shaking pan once.

Nutrition facts per serving: 116 cal., 3 g total fat (0 g sat. fat), 0 mg chol., 108 mg sodium, 20 g carbo., 1 g fiber, 4 g pro.
Daily values: 2% vit. A, 0% vit. C, 7% calcium, 8% iron

A Germ to Behold

Wheat germ—the toasted and ground "germ" of the wheat kernel—is concentrated in protein and minerals. Toasted wheat germ perks up cereals or soups and brings texture to baked goods. It even can bring its nutlike flavor to sandwich spreads—try folding a teaspoon or two into chicken or tuna salad. Look for toasted wheat germ in health food stores and most supermarkets.

whole wheat POPOVERS

Steam causes the batter to rise and "pop over" the sides of the baking cups. For moist popovers, remove from the oven immediately after baking; for crisper results, turn off the oven and let "bake" a few more minutes.

Prep: 20 minutes
Bake: 40 minutes
Makes: 6 popovers

Nonstick spray coating
2 **beaten eggs**
1 **cup fat-free milk**
1 **teaspoon cooking oil**
¾ **cup all-purpose flour**
¼ **cup whole wheat flour**
¼ **teaspoon salt**

① Spray bottoms and sides of six 6-ounce custard cups or cups of a popover pan with nonstick coating. Set aside.

② In a mixing bowl use a wire whisk or rotary beater to beat eggs, milk, and oil until combined. Add all-purpose flour, whole wheat flour, and salt; beat until smooth. Fill prepared cups half full with batter.

③ Bake in a 400° oven about 40 minutes or until very firm. Immediately after removing from oven, prick each popover to allow the steam to escape. (For crisper popovers, turn off the oven; return the popovers to the oven for 5 to 10 minutes or until desired crispness is reached.) Remove popovers from cups; serve immediately.

Nutrition facts per popover: 119 cal., 3 g total fat (1 g sat. fat), 73 mg chol., 131 mg sodium, 17 g carbo., 1 g fiber, 6 g pro.
Daily values: 5% vit. A, 0% vit. C, 5% calcium, 7% iron

breads & rolls

319

vegetables
& SIDES

A great side dish can make the best meal even better. This collection of sidekicks includes inspiring recipes featuring a variety of your favorite vegetables. Try the Thai-Style Asparagus, Lemony Mixed Vegetables, Beans and Caramelized Onions, Roasted Succotash, or Pesto Potatoes to jump-start your dinner.

Vegetable Primavera, *recipe page 322*

vegetable PRIMAVERA

The Italian word "primavera" refers to the use of fresh vegetables, and that is what this recipe features. Squash, carrots, red pepper, and broccoli combine to create a festival of colors.

Start to Finish: 20 minutes
Makes: 6 (¾-cup) servings

- 3 **tablespoons reduced-sodium chicken broth**
- 1 **tablespoon Dijon-style mustard**
- 1 **tablespoon olive oil**
- 2 **teaspoons white wine vinegar**
- **Nonstick spray coating**
- 1½ **cups sliced yellow summer squash**
- 1 **cup packaged, peeled baby carrots**
- 1 **cup chopped red sweet pepper**
- 3 **cups broccoli flowerets**
- 2 **tablespoons snipped parsley**

1 In a small bowl combine 1 tablespoon of the chicken broth, the mustard, olive oil, and vinegar. Set aside.

2 Spray a large nonstick skillet with nonstick coating. Preheat the skillet over medium heat. Cook and stir squash, carrots, and sweet pepper in hot skillet about 5 minutes or until nearly tender. Add broccoli and remaining chicken broth to skillet. Cook, covered, about 3 minutes or until broccoli is crisp-tender.

3 Stir in the mustard mixture; heat through. To serve, sprinkle with parsley.

Nutrition facts per serving: 56 cal., 3 g total fat (0 g sat. fat), 0 mg chol., 114 mg sodium, 7 g carbo., 3 g fiber, 2 g pro.
Daily values: 75% vit. A, 99% vit. C, 3% calcium, 5% iron

vegetables & sides

Spray for Success

Nonstick spray coating not only eliminates the mess of greasing pans, it also saves on fat and calories. For added pizzazz, look for roasted garlic-, olive oil-, and butter-flavored sprays. Compare the difference of using nonstick spray in place of oil, margarine, or butter:

Nonstick spray coating (1-second spray)	<1 g fat	7 calories
Butter/margarine (1 teaspoon)	4 g fat	35 calories
Oil (1 teaspoon)	5 g fat	41 calories

beans & CARAMELIZED ONIONS

No more boring beans! In this recipe, the familiar green bean takes on an exciting new flavor. Onions, sugar, and balsamic vinegar coat the beans in a sweet, but tangy sauce.

Start to Finish: 20 minutes
Makes: about 5 (¾-cup) servings

1 tablespoon margarine or butter

1½ cups chopped onion

1 teaspoon sugar

1 tablespoon balsamic vinegar or red wine vinegar

½ of a 7½-ounce jar roasted red sweet peppers, drained and finely chopped (½ cup)

¼ cup quartered pitted ripe olives

2 tablespoons snipped fresh basil

¼ teaspoon salt

¼ teaspoon black pepper

1 pound green beans, cut into 2-inch lengths (about 4 cups)

① In a large heavy skillet heat margarine or butter over medium heat until melted. Cook and stir onion and sugar in margarine or butter about 10 minutes or until the onion is very tender and golden brown. Stir in vinegar. Cook and stir for 1 to 2 minutes more or until liquid evaporates. Stir in the roasted red peppers, olives, basil, salt, and black pepper. Remove skillet from heat; keep warm.

② Meanwhile, in a medium saucepan cook the green beans, covered, in a small amount of boiling water about 10 minutes or until crisp-tender; drain. To serve, stir caramelized onion into green beans.

Nutrition facts per serving: 86 cal., 6 g total fat (1 g sat. fat), 0 mg chol., 169 mg sodium, 14 g carbo., 4 g fiber, 2 g pro.
Daily values: 16% vit. A, 86% vit. C, 4% calcium, 10% iron

vegetables & sides

lemony MIXED VEGETABLES

Be creative with seasonings! The inspired combination of coriander, oregano, and lemon peel adds character to this simple vegetable side dish.

Prep: 20 minutes
Cook: 18 minutes
Makes: 6 (¾-cup) servings

- 1 cup reduced-sodium chicken broth
- ¼ teaspoon ground coriander
- ⅛ teaspoon salt
- ⅛ teaspoon black pepper
- ½ pound green beans, cut into 2-inch lengths (about 2 cups)
- 2 cups thinly bias-sliced carrots
- 1 cup cauliflower flowerets
- ½ of a medium red sweet pepper, cut into 1-inch pieces
- 1 tablespoon snipped fresh oregano or 1 teaspoon dried oregano, crushed
- 1 tablespoon cold water
- 1½ teaspoons cornstarch
- ½ teaspoon finely shredded lemon peel
- 4 teaspoons lemon juice

1 In a large saucepan combine the chicken broth, coriander, salt, and black pepper. Bring to boiling; add green beans. Return to boiling; reduce heat. Simmer, covered, for 10 minutes. Add carrots, cauliflower, and sweet pepper. Return to boiling; reduce heat. Simmer, covered, for 4 to 5 minutes more or until vegetables are crisp-tender.

2 Using a slotted spoon, transfer vegetables to a serving bowl, reserving broth mixture in saucepan. Cover vegetables; keep warm.

3 In a small bowl stir together oregano, water, cornstarch, and lemon peel; stir into broth mixture in saucepan. Cook and stir over medium heat until slightly thickened and bubbly. Cook and stir for 2 minutes more. Stir in lemon juice. Pour thickened broth mixture over vegetables. Toss lightly to coat.

Nutrition facts per serving: 49 cal., 0 g total fat (0 g sat. fat), 0 mg chol., 184 mg sodium, 11 g carbo., 3 g fiber, 2 g pro.
Daily values: 121% vit. A, 48% vit. C, 3% calcium, 6% iron

vegetables & sides

roasted SUCCOTASH

Put away your saucepan! This colorful lima bean, corn, and red pepper succotash is prepared in the oven. Just combine the ingredients in the pan, bake, and finish with a light sprinkling of fresh cilantro.

Prep: 15 minutes
Bake: 25 minutes
Makes: 6 (½-cup) servings

- **1 10-ounce package frozen baby lima beans**
- **1½ cups fresh or frozen whole kernel corn**
- **1½ cups finely chopped red sweet pepper**
- **1 cup chopped onion**
- **1 tablespoon olive oil**
- **1 teaspoon ground cumin**
- **¼ teaspoon salt**
- **⅛ to ¼ teaspoon ground red pepper**
- **1 to 2 tablespoons snipped cilantro**

1 In a 15×10×1-inch baking pan combine lima beans, corn, sweet pepper, onion, olive oil, cumin, salt, and red pepper.

2 Bake in a 400° oven about 25 minutes or until vegetables are tender and lightly browned, stirring after 15 minutes. To serve, sprinkle with cilantro.

Nutrition facts per serving: 210 cal., 3 g total fat (1 g sat. fat), 0 mg chol., 100 mg sodium, 37 g carbo., 5 g fiber, 11 g pro.
Daily values: 19% vit. A, 75% vit. C, 3% calcium, 23% iron

vegetables & sides

orange-ginger CARROTS

Consider keeping fresh ginger on hand to add zesty flavor to vegetables. The knobby, tan root stays fresh in the refrigerator for at least a week. It also can be frozen for up to two months.

Start to Finish: 10 minutes
Makes: 4 (¾-cup) servings

- 1 **16-ounce package peeled baby carrots**
- 2 **tablespoons orange juice**
- 1 **tablespoon honey**
- ½ **teaspoon grated fresh ginger**
- 1 **tablespoon snipped parsley**
  Finely shredded orange peel (optional)

1 In a large saucepan cook the carrots, covered, in a small amount of boiling water for 3 to 5 minutes or until crisp-tender. Drain well.

2 Meanwhile, in a small bowl stir together the orange juice, honey, and ginger; drizzle over warm carrots. Toss to coat. To serve, sprinkle with parsley and, if desired, orange peel.

Nutrition facts per serving: 67 cal., 0 g total fat (0 g sat. fat), 0 mg chol., 70 mg sodium, 16 g carbo., 4 g fiber, 1 g pro.
Daily values: 256% vit. A, 12% vit. C, 2% calcium, 4% iron

vegetables & sides

orzo-broccoli PILAF

Orzo is a tiny, rice-shaped pasta, larger than a grain of rice, but slightly smaller than a pine nut. It is a great substitute for rice in this vegetable-filled pilaf.

Prep: 20 minutes
Cook: 15 minutes
Stand: 5 minutes
Makes: 6 (⅔-cup) servings

- 2 teaspoons olive oil
- 1 cup sliced fresh mushrooms
- ½ cup chopped onion
- ⅔ cup orzo (rosamarina)
- 1 14½-ounce can reduced-sodium chicken broth
- ½ cup shredded carrot
- 1 teaspoon dried marjoram, crushed
- ⅛ teaspoon pepper
- 2 cups small broccoli flowerets

1 In a large saucepan heat olive oil over medium-high heat. Cook and stir the mushrooms and onion in hot oil until onion is tender. Stir in the orzo. Cook and stir about 2 minutes more or until orzo is lightly browned. Remove from heat.

2 Carefully stir in the chicken broth, carrot, marjoram, and pepper. Bring to boiling; reduce heat. Simmer, covered, about 15 minutes or until orzo is tender but still firm. Remove saucepan from heat; stir in broccoli. Let stand, covered, for 5 minutes.

Nutrition facts per serving: 113 cal., 2 g total fat (0 g sat. fat), 0 mg chol., 209 mg sodium, 19 g carbo., 2 g fiber, 4 g pro.
Daily values: 30% vit. A, 37% vit. C, 2% calcium, 9% iron

vegetables & sides

barley-TOMATO PILAF

Pearl barley is featured in this pilaf. Barley is said to be "pearled" after the outer husk and bran are removed, and the remaining grain is steamed and polished. This process gives barley a unique texture.

Prep: 20 minutes
Cook: 45 minutes
Makes: four ⅔-cup servings

Nonstick spray coating

½ **cup chopped onion**

2 **cloves garlic, minced**

1 **14½-ounce can reduced-sodium chicken broth**

¼ **cup water**

1 **teaspoon dried oregano, crushed**

½ **teaspoon paprika**

¼ **teaspoon ground turmeric**

⅛ **teaspoon black pepper**

½ **cup pearl barley**

1 **medium red or green sweet pepper, cut into matchstick strips (1 cup)**

3 **medium plum tomatoes, chopped (1 cup)**

1 Spray a large saucepan with nonstick coating. Preheat over medium heat. Cook and stir onion and garlic in hot saucepan until onion is tender. Carefully stir in chicken broth, water, oregano, paprika, turmeric, and black pepper. Bring to boiling; stir in the barley. Return to boiling; reduce heat. Simmer, covered, for 40 minutes.

2 Stir in sweet pepper. Cook, uncovered, over medium heat for 5 to 10 minutes more or until liquid is evaporated, stirring occasionally. Stir in tomatoes.

Nutrition facts per serving: 119 cal., 2 g total fat (0 g saturated fat), 0 mg chol., 289 mg sodium, 24 g carbo., 5 g fiber, 5 g pro.
Daily values: 18% vit. A, 72% vit. C, 1% calcium, 9% iron

vegetables & sides

santa fe VEGETABLES

In mid- and late summer, when tomatoes and zucchini are plentiful and corn is at its sweetest, be sure to try this colorful vegetable dish. Cumin, cilantro, and pepper sauce add a touch of Southwestern pizzazz.

Start to Finish: 25 minutes
Makes: 6 (⅔-cup) servings

1 tablespoon olive oil or cooking oil

2 cups fresh or frozen whole kernel corn

¾ cup chopped onion

1½ cups finely chopped zucchini

1 teaspoon ground cumin

2 cups chopped, seeded tomatoes

¼ cup snipped cilantro

¼ teaspoon salt

Few dashes bottled hot pepper sauce

1 In a large heavy skillet heat oil over medium-high heat. Cook and stir the corn and onion in hot oil for 5 minutes. Stir in the zucchini and cumin. Cook and stir about 3 minutes more or until the corn is just tender.

2 Remove from heat. Stir in tomatoes, cilantro, salt, and hot pepper sauce.

Nutrition facts per serving: 130 cal., 3 g total fat (0 g sat. fat), 0 mg chol., 102 mg sodium, 25 g carbo., 4 g fiber, 4 g pro.
Daily values: 7% vit. A, 34% vit. C, 1% calcium, 9% iron

pesto POTATOES

A surefire dinner favorite, these mashed potatoes are lightened with reduced-fat cream cheese, skim milk, and a homemade, lower-fat pesto featuring basil and spinach.

Start to Finish: 35 minutes
Makes: 8 (¾-cup) servings

- **2 pounds medium yellow fleshed potatoes, such as Yukon gold**
- **½ of an 8-ounce package fat-free cream cheese**
- **Salt and pepper**
- **2 to 3 tablespoons skim milk**
- **8 teaspoons Pesto**

1 Peel and quarter potatoes. Cook, covered, in a small amount of boiling lightly salted water for 15 to 20 minutes or until tender; drain. Mash with a potato masher or an electric mixer on low speed. Add cream cheese. Season to taste with salt and pepper. Gradually beat in enough milk to make potatoes light and fluffy. Top each serving with 1 teaspoon Pesto.

Pesto: In a food processor bowl combine 1 cup firmly packed fresh basil leaves; ½ cup torn fresh spinach; ¼ cup grated Parmesan cheese; ¼ cup pine nuts or almonds; 2 cloves garlic, quartered; and, if desired, ¼ teaspoon salt. Cover and process with several on-off turns until a paste forms, stopping the machine several times and scraping down the sides. With machine running, gradually add 2 tablespoons olive oil or cooking oil and 2 tablespoons water. Process to the consistency of soft butter. Cover and chill for up to 2 days or freeze for up to 1 month. Makes about ½ cup.

Nutrition facts per serving: 134 cal., 2 g total fat (1 g sat. fat), 3 mg chol., 45 mg sodium, 24 g carbo., 2 g fiber, 5 g pro.
Daily values: 6% vit. A, 14% vit. C, 6% calcium, 3% iron

vegetables & sides

garlic POTATOES & CARROTS

Is convenience a priority? Then remember this recipe—it starts with a package of refrigerated mashed potatoes. Stir in shredded carrots and roasted garlic for plenty of made-from-scratch flavor.

Start to Finish: 10 minutes
Makes: 4 (¾-cup) servings

1 **20-ounce package refrigerated country-style or regular mashed potatoes**
1 **teaspoon olive oil**
1 **cup finely shredded carrots**
2 **teaspoons bottled minced roasted garlic**
⅛ **teaspoon pepper**

1 Prepare potatoes according to package directions, except use olive oil in place of any butter or margarine.

2 Stir in the carrots, garlic, and pepper. Heat through.

Nutrition facts per serving: 138 cal., 3 g total fat (0 g sat. fat), 0 mg chol., 223 mg sodium, 23 g carbo., 2 g fiber, 4 g pro.
Daily values: 77% vit. A, 46% vit. C, 2% calcium, 5% iron

vegetables & sides

Q: Are potatoes fattening?

A: Only if you load them with butter, sour cream, or other fat-filled condiments. The truth is, the humble potato by itself is virtually fat free. It is also one of the best sources of necessary complex carbohydrates, not to mention one of the tastiest. And if you've used up your fat allotment for the day before you get to the potatoes, don't sulk. Flavor mashed potatoes with snipped fresh herbs, roasted garlic, shredded lemon peel, or skinny gravy (cornstarch-thickened broth). You won't even miss the butter or sour cream!

artichokes WITH BALSAMIC SAUCE

What a treat! Tender artichoke leaves are dipped in a sauce featuring Italian balsamic vinegar. Made from white grape juice and aged in wooden barrels, this vinegar is typically dark, pungent, and sweet.

Start to Finish: 35 minutes
Makes: 2 servings

- 1 **lemon**
- 2 **artichokes (about 10 ounces each)**
- 6 **cups water**
- ⅓ **cup dry white wine (optional)**
- 1 **bay leaf**
- 1 **tablespoon olive oil**
- 1 **tablespoon water**
- 1 **tablespoon balsamic vinegar**
- 2 **teaspoons Dijon-style mustard**
- 1 **small clove garlic, minced**

1 Halve lemon; cut one half into thin slices. Set lemon half and lemon slices aside.

2 Wash artichokes; trim stems and remove loose outer leaves. Cut off 1 inch from each top; snip off the sharp leaf tips. Rub lemon half over the cut edges of the artichoke.

3 In a large saucepan combine the 6 cups water, the wine (if desired), bay leaf, and reserved lemon slices. Bring to boiling. Add the artichokes and return to boiling; reduce heat. Simmer, covered, for 20 to 30 minutes or until a leaf pulls out easily. Drain artichokes upside down on paper towels.

4 Meanwhile, for the dipping sauce, stir together the olive oil, the 1 tablespoon water, the vinegar, mustard, and garlic. Serve artichokes with dipping sauce.

Nutrition facts per serving (with 2 tablespoons dipping sauce): 137 cal., 7 g total fat (1 g sat. fat), 0 mg chol., 219 mg sodium, 16 g carbo., 4 g fiber, 5 g pro.
Daily values: 2% vit. A, 24% vit. C, 5% calcium, 12% iron

vegetables & sides

pasta & FRESH TOMATO SAUCE

This pasta sauce is the essence of simplicity—chopped Roma tomatoes lightly sautéed in a little olive oil and seasoned with basil. Served on the side, it's the ideal accompaniment to beef, chicken, or seafood.

Start to Finish: 20 minutes
Makes: 4 servings

- 4 ounces dried rotini or fusilli
- 2 cups coarsely chopped plum tomatoes
- 2 teaspoons olive oil
- ¼ teaspoon salt
- 3 tablespoons shredded fresh basil
- ¼ cup shaved or grated Parmesan or Romano cheese
- ¼ teaspoon pepper

1 Cook the pasta according to package directions; drain.

2 Meanwhile, in a saucepan combine tomatoes, olive oil, and salt. Cook over medium-low heat until heated through and tomatoes start to juice-out slightly. Stir in the basil.

3 Divide pasta among 4 plates. Top each serving with some of the tomato mixture. Sprinkle with Parmesan cheese and pepper.

Nutrition facts per 1⁄2 cup pasta and 3⁄8 cup sauce: 184 cal., 5 g total fat (2 g sat. fat), 5 mg chol., 260 mg sodium, 28 g carbo., 2 g fiber, 7 g pro. **Daily values:** 8% vit. A, 35% vit. C, 8% calcium, 11% iron

vegetables & sides

asparagus & ROASTED PEPPERS

If you grow your own sweet peppers, you can roast them yourself. However, convenient roasted peppers from a jar provide a jump-start on this dish. Here, they are pureed into a colorful sauce for asparagus or broccoli.

Start to Finish: 25 minutes
Makes: 4 servings

½ of a 7¼-ounce jar (about ½ cup) roasted red sweet peppers, drained

¼ cup water

1 teaspoon snipped fresh thyme or savory or ¼ teaspoon dried thyme or savory, crushed

1 teaspoon lemon juice

½ teaspoon cornstarch

¼ teaspoon instant chicken bouillon granules

⅛ teaspoon black pepper

¾ pound asparagus or broccoli, cut lengthwise into spears

❶ For sauce, in a blender container or food processor bowl combine the sweet peppers, water, thyme or savory, lemon juice, cornstarch, bouillon granules, and black pepper. Cover and blend or process until smooth. Pour into a small saucepan. Cook and stir until thickened and bubbly. Cook and stir for 2 minutes more. Cover and keep warm.

❷ In a large saucepan cook the asparagus, covered, in a small amount of boiling water for 4 to 6 minutes or until crisp-tender. (Or, cook broccoli for 8 to 10 minutes or until crisp-tender.) Drain well. To serve, spoon the sauce over the asparagus or broccoli.

Nutrition facts per serving (with 2 tablespoons sauce): 27 cal., 0 g total fat (0 g sat. fat), 0 mg chol., 58 mg sodium, 5 g carbo., 2 g fiber, 2 g pro.
Daily values: 15% vit. A, 121% vit. C, 1% calcium, 5% iron

One Sweet Pepper

Roasting sweet peppers draws out their natural sweetness and flavor. To roast the peppers, cut them into quarters. Remove stems, membranes, and seeds. Place the pepper pieces, cut side down, on a foil-lined baking sheet. Bake in a 425° oven for 20 to 25 minutes or until skins are bubbly and very dark. Wrap pepper pieces tightly in foil and let stand for 10 to 15 minutes or until cool enough to handle. Using a paring knife, pull the skin off gently. Use the peppers as directed in recipes, or cut into strips and toss with salads, layer on sandwiches, or stir into vegetable dishes.

thai-style ASPARAGUS

The nutty taste of sesame oil and pungent fresh ginger—favorites for flavoring Asian foods—team perfectly with fresh asparagus and orange sections. A sprinkling of sesame seeds tops this pretty side dish.

Start to Finish: 20 minutes
Makes: 4 servings

- 2 **tablespoons orange juice**
- 1 **tablespoon white wine vinegar**
- 1½ **teaspoons reduced-sodium soy sauce**
- ½ **teaspoon toasted sesame oil**
- ½ **teaspoon grated fresh ginger**
- 1 **large clove garlic, minced**
- **Dash to ⅛ teaspoon ground red pepper**
- 1 **teaspoon cooking oil**
- 1 **pound asparagus spears**
- 2 **oranges, peeled and sectioned**
- 2 **teaspoons toasted sesame seeds (optional)**

1. For vinaigrette, in a screw-top jar combine orange juice, vinegar, soy sauce, sesame oil, ginger, garlic, and red pepper. Cover and shake well; set aside.

2. In a large nonstick skillet heat oil over medium-high heat. Cook asparagus in hot oil for 3 to 4 minutes or until just tender, turning asparagus occasionally.

3. Shake the vinaigrette; pour over asparagus in skillet. Cook the asparagus for 30 seconds more. Gently stir in the orange sections. To serve, if desired, sprinkle with sesame seeds.

Nutrition facts per serving (with 2 tablespoons vinaigrette): 55 cal., 2 g total fat (0 g sat. fat), 0 mg chol., 69 mg sodium, 9 g carbo., 2 g fiber, 3 g pro.
Daily values: 7% vit. A, 69% vit. C, 2% calcium, 4% iron

vegetables & sides

desserts
& TREATS

Unless you have been misbehaving, there's no need to go to bed without dessert. True, desserts are where moderation and temptation often come head-to-head, but with a little planning, desserts can be enjoyed as a well-deserved treat. Aim for reasonable portion sizes, and for those times you are simply seeking to satisfy a sweet tooth, remember fruit—all on its own, au naturel.

Berry-Ginger Shortcakes, *recipe page 342*

berry ginger SHORTCAKES

Like classic shortcakes, but better! These sweet biscuits are split in half, filled with low-calorie sweetened berries, and topped with sour cream-flavored whipped topping. Heavenly!

desserts & treats

Prep: 25 minutes
Bake: 8 minutes
Makes: 10 servings

3 cups berries (sliced strawberries, blueberries, raspberries, and/or blackberries)

Low-calorie liquid sweetener equal to 2 tablespoons sugar (optional)

2 tablespoons finely chopped crystallized ginger

1 recipe Shortcakes

½ of an 8-ounce container frozen fat-free whipped dessert topping, thawed

¼ cup fat-free dairy sour cream

1 In a small mixing bowl combine the berries, the liquid sweetener (if desired), and the crystallized ginger. Set aside.

2 Meanwhile, prepare Shortcakes.

3 To serve, in a small bowl combine the whipped topping and sour cream. Split shortcakes in half. Place bottoms on dessert plates. Divide the berry mixture among bottoms. Top each with some of the whipped topping mixture. Replace the shortcake tops.

Shortcakes: In a medium bowl stir together 1⅔ cups all-purpose flour, 1 tablespoon sugar, 2 teaspoons baking powder, and ¼ teaspoon baking soda. Using a pastry blender, cut in 3 tablespoons butter or margarine until the mixture resembles coarse crumbs. Combine ½ cup buttermilk and ¼ cup refrigerated or frozen egg product (thawed) or 1 egg. Add to the flour mixture all at once, stirring just until mixture is moistened. Spray a baking sheet with nonstick coating. On a lightly floured surface pat the dough to ½-inch thickness. Cut the dough with a floured 2½-inch star-shaped or heart-shaped cookie cutter or a round biscuit cutter, rerolling scraps as necessary. Place shortcakes on prepared baking sheet. Bake in a 425° oven for 8 to 10 minutes or until golden. Cool the shortcakes slightly on a wire rack.

Nutrition facts per serving: 166 cal., 4 g total fat (2 g sat. fat), 10 mg chol., 176 mg sodium, 28 g carbo., 2 g fiber, 4 g pro.
Daily values: 5% vit. A, 23% vit. C, 9% calcium, 11% iron

cherry bread PUDDING

Leftover French bread never tasted so good! Toss the cubed bread with bits of dried cherries, saturate with a custard mixture, and bake. You'll soon be spooning into a rich-tasting bread pudding.

Prep: 20 minutes
Bake: 35 minutes
Makes: 6 servings

2 **cups fat-free milk**

⅓ **cup refrigerated or frozen egg product, thawed**

¼ **cup packed brown sugar**

1 **teaspoon vanilla**

¼ **teaspoon ground cinnamon**

4 **cups dry French bread cubes**

½ **cup snipped dried cherries**

❶ In a medium bowl beat together the milk, egg product, brown sugar, vanilla, and cinnamon. In an ungreased 1½-quart casserole toss together bread cubes and cherries; pour egg mixture evenly over bread mixture.

❷ Bake in a 350° oven for 35 to 40 minutes or until a knife inserted near the center comes out clean. Cool slightly. Serve pudding warm.

Nutrition facts per serving: 208 cal., 2 g total fat (1 g sat. fat), 6 mg chol., 264 mg sodium, 39 g carbo., 0 g fiber, 7 g pro.
Daily values: 17% vit. A, 1% vit. C, 11% calcium, 8% iron

strawberry CREAM PIE

In the mood for an elegant dessert? Try this creamy mousse of pureed fresh strawberries, fluffy egg whites, gelatin, and whipped topping surrounded by delicate ladyfingers.

Prep: 30 minutes
Chill: 4 hours
Makes: 8 servings

2½ cups strawberries

¼ cup sugar

1 envelope unflavored gelatin

2 tablespoons frozen limeade concentrate or frozen lemonade concentrate, thawed

3 slightly beaten egg whites

1 tablespoon tequila or orange juice

1 3-ounce package ladyfingers, split

2 tablespoons orange juice

½ of an 8-ounce container frozen light whipped dessert topping, thawed

Sliced strawberries (optional)

Fresh mint (optional)

❶ Place the 2½ cups strawberries in a blender container or food processor bowl. Cover and blend or process until nearly smooth. Measure strawberries (you should have about 1½ cups).

❷ In a medium saucepan stir together the sugar and gelatin. Stir in the blended strawberries and limeade or lemonade concentrate. Cook and stir over medium heat until the mixture bubbles and the gelatin is dissolved. Gradually stir about half of the gelatin mixture into the egg whites. Return mixture to the saucepan. Cook, stirring constantly, over low heat about 3 minutes or until mixture is slightly thickened. Do not boil. Pour into a medium bowl; stir in tequila or orange juice. Chill until mixture mounds when spooned, stirring occasionally (about 2 hours).

❸ Meanwhile, cut half of the split ladyfingers in half crosswise; stand on end around the outside edge of a 9-inch tart pan with a removable bottom or a 9-inch springform pan. Arrange remaining split ladyfingers in the bottom of the pan. Drizzle the 2 tablespoons orange juice over the ladyfingers.

❹ Fold whipped topping into strawberry mixture. Spoon into prepared pan. Cover and chill about 2 hours or until set. If desired, garnish with the sliced strawberries and mint.

Nutrition facts per serving: 130 cal., 3 g total fat (2 g sat. fat), 39 mg chol., 48 mg sodium, 22 g carbo., 1 g fiber, 4 g pro.
Daily values: 3% vit. A, 49% vit. C, 1% calcium, 4% iron

desserts & treats

pumpkin-maple PIE

It tastes like Grandmother's, but it's better for you! Our special lower-fat pastry is filled with a maple-flavored pumpkin mixture that is lower in calories and fat than old-fashioned recipes—but it is every bit as good!

desserts & treats

Prep: 25 minutes
Bake: 45 minutes
Makes: 8 servings

- 1 recipe Lower-Fat Oil Pastry
- 1 15-ounce can pumpkin
- ⅓ cup maple-flavored syrup
- 1 tablespoon all-purpose flour
- 2 packets heat-stable sugar substitute
- 1½ teaspoons pumpkin pie spice
- ¾ cup refrigerated or frozen egg product, thawed
- 1 cup evaporated fat-free milk
- 1½ teaspoons vanilla
  Frozen light whipped dessert topping, thawed (optional)

1 Prepare Lower-Fat Oil Pastry. On a lightly floured surface, flatten pastry. Roll into a 12-inch circle. Wrap pastry circle around the rolling pin; unroll into a 9-inch pie plate. Ease pastry into pan, being careful not to stretch pastry. Trim to ½ inch beyond edge of pie plate. Fold under extra pastry. Crimp the edge as desired. Do not prick pastry.

2 For the filling, in a medium bowl combine the pumpkin, maple-flavored syrup, flour, sugar substitute, and pumpkin pie spice; add egg product. Beat lightly with a rotary beater or fork until just combined. Gradually stir in evaporated milk and vanilla; mix well.

3 Place pastry-lined pie plate on oven rack. Carefully pour filling into pastry shell. To prevent overbrowning, cover edge of pie with foil. Bake in a 375° oven for 25 minutes. Remove the foil. Bake 20 to 25 minutes more or until a knife inserted near the center comes out clean. Cool on a wire rack. Cover and refrigerate within 2 hours. If desired, serve with whipped dessert topping.

Lower-Fat Oil Pastry: In a medium bowl stir together 1¼ cups all-purpose flour and ¼ teaspoon salt. Combine ¼ cup fat-free milk and 3 tablespoons cooking oil; add all at once to flour mixture. Stir with a fork until dough forms. If necessary, add 1 to 2 teaspoons additional milk. Shape the dough into a ball.

Nutrition facts per serving: 216 cal., 6 g total fat (1 g sat. fat), 1 mg chol., 153 mg sodium, 32 g carbo., 2 g fiber, 8 g pro.
Daily values: 126% vit. A, 4% vit. C, 11% calcium, 15% iron

peach-berry COBBLER

Cobbler is the ultimate comfort food. You'll agree when you spoon into syrupy peaches and raspberries covered with spicy biscuit topping, served hot with a scoop of low-fat vanilla ice cream.

Prep: 30 minutes
Cook: 25 minutes
Makes: 8 servings

- **4 cups fresh or frozen unsweetened peach slices, thawed**
- **¼ cup sugar**
- **¼ cup water**
- **4 teaspoons cornstarch**
- **1 tablespoon lemon juice**
- **¼ teaspoon ground allspice or ground cardamom**
- **1 recipe Biscuit Topping**
- **1½ cups fresh raspberries or frozen raspberries, thawed**

1 For filling, in a medium saucepan combine the peaches, 2 tablespoons of the sugar, the water, cornstarch, lemon juice, and allspice or cardamom. Let stand for 10 minutes.

2 Meanwhile, prepare Biscuit Topping.

3 Cook and stir the peach mixture over medium heat until thickened and bubbly. Stir in the raspberries. Transfer the hot filling to a 2-quart square baking dish.

4 Immediately drop the Biscuit Topping into 8 small mounds on the hot filling. Sprinkle topping with the remaining sugar.

5 Bake in a 400° oven about 25 minutes or until a toothpick inserted into topping comes out clean.

Biscuit Topping: In a large bowl combine 1¼ cups all-purpose flour, 2 tablespoons sugar, ¾ teaspoon baking powder, ¼ teaspoon baking soda, ¼ teaspoon ground allspice or ground cardamom, and ⅛ teaspoon salt. In a small bowl stir together ½ cup lemon or plain fat-free yogurt; ¼ cup refrigerated or frozen egg substitute, thawed, or 1 large beaten egg; and 2 tablespoons melted butter or margarine. Add egg mixture to flour mixture, stirring just to moisten.

Nutrition facts per serving: 202 cal., 4 g total fat (2 g sat. fat), 8 mg chol., 159 mg sodium, 40 g carbo., 3 g fiber, 4 g pro.
Daily values: 9% vit. A, 20% vit. C, 5% calcium, 8% iron

nectarine TART

The filling in this low-fat dessert tastes deceivingly rich. Fat-free cream cheese is the key. For a pretty finish, arrange the nectarines or peaches and blueberries in a pinwheel design before adding the apricot spread.

Prep: 35 minutes
Bake: 12 minutes
Chill: 2 hours
Makes: 12 servings

1 cup all-purpose flour

¼ teaspoon salt

¼ cup margarine or butter

4 to 5 tablespoons cold water

1 8-ounce package fat-free cream cheese, softened

Sugar substitute equal to ¼ cup sugar, or ¼ cup sugar

1 teaspoon vanilla

4 or 5 nectarines or peeled peaches, pitted and sliced, or one 16-ounce package frozen unsweetened peach slices, thawed and drained

½ cup blueberries

½ cup low-calorie apricot spread

① For pastry, in a medium bowl combine flour and salt. Using a pastry blender, cut in margarine or butter until pieces are the size of small peas. Sprinkle 1 tablespoon of the cold water over a portion of the mixture. Toss with a fork. Push to side of bowl. Repeat until mixture is moistened. Form into a ball.

② On a lightly floured surface, flatten pastry. Roll pastry into a 12-inch circle. Ease pastry into a 10-inch tart pan with a removable bottom, being careful not to stretch pastry. Press pastry about ½ inch up the sides of pan. Prick the bottom well with the tines of a fork. Bake in a 450° oven for 12 to 15 minutes or until golden. Cool on a wire rack. Remove sides of tart pan.

③ Meanwhile, in a medium bowl combine the cream cheese, sugar substitute or sugar, and vanilla. Beat with an electric mixer until smooth; spread over the cooled pastry. Arrange the nectarines or peaches over cream cheese layer. Sprinkle with the blueberries.

④ In a small saucepan heat apricot spread until melted; cut up any large pieces. Spoon melted spread over fruit. Chill for at least 2 hours or up to 3 hours.

Nutrition facts per serving: 140 cal., 4 g total fat (1 g sat. fat), 3 mg chol., 90 mg sodium, 23 g carbo., 1 g fiber, 4 g pro.
Daily values: 14% vit. A, 5% vit. C, 5% calcium, 3% iron

Using the ¼ cup sugar option: 156 cal. and 27 g carbo.

fruit PARFAIT

Parfait, in French, means "perfect," which is what you'll think of this dessert. Served in tall parfait glasses, the layers of fruit and cream look striking, especially when sprinkled with grated chocolate.

desserts & treats

Prep: 20 minutes
Makes: 4 servings

½ cup fat-free dairy sour cream
Low-calorie powdered sweetener equal to 1½ teaspoons sugar, or 1 tablespoon powdered sugar

1 tablespoon orange liqueur, raspberry liqueur, melon liqueur, or orange juice

¼ of an 8-ounce container frozen light whipped dessert topping, thawed

1½ cups sliced, peeled peaches

1 cup raspberries

1 cup blueberries

Grated chocolate (optional)

① In a medium bowl stir together the sour cream, powdered sweetener or powdered sugar, and liqueur or orange juice. Gently fold in dessert topping.

② In 4 parfait glasses, layer half of the peaches, raspberries, blueberries, and sour cream mixture. Repeat layering. If desired, sprinkle grated chocolate over each serving. Serve parfaits immediately or cover and chill for up to 2 hours.

Nutrition facts per serving: 134 cal., 2 g total fat (2 g sat. fat), 0 mg chol., 33 mg sodium, 25 g carbo., 3 g fiber, 3 g pro.
Daily values: 10% vit. A, 27% vit. C, 5% calcium, 2% iron

Using the 1 tablespoon powdered sugar option: 142 calories and 27 g carbohydrate

Whipped Wonders

Whipped topping for dessert is a luxury we all appreciate. Which is best? Compare the differences of the various types (per tablespoon) to determine the one that's best for you.

Topping	Fat (g)	Sat. Fat (g)	Calories
Whipped cream	6	4	52
Frozen whipped dessert topping	2	2	25
Light frozen whipped dessert topping	1	1	20
Nonfat frozen whipped dessert topping	0	0	15
Reduced-calorie whipped topping	1	0	7

berry cheesecake DESSERT

Fat-free cream cheese and low-fat ricotta cheese lend rich taste to this cheesecake. Serve it when fresh berries are in season, as a tempting finale to a festive dinner.

desserts & treats

Prep: 20 minutes
Chill: 4 to 24 hours
Makes: 4 servings

½ **of an 8-ounce tub (about
½ cup) fat-free cream cheese**

½ **cup low-fat ricotta cheese**

**Low-calorie powdered
sweetener equal to
3 tablespoons sugar, or
3 tablespoons sugar**

½ **teaspoon finely shredded
orange peel or lemon peel**

1 **tablespoon orange juice**

3 **cups sliced strawberries,
raspberries, and/or
blueberries**

4 **gingersnaps or chocolate
wafers, broken**

1 In a blender container or food processor bowl combine cream cheese, ricotta cheese, powdered sweetener or sugar, orange or lemon peel, and orange juice. Cover and blend or process until smooth. Cover and chill for 4 to 24 hours.

2 To serve, divide the fruit among dessert dishes. Top each serving with the cream cheese mixture and sprinkle with the broken cookies.

Nutrition facts per serving: 115 cal., 2 g total fat (1 g sat. fat), 9 mg chol.,
61 mg sodium, 17 g carbo., 2 g fiber, 8 g pro.
Daily values: 11% vit. A, 109% vit. C, 12% calcium, 4% iron

Using sugar option: 152 cal. and 26 g carbo.

351

brownie BITES

These snack bites will do little harm to your waistline—especially if you share.

Prep: 12 minutes
Bake: 20 minutes
Cool: 1 hour
Oven: 350°F
Makes: 8 bars

2 **tablespoons butter**

⅓ **cup granulated sugar**

¼ **cup cold water**

½ **teaspoon vanilla**

½ **cup all-purpose flour**

2 **tablespoons unsweetened cocoa powder**

½ **teaspoon baking powder**

2 **tablespoons chopped walnuts or pecans**

Nonstick cooking spray

1 **teaspoon powdered sugar**

1 In a small saucepan melt butter; remove from heat. Stir in granulated sugar, cold water, and vanilla. Stir in flour, cocoa powder, and baking powder until thoroughly combined. Stir in 1 tablespoon of the nuts.

2 Spray the bottom of an 8×4×2-inch loaf pan with nonstick cooking spray. Pour batter into pan. Sprinkle with remaining 1 tablespoon chopped nuts.

3 Bake in a 350° oven about 20 minutes or until a toothpick inserted near center comes out clean. Cool completely in pan on wire rack. Remove from pan. Cut into 8 bars. Sprinkle with the powdered sugar.

Nutrition Facts per bar: 104 cal., 4 g total fat (1 g sat. fat), 0 mg chol., 57 mg sodium, 15 g carbo., 1 g pro.
Daily Values: 2% vit. A, 3% calcium, 3% iron

honey-ginger COMPOTE

Imagine the impression this spicy fruit compote will make when you bring it to the table in tall, stemmed glasses! Add a sprig of fresh mint to each serving for a cool summertime accent.

Prep: 20 minutes
Chill: 4 to 48 hours
Makes: 4 servings

½ **cup apple juice or unsweetened pineapple juice**

2 **tablespoons honey**

1 **tablespoon finely chopped crystallized ginger**

1 **tablespoon lemon juice**

2 **cups cubed cantaloupe, sliced starfruit, and/or chopped pineapple**

1 **cup blueberries or quartered strawberries**

1 In a small saucepan combine apple juice or pineapple juice, honey, crystallized ginger, and lemon juice. Cook and stir over medium heat until boiling. Remove from heat; cool slightly. Cover and chill for 4 to 48 hours.

2 To serve, toss together the cantaloupe, starfruit, and/or pineapple and blueberries or strawberries; spoon into 4 tall stemmed glasses or dessert dishes. Pour apple juice mixture over fruit.

Nutrition facts per serving: 102 cal., 0 g total fat (0 g sat. fat), 0 mg chol., 12 mg sodium, 26 g carbo., 2 g fiber, 1 g pro.
Daily values: 26% vit. A, 68% vit. C, 1% calcium, 5% iron

gingered sauce & FRUIT

It's hard to believe this custard sauce is low in fat and calories because it looks and tastes so rich. Prepare the custard ahead and store it in the refrigerator for up to 24 hours. Spoon over the fruit just before serving.

Prep: 25 minutes
Chill: 1 to 24 hours
Makes: 6 servings

⅓ **cup fat-free milk**

2 **tablespoons sugar**

1 **tablespoon chopped crystallized ginger**

1 **beaten egg**

⅓ **cup fat-free milk**

½ **teaspoon vanilla**

3 **cups sliced fresh strawberries, kiwifruit, peaches, or pears**

2 **tablespoons slivered almonds, toasted**

❶ In a blender container combine the ½ cup milk, the sugar, and crystallized ginger. Cover; blend until mixture is smooth.

❷ For sauce, in a small heavy saucepan combine the egg and the ⅓ cup milk. Add blended mixture. Cook and stir over medium heat about 10 minutes or until mixture just coats a metal spoon. Remove saucepan from heat. Stir in vanilla.

❸ Quickly cool custard sauce by placing the saucepan in a sink of ice water for 1 to 2 minutes, stirring constantly. Pour custard sauce into a bowl. Cover the surface with plastic wrap. Refrigerate for at least 1 hour or up to 24 hours.

❹ Place fruit in 6 dessert dishes. Spoon custard sauce over fruit. Sprinkle with almonds.

Nutrition facts per serving: 83 cal., 3 g total fat (0 g sat. fat), 36 mg chol., 48 mg sodium, 13 g carbo., 2 g fiber, 3 g pro.
Daily values: 3% vit. A, 71% vit. C, 4% calcium, 5% iron

Ending on a Sweet Note

When preparing desserts, experiment using the minimum amount of sweetener possible to get the desired results and the flavor you crave. Make the sweetness of sugar work harder by magnifying it with vanilla or spices, such as cinnamon and cloves. And you don't always have to use bar chocolate, either. When a recipe calls for unsweetened chocolate and when it is feasible, substitute unsweetened cocoa powder, a lower-fat alternative to bar chocolate. For each ounce of bar chocolate, stir together 3 tablespoons of cocoa powder and 1 tablespoon water.

yo-yos

Like the toy, this goodie has two outsides with something in between: in this case, chocolate and sorbet. Play with different flavor options.

Prep: 30 minutes
Freeze: 1 hour
Makes: 12 cookie sandwiches

¼ **cup semisweet chocolate pieces**

¼ **teaspoon shortening**

24 **amaretti cookies (4.6 ounces total) or vanilla wafers**

⅓ **cup mango, orange, lemon, or raspberry sorbet**

1 In a heavy small saucepan heat chocolate pieces and shortening over low heat just until melted. Cool slightly. Using a narrow metal spatula, spread about 1 teaspoon chocolate mixture on the flat side of half of the cookies. Place coated cookies, chocolate side up, on a wire rack until chocolate mixture is set.

2 Using a melon baller, place a small scoop of sorbet (about 1 rounded teaspoon) on top of the chocolate side of each coated cookie. Dip the melon baller into water between scoops to make the scoops come out neatly. Top sorbet with another cookie to make a sandwich. Cover and freeze for 1 to 4 hours.

Nutrition Facts per cookie sandwich: 71 cal., 2 g total fat (0 g sat. fat), 6 mg chol., 7 mg sodium, 12 g carbo., 0 g fiber, 1 g pro.
Daily Values: 1% vit. C, 1% iron

desserts & treats

357

mango MOUSSE

How do you tell if a mango is ripe? Look for fruit that has a colorful green or gold skin with a blush of red or purple. Mangoes are ready to eat when they are soft enough to yield to gentle pressure.

desserts & treats

Prep: 20 minutes
Freeze: 45 minutes
Chill: 2 hours
Makes: 6 servings

2 ripe mangoes, peeled, seeded, and chopped

2 tablespoons sugar

1 envelope unflavored gelatin

2 teaspoons lemon juice

1 8-ounce container frozen light whipped dessert topping, thawed

❶ Place mangoes in a food processor bowl or blender container. Cover and process or blend until smooth. Add enough water to make 2 cups total. Transfer the mango mixture to a medium saucepan. Bring to boiling.

❷ Meanwhile, in a large bowl stir together sugar and gelatin. Pour mango mixture over gelatin mixture; stir until gelatin dissolves. Stir in lemon juice. Cover; freeze for 45 to 60 minutes or until mixture mounds, stirring occasionally. Beat mango mixture with an electric mixer for 2 to 3 minutes or until thick and light. Fold in whipped topping.

❸ Spoon or pipe mango mixture into 6 dessert dishes or parfait glasses. Cover and refrigerate for 2 hours or until set.

Nutrition facts per serving: 149 cal., 5 g total fat (0 g sat. fat), 1 mg chol., 31 mg sodium, 25 g carbo., 2 g fiber, 1 g pro.
Daily values: 31% vit. A, 34% vit. C, 2% calcium, 1% iron

Managing a Mango

Removing the large seed of a mango takes a little cutting know-how. Place the fruit on its blossom end and align a sharp knife slightly off-center of the stemmed end of the fruit. Slice down through the peel and flesh, next to the pit. Repeat on other side. Cut off the remaining flesh around the seed. Cut off the peel; cut the mango into pieces as directed.

mint chocolate CREAM PUFFS

These cream puffs are hard to resist! The small, hollow puffed pastries are filled with reduced-calorie chocolate pudding that's dressed up with a dash of peppermint extract.

Prep: 25 minutes
Bake: 30 minutes
Cool: 1 hour
Chill: 2 to 24 hours
Makes: 8 servings

Nonstick spray coating

½ **cup water**

2 **tablespoons margarine or butter**

½ **cup all-purpose flour**

2 **eggs**

1 **4-serving-size package reduced-calorie regular chocolate pudding mix**

⅛ **teaspoon peppermint extract**

1 **cup sliced strawberries**

1 Spray a baking sheet with nonstick coating; set aside.

2 In a small saucepan combine the water and margarine or butter. Bring to boiling. Add the flour all at once, stirring vigorously. Cook and stir until mixture forms a ball that doesn't separate. Remove from heat. Cool for 5 minutes. Add eggs, one at a time, beating after each addition until mixture is shiny and smooth. Drop dough in 8 mounds 3 inches apart on the prepared baking sheet.

3 Bake in a 400° oven about 30 minutes or until golden brown. Cool completely on a wire rack. Split puffs; remove any soft dough from inside.

4 Meanwhile, for the filling, prepare pudding mix according to package directions. Stir in the peppermint extract. Cover surface with plastic wrap. Chill for 2 to 24 hours.

5 To serve, spoon about ¼ cup of the filling into the bottom half of each cream puff. Top with strawberries. Replace tops.

Nutrition facts per serving: 126 cal., 4 g total fat (1 g sat. fat), 53 mg chol., 225 mg sodium, 20 g carbo., 1 g fiber, 2 g pro.
Daily values: 5% vit. A, 17% vit. C, 0% calcium, 5% iron

carrot SNACK CAKE

Usually you find carrot cake under a slathering of cream cheese frosting. Here powdered sugar steps in, cutting back on fat and calories.

desserts & treats

Prep: 15 minutes
Bake: 30 minutes
Oven: 350°F
Makes: 12 servings

Nonstick cooking spray

1 **cup all-purpose flour**

¾ **cup granulated sugar**

1½ **teaspoons apple pie spice**

½ **teaspoon baking powder**

½ **teaspoon baking soda**

⅛ **teaspoon salt**

1 **cup finely shredded carrot**

⅓ **cup cooking oil**

¼ **cup low-fat milk**

3 **egg whites**

1 **teaspoon sifted powdered
   sugar**

Fresh raspberries (optional)

1 Lightly coat an 8×8×2-inch baking pan with nonstick cooking spray. Set aside.

2 In a large bowl combine flour, granulated sugar, apple pie spice, baking powder, baking soda, and salt. Add carrot, oil, and milk. Stir to moisten. In a medium mixing bowl beat egg whites with an electric mixer on medium to high speed until stiff peaks form (tips stand straight). Fold egg whites into carrot mixture.

3 Pour batter into the prepared pan. Bake in a 350° oven for 30 to 35 minutes or until a wooden toothpick inserted near center comes out clean. Cool completely in pan on a wire rack.

4 To serve, sprinkle with powdered sugar and, if desired, garnish with raspberries.

Nutrition Facts per serving: 147 cal., 6 g total fat (1 g sat. fat), 0 mg chol., 114 mg sodium, 21 g carbo., 1 g fiber, 2 g pro.
Daily Values: 57% vit. A, 2% vit. C, 3% calcium, 4% iron

melon ICE

Summer is synonymous with fresh melons. This honeydew melon ice will be a welcome treat when the temperature soars. It will satisfy your sweet tooth with a mere 47 calories and zero grams fat.

Prep: 25 minutes
Freeze: 8 hours
Stand: 5 minutes
Makes: 16 (½-cup) servings

1 **large ripe honeydew melon, seeded, peeled, and chopped (about 8 cups)**

2 **cups water**

⅓ **cup powdered fructose or 23 packets powdered fructose**

1 **teaspoon ground ginger**

❶ In a large bowl combine melon, water, fructose, and ginger. Place melon mixture, a portion at a time, in a food processor bowl or blender container. Cover and process or blend until smooth.

❷ Pour melon mixture into a 13×9×2-inch baking pan; cover with foil. Freeze about 4 hours or until almost firm. Break the mixture into small chunks; transfer to a chilled, large bowl. Beat with an electric mixer until slushy. Return mixture to pan. Cover; freeze at least 4 hours more.

❸ Before serving, let stand at room temperature about 5 minutes.

Nutrition facts per serving: 47 cal., 0 g total fat (0 g sat. fat), 0 mg chol., 9 mg sodium, 12 g carbo., 1 g fiber, 0 g pro.
Daily values: 0% vit. A, 35% vit. C, 0% calcium, 0% iron

lemon-BLUEBERRY FREEZE

Give yogurt a whirl! Place a blend of lemonade drink mix, blueberries, and vanilla yogurt in the freezer container of an ice cream freezer, and churn it into flavorful frozen yogurt. Simple, but tasty.

Prep: 10 minutes
Freeze: 25 minutes
Ripen: 4 hours
Makes: 12 (½-cup) servings

3 **cups prepared lemonade from sugar-free lemonade mix**

2 **cups fresh or frozen blueberries**

3 **tablespoons sugar**

2 **8-ounce cartons vanilla low-fat yogurt**

1 In a blender container or food processor bowl combine 1½ cups of the lemonade, the blueberries, and sugar. Cover and blend or process until smooth.

2 Place the yogurt in the freezer container of a 4-quart ice-cream freezer. Stir in berry mixture and remaining 1½ cups lemonade. Freeze mixture according to the manufacturer's directions. Ripen 4 hours.

Nutrition facts per serving: 62 cal., 1 g total fat (0 g sat. fat), 2 mg chol., 25 mg sodium, 13 g carbo., 1 g fiber, 2 g pro.
Daily values: 1% vit. A, 5% vit. C, 5% calcium, 0% iron

Fructose Facts

Found in fruits and honey, fructose is sweeter than any other type of sugar in an equal amount. It often is called high-fructose syrup or high-fructose corn syrup on food labels. These are very concentrated forms of fructose. Fructose can be purchased in a crystalline form or in individual packets. Fructose causes a lower rise in blood glucose than sucrose (table sugar) or starches. It is best to limit your intake of large amounts of this sweetener in the form of fructose-sweetened foods. If eaten often, fructose has been shown to increase total cholesterol, triglycerides, and LDL cholesterol ("bad" cholesterol) levels. Moderation, as with regular sugar, is key.

tiramisu CUPS

This lightened version of the popular Italian-inspired dessert is a snap to make at home.

desserts & treats

Prep: 20 minutes
Chill: 1 hour
Makes: 4 servings

½ of a 3-ounce package
  ladyfingers, cubed
  (12 halves)

¼ cup espresso or strong coffee

¼ of an 8-ounce package
  reduced-fat cream cheese
  (Neufchâtel), softened

½ cup light dairy sour cream

  Sugar substitute to equal
  3 tablespoons sugar

1 teaspoon vanilla

½ teaspoon unsweetened cocoa
  powder

① Divide half of the ladyfinger cubes among four 4- to 6-ounce dessert dishes. Drizzle ladyfinger cubes with half of the espresso. Set aside.

② In a medium bowl stir cream cheese to soften. Stir in sour cream, sugar substitute, and vanilla. (Beat smooth with a wire whisk, if necessary.) Spoon half of the cream cheese mixture over ladyfinger cubes. Add remaining ladyfinger cubes and drizzle with remaining espresso. Cover and chill for 1 to 24 hours. Just before serving, top with remaining cream cheese mixture and sprinkle with cocoa powder.

Nutrition Facts per serving: 124 cal., 8 g total fat (5 g sat. fat), 61 mg chol., 85 mg sodium, 9 g carbo., 0 g fiber, 3 g pro.
Daily Values: 9% vit. A, 3% vit. C, 7% calcium, 5% iron

mixed berry TRIFLE CAKES

Good things happen when the English trifle meets the all-American shortcake. Use any berries you like in this beautiful, bountiful dessert, but a combination of two or three kinds is best.

desserts & treats

Start to Finish: 20 minutes
Makes: 8 servings

- 2 **4.5-ounce packages individual shortcake cups (8 cups)**
- 2 **tablespoons sugar-free apricot preserves**
- 2 **tablespoons orange juice**
- 1 **6-ounce carton vanilla fat-free yogurt with sweetener**
- ½ **teaspoon vanilla**
- ¼ **of an 8-ounce container frozen light whipped dessert topping, thawed**
- 1½ **cups mixed fresh berries such as sliced strawberries, blueberries, raspberries, and/or blackberries**

① Arrange shortcake cups on a serving platter; set aside. In a small bowl stir together preserves and orange juice. Spoon some of the mixture over each shortcake cup. In another small bowl stir together yogurt and vanilla. Fold in whipped topping. Spoon yogurt mixture onto cake over preserves mixture. Top with berries.

Nutrition Facts per serving: 153 cal., 3 g total fat (1 g sat. fat), 15 mg chol., 13 mg sodium, 28 g carbo., 1 g fiber, 2 g pro.
Daily Values: 1% vit. A, 21% vit. C, 4% calcium, 3% iron

More Flavor

Fat-free, sugar-free yogurts are great multipurpose ingredients in healthy cooking. In addition to the flavor they provide, they add creaminess and moisture to recipes, both of which can be lost when fat is taken out. And, without much extra calories or fat, these yogurts add a protein and calcium boost. Vanilla and plain yogurts are neutral and mix well with any recipe, but why not get creative? Try a berry-flavor yogurt in this trifle recipe or coffee-flavor yogurt in a chocolate-based recipe.

honey-ricotta CHEESECAKE

With a graham cracker crust, sweet honey filling, and mild lemon undertones, this dessert will satisfy any cheesecake lover's craving.

Prep: 30 minutes
Bake: 35 minutes
Cool: 1¾ hours
Chill: 4 hours
Oven: 350°F
Makes: 16 servings

Butter

⅓ **cup finely crushed graham crackers**

2 **8-ounce packages reduced-fat cream cheese (Neufchâtel), softened**

1 **cup fat-free ricotta cheese**

¾ **cup no-calorie, heat-stable granular sugar substitute**

2 **tablespoons honey**

2 **tablespoons all-purpose flour**

¼ **cup fat-free milk**

1 **teaspoon vanilla**

3 **slightly beaten eggs**

1 **teaspoon finely shredded lemon peel**

1 Generously butter the bottom and sides of an 8-inch springform pan. Sprinkle crushed graham crackers on bottom of pan; set aside.

2 For filling, in a large mixing bowl beat cream cheese, ricotta cheese, sugar substitute, honey, and flour with an electric mixer on low speed until smooth. Beat in milk and vanilla. Stir in eggs and lemon peel just until combined.

3 Pour filling into the prepared pan. Bake in a 350° oven for 35 to 40 minutes or until center appears nearly set when cake is gently shaken.

4 Cool in pan on a wire rack for 15 minutes. Using a small sharp knife, loosen the cheesecake from sides of pan; cool for 30 minutes more. Remove the sides of the pan; cool cheesecake completely on rack. Cover and chill at least 4 hours before serving.

Nutrition Facts per serving: 130 cal., 8 g total fat (5 g sat. fat), 64 mg chol., 179 mg sodium, 7 g carbo., 0 g fiber, 7 g pro.
Daily Values: 11% vit. A, 3% vit. C, 12% calcium, 4% iron

chocolate-CHERRY BISCOTTI

These Italian cookies are made by first baking the dough in a loaf, then slicing the loaf and baking the slices. The result is an ultra-crunchy cookie that is perfect for dipping into coffee.

Prep: 25 minutes
Bake: 18 minutes/16 minutes
Cool: 1 hour
Makes: 40 cookies

Nonstick spray coating
¼ **cup margarine or butter**
½ **cup sugar**
1 **teaspoon baking powder**
¼ **teaspoon baking soda**
½ **cup refrigerated or frozen egg product, thawed**
½ **teaspoon vanilla**
2 **cups all-purpose flour**
¼ **cup unsweetened cocoa powder**
⅓ **cup finely chopped dried tart cherries**

1 Spray a cookie sheet with nonstick coating; set aside.

2 In a medium bowl beat margarine or butter on medium speed with an electric mixer for 30 seconds. Add sugar, baking powder, and baking soda; beat until combined. Beat in egg product and vanilla. In a small bowl stir together flour and cocoa powder; beat as much of the flour mixture as you can into the margarine mixture. Stir in the remaining flour mixture and cherries.

3 On waxed paper, shape dough into two 12-inch-long logs. Place on prepared cookie sheet; flatten the logs slightly to 1½-inch width. Bake in a 375° oven for 18 to 20 minutes or until firm and a wooden toothpick inserted near the center of each log comes out clean. Cool on sheet for 1 hour.

4 Cut each log into ½-inch slices. Arrange the slices, cut sides down, on the cookie sheet. Bake in a 325° oven for 8 minutes; turn and bake for 8 minutes more or until crisp. Transfer cookies to a wire rack; cool.

Nutrition facts per cookie: 48 cal., 1 g total fat (0 g sat. fat), 0 mg chol., 35 mg sodium, 8 g carbo., 0 g fiber, 1 g pro.
Daily values: 3% vit. A, 0% vit. C, 1% calcium, 2% iron

spiced CORNMEAL COOKIES

These finger-shaped cookies contain cornmeal, which adds a bit of toasty crunch. Cinnamon and hazelnuts contribute spicy, sweet flavor, making these cookies the ultimate treat.

Prep: 30 minutes
Bake: 10 minutes
Makes: 24 cookies

¼ **cup margarine or butter**

¾ **cup all-purpose flour**

¼ **cup yellow cornmeal**

¼ **cup sugar**

1 **egg white**

¼ **teaspoon finely shredded lemon peel**

¼ **teaspoon vanilla**

⅛ **teaspoon salt**

⅛ **teaspoon ground cinnamon**

2 **tablespoons finely chopped hazelnuts or almonds**

1 In a large bowl beat the margarine or butter with an electric mixer on medium to high speed for 30 seconds. Add about half of the flour, the cornmeal, sugar, egg white, lemon peel, vanilla, salt, and cinnamon. Beat until combined. Beat or stir in remaining flour. Stir in hazelnuts or almonds.

2 Shape the dough into 24 fingers, about 2½ inches long. Place on an ungreased baking sheet. Bake in a 375° oven about 10 minutes or until the bottoms are golden. Transfer to a wire rack; cool.

Nutrition facts per cookie: 48 cal., 2 g total fat (0 g sat. fat), 0 mg chol., 36 mg sodium, 6 g carbo., 0 g fiber, 1 g pro.
Daily values: 2% vit. A, 0% vit. C, 0% calcium, 1% iron

desserts & treats

369

chocolate chip COOKIES

With this reduced-sugar recipe there's no need to deprive yourself or your family of this beloved snack.

desserts & treats

Prep: 25 minutes
Bake: 8 minutes per batch
Oven: 375°F
Makes: about 40 cookies

½ **cup shortening**

½ **cup butter, softened**

¾ **cup no-calorie, heat-stable granular sugar substitute**

½ **cup packed brown sugar**

½ **teaspoon baking soda**

  Dash salt

2 **eggs**

2 **teaspoons vanilla**

2¼ **cups all-purpose flour**

6 **ounces bittersweet chocolate, coarsely chopped**

❶ In a large mixing bowl beat shortening and butter with an electric mixer on medium to high speed for 30 seconds. Add sugar substitute, brown sugar, baking soda, and salt. Beat until combined, scraping sides of bowl occasionally. Beat in eggs and vanilla until combined. Beat in as much of the flour as you can with the mixer. Stir in any remaining flour. Stir in chocolate.

❷ Drop dough by rounded teaspoons 2 inches apart onto an ungreased cookie sheet. Bake in a 375° oven about 8 minutes or until edges are lightly browned. Transfer cookies to a wire rack; cool.

Nutrition Facts per cookie: 106 cal., 7 g total fat (3 g sat. fat), 17 mg chol., 49 mg sodium, 11 g carbo., 1 g fiber, 1 g pro.
Daily Values: 3% vit. A, 1% vit. C, 2% calcium, 4% iron

special OCCASIONS

Birthdays, Christmas, and other celebrations are a time to indulge in your favorite foods. The recipes in this chapter include the favorite foods you love plus some delicious surprises. There are even treats for kids' parties, like cupcakes and punch!

Birthday Cake with Frosting, *recipe page 394*

holiday cherry CHUTNEY

This thick, tart-sweet fruit mixture deserves a place on your holiday menu. Try it with slices of ham or turkey.

special occasions

Prep: 10 minutes
Cook: 15 minutes
Chill: 4 hours
Makes: 8 (2-tablespoon)
servings

⅔ **cup light cranberry juice cocktail**

⅓ **cup no-calorie, heat-stable granular sugar substitute**

2 **tablespoons packed brown sugar**

1½ **cups fresh cranberries**

½ **cup dried tart or sweet cherries**

⅛ **teaspoon ground allspice**

Dash salt

① In a medium saucepan combine cranberry juice, sugar substitute, and brown sugar; stir to dissolve sugar. Add cranberries, dried cherries, allspice, and salt. Bring to boiling; reduce heat. Simmer, uncovered, for 15 minutes or until mixture thickens (the mixture will thicken further upon chilling). Transfer to a bowl. Cover and chill for 4 hours or up to 3 days.

Nutrition Facts per serving: 55 cal., 0 g total fat (0 g sat. fat), 0 mg chol., 23 mg sodium, 14 g carbo., 1 g fiber, 0 g pro.
Daily Values: 2% vit. A, 17% vit. C, 2% calcium, 3% iron

Winter Berries

Cranberries pack a real nutritional punch. A half-cup of raw berries has only 25 calories and 7 grams of carbohydrates. They've been shown to possibly play a role in preventing heart disease and some cancers, and they may slow down the development of ulcers and gum disease. And, after years of folklore, it seems as though cranberry juice really can help prevent urinary tract infections.

fennel-herb BREAD STUFFING

Whole grain bread yields stuffing that's moist but not mushy. Aromatic fennel and tender vegetables take it to flavorful heights.

Prep: 35 minutes
Bake: 40 minutes
Oven: 300°F/325°F
Makes: 12 to 14 servings

8 **cups whole grain bread cubes (about 9 slices)**

1 **medium fennel bulb with tops**

1 **cup chopped carrot**

1 **cup chopped onion**

2 **cloves garlic, minced**

2 **tablespoons olive oil**

1 **teaspoon dried Italian seasoning, crushed**

¼ **teaspoon black pepper**

⅛ **teaspoon salt**

1 **to 1½ cups reduced-sodium chicken broth**

① Spread bread cubes in a large shallow roasting pan. Bake in a 300° oven for 10 to 15 minutes or until bread cubes are dry, stirring twice. Cool. Increase oven to 325°.

② Remove green leafy tops from fennel; snip enough of the tops to make 1 to 2 tablespoons. Set aside. Cut off and discard upper stalks. Remove any wilted outer layers and cut a thin slice from the fennel base. Cut fennel bulb into wedges, removing the core. Coarsely chop fennel.

③ In a large skillet cook chopped fennel bulb, carrot, onion, and garlic in hot oil over medium heat until tender, stirring occasionally. Stir in snipped fennel tops, Italian seasoning, pepper, and salt. Place fennel mixture in a very large bowl. Stir in bread cubes. Drizzle with enough broth to moisten; toss gently to coat. Transfer mixture to a 2-quart casserole. Bake, covered, in the 325° oven for 20 minutes. Uncover; bake about 20 minutes more or until heated through.

Nutrition Facts per serving: 94 cal., 3 g total fat 0 mg chol., 212 mg sodium, 17 g carbo., 3 g fiber, 4 g pro.
Daily Values: 52% vit. A, 7% vit. C, 12% calcium, 12% iron

turkey and VEGETABLE BAKE

Rice and vegetables win an encore for the last of the holiday turkey. This creamy main dish gives leftovers a good name.

Prep: 35 minutes
Bake: 30 minutes
Stand: 15 minutes
Oven: 350°F
Makes: 6 servings

- 2 **cups sliced fresh mushrooms**
- ¾ **cup chopped red or yellow sweet pepper**
- ½ **cup chopped onion**
- 2 **cloves garlic, minced**
- 2 **tablespoons butter or margarine**
- ¼ **cup all-purpose flour**
- ¾ **teaspoon salt**
- ½ **teaspoon dried thyme, crushed**
- ¼ **teaspoon black pepper**
- 2 **cups fat-free milk**
- 1 **10-ounce package frozen chopped spinach, thawed and well drained**
- 2 **cups cooked brown or white rice**
- 2 **cups chopped cooked turkey or chicken**
- ½ **cup finely shredded Parmesan cheese (2 ounces)**

1 In a 12-inch skillet cook and stir mushrooms, sweet pepper, onion, and garlic in hot butter over medium heat until tender. Stir in flour, salt, thyme, and black pepper. Add milk all at once; cook and stir until thickened and bubbly. Stir in spinach, rice, turkey, and ¼ cup of the Parmesan cheese.

2 Spoon mixture into a 2-quart rectangular baking dish. Sprinkle with remaining Parmesan cheese. Bake, covered, in a 350° oven for 20 minutes. Uncover and bake about 10 minutes more or until heated through. Let stand 15 minutes before serving.

Nutrition Facts per serving: 297 cal., 10 g total fat (5 g sat. fat), 53 mg chol., 602 mg sodium, 28 g carbo., 3 g fiber, 24 g pro.
Daily Values: 165% vit. A, 59% vit. C, 26% calcium, 11% iron

apricot-almond COFFEE CAKE

Welcome guests to a weekend brunch buffet that includes this moist, fruity coffee cake.

special occasions

Prep: 15 minutes
Bake: 25 minutes
Cool: 10 minutes
Oven: 350°F
Makes: 10 servings

Nonstick cooking spray

1½ **cups all-purpose flour**

1 **teaspoon baking powder**

¼ **teaspoon salt**

¼ **teaspoon ground cinnamon**

⅛ **teaspoon ground ginger**

1 **slightly beaten egg**

½ **cup snipped dried apricots**

½ **cup fat-free milk**

¼ **cup no-calorie, heat-stable granular sugar substitute**

¼ **cup unsweetened applesauce**

3 **tablespoons butter, melted**

2 **tablespoons honey**

1 **teaspoon vanilla**

2 **tablespoons reduced-sugar apricot preserves, melted**

2 **tablespoons toasted sliced almonds**

1 Lightly coat an 8×1½-inch round baking pan with nonstick cooking spray; set aside. In a medium bowl stir together flour, baking powder, salt, cinnamon, and ginger.

2 In a medium bowl combine egg and apricots. Stir in milk, sugar substitute, applesauce, melted butter, honey, and vanilla. Add fruit mixture all at once to flour mixture; stir to combine. Pour batter into the prepared baking pan.

3 Bake in a 350° oven for 25 to 30 minutes or until a toothpick inserted near center comes out clean. Cool in pan on a wire rack for 10 minutes. Cut up any large pieces of fruit in preserves; spoon over cake. Sprinkle with toasted almonds. Serve warm.

Nutrition Facts per serving: 157 cal., 5 g total fat (3 g sat. fat), 31 mg chol., 150 mg sodium, 24 g carbo., 1 g fiber, 3 g pro.
Daily Values: 10% vit. A, 7% vit. C, 7% calcium, 8% iron

cranberry-pecan MUFFINS

The dynamic duo of orange peel and cranberries leaves a memorable impression. Serve these tender muffins warm at a holiday brunch.

Prep: 20 minutes
Bake: 12 minutes
Oven: 400°F
Makes: 12 muffins

1¾ **cups all-purpose flour**

2 **teaspoons baking powder**

¼ **teaspoon salt**

¼ **teaspoon ground cinnamon**

1 **slightly beaten egg**

¾ **cup fat-free milk**

½ **cup no-calorie, heat-stable granular sugar substitute**

¼ **cup sugar**

3 **tablespoons cooking oil**

1 **teaspoon finely shredded orange peel**

¾ **cup coarsely chopped cranberries**

¼ **cup chopped pecans, toasted**

1 Grease twelve 2½-inch muffin cups; set aside. In a medium bowl stir together flour, baking powder, salt, and cinnamon. Make a well in center of the flour mixture; set aside.

2 In another medium bowl combine egg, milk, sugar substitute, sugar, oil, and orange peel. Add milk mixture all at once to flour mixture. Stir just until moistened (batter should be lumpy). Gently stir in cranberries and pecans.

3 Spoon batter into prepared muffin cups, filling each about two-thirds full. Bake in a 400° oven for 12 to 15 minutes or until muffins are lightly golden and a wooden toothpick inserted in centers comes out clean. Cool in muffin cups on wire rack for 5 minutes. Remove from muffin cups; serve warm.

Nutrition Facts per muffin: 146 cal., 6 g total fat (1 g sat. fat), 18 mg chol., 130 mg sodium, 21 g carbo., 1 g fiber, 3 g pro.
Daily Values: 3% vit. A, 4% vit. C, 9% calcium, 8% iron

special occasions

379

apple CRANBERRY CRISP

As tasty as it is simple to fix, this down-home recipe will remind you of one of your Grandma's old-fashioned autumn desserts.

Prep: 15 minutes
Bake: 30 minutes
Oven: 375°F
Makes: 6 servings

5 **cups thinly sliced peeled apples**

1 **cup cranberries**

2 **tablespoons granulated sugar**

½ **teaspoon apple pie spice or ground cinnamon**

½ **cup quick-cooking rolled oats**

3 **tablespoons packed brown sugar**

2 **tablespoons all-purpose flour**

½ **teaspoon apple pie spice or ground cinnamon**

2 **tablespoons butter**

1 In a 2-quart baking dish combine apples and cranberries. Stir together granulated sugar and ½ teaspoon apple pie spice. Sprinkle over fruit mixture in dish; toss to coat.

2 In a small bowl combine oats, brown sugar, flour, and ½ teaspoon apple pie spice. Cut in butter until crumbly. Sprinkle oat mixture evenly over apple mixture.

3 Bake in a 375° oven for 30 to 35 minutes or until apples are tender. Serve warm.

Nutrition Facts per serving: 189 cal., 5 g total fat (3 g sat. fat), 11 mg chol., 45 mg sodium, 37 g carbo., 4 g fiber, 2 g pro.
Daily Values: 4% vit. A, 10% vit. C, 2% calcium, 5% iron

special occasions

maple-nut BAKED APPLES

These apples are pleasers alone or topped with frozen yogurt.

special occasions

Prep: 15 minutes
Bake: 25 minutes
Oven: 350°F
Makes: 4 servings

- 2 **medium cooking apples, such as Rome Beauty, Granny Smith, or Jonathan**
- 3 **tablespoons water**
- 3 **tablespoons sugar-free maple-flavor syrup with no-calorie, heat-stable granular sugar substitute**
- ¼ **cup snipped dried figs, snipped pitted whole dates, raisins, or mixed dried fruit bits**
- ¼ **teaspoon apple pie spice or ground cinnamon**
- 2 **tablespoons chopped toasted pecans or walnuts**

  Low-fat vanilla frozen yogurt (optional)

1 Core apples; peel a strip from the top of each. In a 2-quart square baking dish stir together the water and 2 tablespoons of the maple-flavor syrup. Add apples to dish. In a small bowl combine dried fruit, remaining 1 tablespoon syrup, and apple pie spice; spoon into center of apples. Cover dish with foil; fold back one corner of foil to vent. Bake in a 350° oven for 25 to 30 minutes or until the apples are tender, spooning syrup mixture over apples once halfway through baking.

2 To serve, halve warm apples lengthwise. Transfer apple halves to dessert dishes. Spoon some of the cooking liquid over apples. Sprinkle with nuts. If desired, top with a small scoop of frozen yogurt.

Nutrition Facts per serving: 103 cal., 3 g total fat (1 g sat. fat), 0 mg chol., 21 mg sodium, 22 g carbo., 4 g fiber, 1 g pro.
Daily Values: 1% vit. A, 6% vit. C, 3% calcium, 3% iron

Healthy Holiday Eating

The challenge of healthy eating grows more difficult during the holidays when high-fat, sugar-laden foods are everywhere. Keeping the principles of a healthy lifestyle at the forefront is especially important. In addition to sticking with your exercise routine, continue to eat scheduled meals. Eating regularly keeps you from getting hungry and makes it easier to say no. When faced with something you can't or don't want to say no to, find a way to make it fit into your meal plan. Try eating a small amount with a meal or eating just a little bit less of everything to make room for the extra calories.

pumpkin PIE

The tender pastry, pleasant sweetness, and piquant spices are enough to make you forget that you're watching what you eat.

Prep: 30 minutes
Bake: 45 minutes
Oven: 375°F
Makes: 8 servings

1 **recipe Easy Oil Pastry**

1 **15-ounce can pumpkin**

⅓ **cup no-calorie, heat-stable granular sugar substitute**

2 **tablespoons honey**

1 **teaspoon ground cinnamon**

½ **teaspoon ground ginger**

¼ **teaspoon ground nutmeg**

2 **slightly beaten eggs**

1 **teaspoon vanilla**

¾ **cup fat-free milk**

❶ Prepare Easy Oil Pastry. Press dough firmly onto bottom and up sides of a 9-inch pie plate.

❷ For filling, in a medium bowl combine pumpkin, sugar substitute, honey, cinnamon, ginger, and nutmeg. Add eggs and vanilla. Beat lightly with a fork just until combined. Gradually add milk; stir until combined.

❸ Place the pastry-lined pie plate on the oven rack. Carefully pour filling into pastry shell.

❹ To prevent overbrowning, cover edge of the pie with foil. Bake in a 375° oven for 25 minutes. Remove foil. Bake 20 to 25 minutes more or until a knife inserted near center comes out clean (edges of filling may crack slightly). Cool on a wire rack. Cover and refrigerate within 2 hours.

Easy Oil Pastry: In a medium bowl stir together 1¼ cups all-purpose flour and ¼ teaspoon salt. Add ¼ cup cooking oil and 3 tablespoons fat-free milk all at once to flour mixture. Stir lightly with a fork. Form into a ball.

Nutrition Facts per serving: 201 cal., 9 g total fat (2 g sat. fat), 54 mg chol., 108 mg sodium, 26 g carbo., 2 g fiber, 5 g pro.
Daily Values: 239% vit. A, 7% vit. C, 9% calcium, 14% iron

special occasions

pumpkin CHEESECAKE

A blend of low-fat ricotta cheese and fat-free cream cheese keeps this cheesecake light.

Prep: 25 minutes
Chill: 4 hours
Makes: 12 servings

¾ **cup finely crushed graham crackers**

2 **tablespoons butter, melted**

1 **15-ounce carton low-fat ricotta cheese**

1 **8-ounce tub fat-free cream cheese**

1 **cup canned pumpkin**

½ **cup fat-free milk**

1 **envelope unflavored gelatin**

½ **cup orange juice**

2 **teaspoons finely shredded orange peel**

⅓ **cup granulated sugar**

⅓ **cup packed brown sugar**

2 **teaspoons vanilla**

1 **teaspoon pumpkin pie spice**

Light whipped dessert topping (optional)

Pumpkin pie spice (optional)

① For crust, in a medium bowl stir together crushed graham crackers and melted butter until crackers are moistened. Press mixture onto bottom of a 9-inch springform pan. Refrigerate while preparing filling.

② For filling, in a food processor bowl or blender container combine half of the ricotta cheese, half of the cream cheese, half of the pumpkin, and half of the milk. Cover and process or blend until smooth. Transfer to a large bowl. Repeat with remaining ricotta, cream cheese, pumpkin, and milk.

③ In a small saucepan sprinkle gelatin over orange juice; let stand for 5 minutes. Cook and stir over low heat until gelatin is dissolved. Stir into pumpkin mixture. Stir in orange peel, granulated sugar, brown sugar, vanilla, and pumpkin pie spice. Pour mixture into chilled crust. Cover and chill for at least 4 hours or until firm.

④ To serve, using a small sharp knife, loosen crust from sides of pan; remove sides of pan. Cut into wedges. If desired, garnish with whipped topping and sprinkle with additional pumpkin pie spice.

Nutrition Facts per serving: 160 cal., 4 g total fat (2 g sat. fat), 15 mg chol., 116 mg sodium, 22 g carbo., 1 g fiber, 10 g pro.
Daily Values: 93% vit. A, 11% vit. C, 26% calcium, 4% iron

pumpkin BREAD

Plan to bake this bread a day before you want to serve it. Like most quick breads it slices best if wrapped and stored overnight.

special occasions

Prep: 15 minutes
Bake: 65 minutes
Oven: 350°F
Makes: 1 loaf (16 servings)

- **2 cups all-purpose flour**
- **¾ cup no-calorie, heat-stable granular sugar substitute**
- **1 tablespoon baking powder**
- **1½ teaspoons ground cinnamon**
- **¼ teaspoon baking soda**
- **¼ teaspoon salt**
- **¼ teaspoon ground nutmeg**
- **¼ teaspoon ground ginger or ⅛ teaspoon ground cloves**
- **2 beaten eggs**
- **1 cup canned pumpkin**
- **1 cup fat-free milk**
- **⅓ cup cooking oil**
- **¼ cup packed brown sugar**
- **1 teaspoon vanilla**

1 Grease the bottom and ½ inch up the sides of an 8×4×2 inch loaf pan; set aside.

2 In a large bowl combine flour, sugar substitute, baking powder, cinnamon, baking soda, salt, nutmeg, and ginger. In a medium bowl stir together eggs, pumpkin, milk, oil, brown sugar, and vanilla. Add egg mixture all at once to flour mixture. Stir just until moistened.

3 Spoon batter into prepared pan. Bake in a 350° oven for 65 to 70 minutes or until a wooden toothpick inserted near center comes out clean. Cool in pan on a wire rack for 10 minutes. Remove loaf from pan. Cool completely on a wire rack. For easier slicing, wrap and store overnight.

Nutrition Facts per serving: 135 cal., 5 g total fat (1 g sat. fat), 27 mg chol., 150 mg sodium, 19 g carbo., 1 g fiber, 3 g pro.
Daily Values: 71% vit. A, 4% vit. C, 10% calcium, 9% iron

chocolate CREAM CHEESE PIE

Like cheesecake? Crave chocolate? Put them together to form a luscious union.

Prep: 20 minutes
Chill: 4 hours
Makes: 8 servings

- 1 **4-serving-size package fat-free, sugar-free instant chocolate pudding mix**
- 1¾ **cups fat-free milk**
- 1 **teaspoon vanilla**
- ½ **of an 8-ounce package reduced-fat cream cheese (Neufchâtel), softened**
- ½ **of an 8-ounce container frozen light whipped dessert topping, thawed**
- 1 **6-ounce chocolate-flavor crumb pie shell**
- 1 **cup fresh raspberries**
- 1 **tablespoon grated semisweet chocolate**

❶ In a medium bowl prepare pudding mix according to package directions using the 1¾ cups milk. Stir in vanilla; set aside.

❷ In a large microwave-safe mixing bowl microwave cream cheese, uncovered, on 100 percent power (high) for 15 seconds; stir. Microwave on high for 15 seconds more. Beat cream cheese with an electric mixer on medium speed for 15 seconds. Add half of the pudding mixture; beat until smooth. Add remaining pudding mixture; beat until smooth. Fold in half of the whipped topping. Spread mixture in pie shell. Chill for 4 hours or until set. (Cover and chill for longer storage up to 24 hours.)

❸ Top individual servings with remaining whipped topping, raspberries, and grated chocolate.

Nutrition Facts per serving: 228 cal., 10 g total fat (5 g sat. fat), 12 mg chol., 350 mg sodium, 27 g carbo., 2 g fiber, 5 g pro.
Daily Values: 6% vit. A, 7% vit. C, 8% calcium, 5% iron

special occasions

Choosing Chocolate

Everyone has a favorite kind of chocolate. The varying amounts of chocolate liquor are the basis for the categorizations. Dark chocolate, which may be bittersweet or semisweet, contains the most. Milk chocolate is a mixture of milk powder, sugar, and flavorings and a smaller amount of chocolate liquor mixed with cocoa butter. White chocolate contains no chocolate liquor, and, for this reason, many don't consider it chocolate. Recent research claims chocolate contains powerful antioxidants that can protect against heart disease. The higher the chocolate liquor content in the product, the more antioxidant power.

sugar cookie CUTOUTS

Edible egg paint bakes right onto the cutouts for hassle-free decorating. The range of paste food coloring available means your color options are almost limitless.

Prep: 45 minutes
Bake: 6 minutes per batch
Oven: 375°F
Makes: about 36 cookies

⅔ **cup butter, softened**

½ **cup no-calorie, heat-stable granular sugar substitute**

¼ **cup sugar**

1 **teaspoon baking powder**

¼ **teaspoon salt**

1 **egg**

2 **teaspoons vanilla**

2 **cups all-purpose flour**

1 **to 2 egg yolks**
Few drops water
Paste food coloring

1 In a large mixing bowl beat butter with an electric mixer on medium to high speed for 30 seconds. Add sugar substitute, sugar, baking powder, and salt. Beat until combined, scraping sides of bowl occasionally. Beat in egg and vanilla until combined. Beat in as much of the flour as you can with the mixer. Stir in any remaining flour with a wooden spoon. Divide dough in half. If necessary, cover and chill dough about 30 minutes or until easy to handle.

2 On a lightly floured surface, roll half the dough at a time until ⅛ inch thick. Using a 2½-inch cookie cutter, cut into desired shapes. Place cutouts 1 inch apart on an ungreased cookie sheet.

3 For egg paint, in a small bowl stir together egg yolk and water. Divide mixture among several small bowls. Mix a little paste food coloring into each. Use a small clean watercolor paintbrush to paint various colors onto unbaked cutout cookies. Clean the brush between colors using plain water. Put only a small amount of paint on the brush. If the egg paint thickens while you're working with it, stir in a little water, a drop at a time. If using more than one color on a cookie, leave a narrow strip of cookie between painted areas so the colors don't run together.

4 Bake in a 375° oven for 6 to 7 minutes or until edges are firm and bottoms are very lightly browned. Transfer cookies to a wire rack; cool.

Nutrition Facts per cookie: 68 cal., 4 g total fat (2 g sat. fat), 21 mg chol., 66 mg sodium, 7 g carbo., 0 g fiber, 1 g pro.
Daily Values: 4% vit. A, 1% vit. C, 2% calcium, 3% iron

special occasions

gossamer spice COOKIES

The word gossamer refers to something light and delicate and aptly describes these crisp, paper-thin cookies of northern European descent.

Prep: 45 minutes
Chill: 1 hour
Bake: 5 minutes per batch
Oven: 375°F
Makes: about 66 cookies

1⅓ **cups all-purpose flour**
½ **teaspoon ground ginger**
½ **teaspoon apple pie spice**
¼ **teaspoon ground cloves**
¼ **teaspoon ground cardamom**
⅛ **teaspoon cayenne pepper**
⅓ **cup butter, softened**
⅓ **cup mild-flavor molasses**
¼ **cup packed dark brown sugar**

1 In a medium bowl stir together flour, ginger, apple pie spice, cloves, cardamom, and cayenne pepper; set flour mixture aside.

2 In a large mixing bowl beat butter with an electric mixer on medium speed for 30 seconds. Add molasses and brown sugar. Beat until combined, scraping sides of bowl occasionally. Beat in flour mixture until just combined. Divide dough in half. Cover and chill dough about 1 hour or until easy to handle.

3 On a lightly floured surface, roll half of the dough at a time until $\frac{1}{16}$ inch thick. Using a floured 2-inch round scalloped cookie cutter, cut out dough. Place cutouts 1 inch apart on an ungreased cookie sheet.

4 Bake in a 375° oven for 5 to 6 minutes or until edges are lightly browned. Transfer cookies to a wire rack; cool.

To store: Place in layers separated by waxed paper in an airtight container; cover. Store at room temperature for up to 3 days or freeze for up to 3 months.

Nutrition Facts per 2 cookies: 50 cal., 2 g total fat (1 g sat. fat), 5 mg chol., 22 mg sodium, 8 g carbo., 1 g pro.
Daily Values: 2% vit. A, 1% calcium, 2% iron

special occasions

chocolate-mint COOKIES

Kids eagerly accept these fudgy treats as an after-school snack along with a cold glass of milk.

Prep: 30 minutes
Bake: 9 minutes per batch
Freeze: 30 minutes
Oven: 350°F
Makes: about 36 cookies

1⅓ **cups all-purpose flour**

1 **cup no-calorie, heat-stable granular sugar substitute**

1½ **teaspoons baking powder**

¼ **teaspoon salt**

1 **cup semisweet chocolate pieces**

⅓ **cup butter, softened**

2 **eggs**

1½ **teaspoons vanilla**

¼ **teaspoon mint extract**

Sifted powdered sugar (optional)

1 In a bowl combine flour, sugar substitute, baking powder, and salt; set aside.

2 In a small saucepan heat chocolate pieces over low heat until melted, stirring constantly.

3 In a large mixing bowl beat butter with an electric mixer on high speed for 1 minute. Beat in melted chocolate, eggs, vanilla, and mint extract.

4 Gradually beat in flour mixture. Wrap dough in plastic wrap. Freeze for 30 minutes or until firm enough to shape into balls. Shape dough into 1-inch balls. Place balls about 1½ inches apart on an ungreased cookie sheet. Bake in a 350° oven for 9 to 11 minutes or until tops are cracked. Transfer cookies to a wire rack; cool.

5 If desired, dust cookies lightly with sifted powdered sugar before serving. Store up to 2 days at room temperature. Freeze for longer storage.

Nutrition Facts per cookie: 63 cal., 4 g total fat (2 g sat. fat), 17 mg chol., 56 mg sodium, 7 g carbo., 0 g fiber, 1 g pro.
Daily Values: 3% vit. A, 1% vit. C, 3% calcium, 4% iron

special occasions

marbled CUPCAKES

These little cakes love to party! Let the holiday, birthday party theme, or school colors (for a graduation party) dictate the cake and frosting colors.

Prep: 30 minutes
Stand: 30 minutes
Bake: 15 minutes
Oven: 350°F
Makes: 18 cupcakes

- **4 egg whites**
- **2 cups all-purpose flour**
- **1¼ cups no-calorie, heat-stable granular sugar substitute**
- **1½ teaspoons baking powder**
- **½ teaspoon baking soda**
- **⅛ teaspoon salt**
- **½ cup butter, softened**
- **½ cup sugar**
- **2 teaspoons vanilla**
- **1⅓ cups buttermilk or sour milk***
- **1 4-serving-size package sugar-free lemon-, orange-, or strawberry-flavor gelatin**
- **Few drops food coloring (optional)**
- **1 8-ounce container frozen light whipped dessert topping, thawed**

1 Allow egg whites to stand at room temperature for 30 minutes. Meanwhile, grease and lightly flour eighteen 2½-inch muffin cups or line with paper or foil bake cups; set aside. In a medium bowl stir together flour, sugar substitute, baking powder, baking soda, and salt; set aside.

2 In a large mixing bowl beat butter with an electric mixer on medium to high speed for 30 seconds. Add sugar and vanilla; beat until combined. Add egg whites, 1 at a time, beating well after each addition. Add flour mixture and buttermilk alternately to beaten mixture, beating on low speed after each addition just until combined. Place half of the batter in a medium bowl; stir in desired gelatin. Spoon some plain and some flavored batter into each muffin cup, filling each cup about half full. Use a knife to swirl batter.

3 Bake in a 350° oven about 15 minutes or until a wooden toothpick inserted near the centers comes out clean. Cool in pans on wire racks for 5 minutes. Carefully loosen and remove cupcakes from muffin cups. Cool on wire racks.

4 For frosting, if desired, fold food coloring into whipped topping. Pipe or spread topping on cupcakes.

*Note: To make 1⅓ cups sour milk, place 4 teaspoons lemon juice or vinegar in a 2-cup glass measuring cup. Add enough fat-free milk to make 1⅓ cups total liquid; stir. Let stand 5 minutes before using.

Nutrition Facts per cupcake: 168 cal., 7 g total fat (5 g sat. fat), 15 mg chol., 187 mg sodium, 21 g carbo., 0 g fiber, 3 g pro.
Daily Values: 8% vit. A, 4% vit. C, 8% calcium, 7% iron

special occasions

birthday cake WITH FROSTING

You'll get a slightly whiter cake if you use shortening instead of butter to prepare this moist, dense treat.

special occasions

Prep: 40 minutes
Stand: 30 minutes
Bake: 20 minutes
Cool: 1 hour
Oven: 350°F
Makes: 16 servings

4 **egg whites**

2 **cups all-purpose flour**

1¼ **cups no-calorie, heat-stable granular sugar substitute**

1½ **teaspoons baking powder**

½ **teaspoon baking soda**

⅛ **teaspoon salt**

½ **cup shortening or butter, softened**

½ **cup sugar**

2 **teaspoons vanilla**

1⅓ **cups buttermilk or sour milk***

1 **4-serving-size package fat-free, sugar-free instant white chocolate pudding mix**

1 **cup fat-free milk**

1 **8-ounce container frozen light whipped dessert topping, thawed**

1 Allow egg whites to stand at room temperature for 30 minutes. Meanwhile, lightly grease bottoms of two 9×1½-inch or 8×1½-inch round cake pans. Line bottoms of pans with waxed paper. Grease and lightly flour bottoms and sides of pans. Set aside. In a medium bowl stir together flour, sugar substitute, baking powder, baking soda, and salt; set aside.

2 In a large mixing bowl beat shortening with an electric mixer on medium to high speed for 30 seconds. Add sugar and vanilla; beat until combined. Add egg whites, 1 at a time, beating well after each addition. Add flour mixture and buttermilk alternately to beaten mixture, beating on low speed after each addition just until combined. Spread batter in prepared pans.

3 Bake in a 350° oven for 20 to 25 minutes for 9-inch pans, 25 to 30 minutes for 8-inch pans, or until a wooden toothpick inserted near centers comes out clean. Cool cakes in pans on wire racks for 10 minutes. Remove cakes from pans; peel off waxed paper. Cool thoroughly on racks.

4 For frosting, in a medium bowl prepare pudding mix according to package directions using the 1 cup milk. Fold in whipped topping. Immediately spread between cake layers and over top and sides of cake. Refrigerate until serving time.

*Note: To make 1⅓ cups sour milk, place 4 teaspoons lemon juice or vinegar in a 2-cup glass measuring cup. Add enough fat-free milk to make 1⅓ cups total liquid; stir. Let stand 5 minutes before using.

Nutrition Facts per serving: 199 cal., 8 g total fat (3 g sat. fat), 1 mg chol., 222 mg sodium, 26 g carbo., 1 g fiber, 4 g pro.
Daily Values: 5% vit. A, 4% vit. C, 11% calcium, 9% iron

brownie fruit PIZZA

Honor the birthday child or say "Happy Valentine's Day" with wedges of this chocolaty fruit pizza.

Prep: 20 minutes
Bake: 15 minutes
Chill: 1 hour
Oven: 350°F
Makes: 12 servings

1 **10¼-ounce package fudge brownie mix**

¼ **cup unsweetened applesauce**

1 **4-serving-size package fat-free, sugar-free instant chocolate fudge or chocolate pudding mix**

1 **cup fat-free milk**

1 **teaspoon vanilla**

1 **cup sliced banana**

1 **cup sliced fresh strawberries**

1 Grease the bottom of a 10-inch springform pan; set aside. Prepare brownie mix according to package directions, except substitute the ¼ cup unsweetened applesauce for cooking oil. Spread batter in prepared pan. Bake in a 350° oven for 15 minutes or until sides begin to pull away from pan. Cool completely on a wire rack. Remove sides of pan.

2 Prepare pudding mix according to package directions, using the 1 cup milk and adding the vanilla with the milk. Cover and chill at least 1 hour.

3 Spread pudding mixture over cooled brownie crust. Arrange fruit on pudding. Cut into wedges and serve immediately.

Nutrition Facts per serving: 141 cal., 2 g total fat (1 g sat. fat), 18 mg chol., 216 mg sodium, 28 g carbo., 2 g fiber, 3 g pro.
Daily Values: 2% vit. A, 14% vit. C, 4% calcium, 7% iron

special occasions

white chocolate PARFAITS

Make these parfaits with blueberries and strawberries for a festive red, white, and blue dessert at a Fourth of July party. Guests will love the contrast of satiny pudding with crisp cookies and fresh berries.

Start to Finish: 20 minutes
Makes: 6 servings

- **1 4-serving-size package fat-free, sugar-free instant white chocolate pudding mix**
- **2 cups fat-free milk**
- **1 teaspoon vanilla**
- **6 chocolate wafers or shortbread cookies, broken into small pieces**
- **½ of an 8-ounce container frozen light whipped dessert topping, thawed**
- **1½ cups fresh blueberries, raspberries, and/or sliced strawberries**

1 In a medium mixing bowl prepare pudding mix according to package directions using the 2 cups milk. Stir in vanilla. Divide pudding mixture among 6 parfait glasses or dessert dishes. Sprinkle with cookie pieces. Top with whipped topping and berries. Serve immediately.

Nutrition Facts per serving: 139 cal., 3 g total fat (3 g sat. fat), 2 mg chol., 309 mg sodium, 22 g carbo., 2 g fiber, 4 g pro.
Daily Values: 4% vit. A, 20% vit. C, 11% calcium, 5% iron

special occasions

sparkling BERRY LEMONADE

These ice cubes require more prep work—but not much, and they're well worth it. They cool, flavor, and garnish all at the same time—great for a kids' party or summertime cooler.

Prep: 15 minutes
Freeze: 4 hours
Makes: 8 (6-ounce) servings

1 **envelope or tub low-calorie lemonade-flavor soft drink mix (enough to make 2 quarts)**

5 **cups water**

8 **medium strawberries, hulled and quartered**

1 **envelope or tub low-calorie cherry- or raspberry-flavor soft drink mix (enough to make 2 quarts)**

1 **1-liter bottle club soda, chilled**

❶ In a 2-quart pitcher stir together lemonade drink mix and the water. Place 1 strawberry quarter in each of 32 compartments of ice cube trays; fill with 3 cups of the lemonade mixture. Freeze about 4 hours or until solid.

❷ Stir cherry or raspberry drink mix into remaining lemonade mixture in pitcher. Cover and chill until serving time.

❸ To serve, slowly pour club soda into lemonade mixture in pitcher. Put 4 ice cubes in each of 8 glasses. Pour lemonade mixture into each glass.

Nutrition Facts per serving: 4 cal., 0 g total fat (0 g sat. fat), 0 mg chol., 31 mg sodium, 1 g carbo., 0 g fiber, 0 g pro.
Daily Values: 31% vit. C, 1% calcium

special occasions

index

Note: **Boldfaced** page references indicate photographs.

metric information

The charts on this page provide a guide for converting measurements from the U.S. customary system, which is used throughout this book, to the metric system.

PRODUCT DIFFERENCES

Most of the ingredients called for in the recipes in this book are available in most countries. However, some are known by different names. Here are some common American ingredients and their possible counterparts:

- Sugar (white) is granulated, fine granulated, or castor sugar.
- Powdered sugar is icing sugar.
- All-purpose flour is enriched, bleached, or unbleached white household flour. When self-rising flour is used in place of all-purpose flour in a recipe that calls for leavening, omit the leavening agent (baking soda or baking powder) and salt.
- Light-colored corn syrup is golden syrup.
- Cornstarch is cornflour.
- Baking soda is bicarbonate of soda.
- Vanilla or vanilla extract is vanilla essence.
- Green, red, or yellow sweet peppers are capsicums or bell peppers.
- Golden raisins are sultanas.

VOLUME AND WEIGHT

The United States traditionally uses cup measures for liquid and solid ingredients. The chart, top right, shows the approximate imperial and metric equivalents. If you are accustomed to weighing solid ingredients, the following approximate equivalents will be helpful.

- 1 cup butter, castor sugar, or rice = 8 ounces = $\frac{1}{2}$ pound = 250 grams
- 1 cup flour = 4 ounces = $\frac{1}{4}$ pound = 125 grams
- 1 cup icing sugar = 5 ounces = 150 grams

Canadian and U.S. volume for a cup measure is 8 fluid ounces (237 ml), but the standard metric equivalent is 250 ml.

1 British imperial cup is 10 fluid ounces.

In Australia, 1 tablespoon equals 20 ml, and there are 4 teaspoons in the Australian tablespoon.

Spoon measures are used for smaller amounts of ingredients. Although the size of the tablespoon varies slightly in different countries, for practical purposes and for recipes in this book, a straight substitution is all that's necessary. Measurements made using cups or spoons always should be level unless stated otherwise.

COMMON WEIGHT RANGE REPLACEMENTS

Imperial / U.S.	Metric
$\frac{1}{2}$ ounce	15 g
1 ounce	25 g or 30 g
4 ounces ($\frac{1}{4}$ pound)	115 g or 125 g
8 ounces ($\frac{1}{2}$ pound)	225 g or 250 g
16 ounces (1 pound)	450 g or 500 g
$1\frac{1}{4}$ pounds	625 g
$1\frac{1}{2}$ pounds	750 g
2 pounds or $2\frac{1}{4}$ pounds	1,000 g or 1 Kg

OVEN TEMPERATURE EQUIVALENTS

Fahrenheit Setting	Celsius Setting*	Gas Setting
300°F	150°C	Gas Mark 2 (very low)
325°F	160°C	Gas Mark 3 (low)
350°F	180°C	Gas Mark 4 (moderate)
375°F	190°C	Gas Mark 5 (moderate)
400°F	200°C	Gas Mark 6 (hot)
425°F	220°C	Gas Mark 7 (hot)
450°F	230°C	Gas Mark 8 (very hot)
475°F	240°C	Gas Mark 9 (very hot)
500°F	260°C	Gas Mark 10 (extremely hot)
Broil	Broil	Grill

*Electric and gas ovens may be calibrated using celsius. However, for an electric oven, increase celsius setting 10 to 20 degrees when cooking above 160°C. For convection or forced air ovens (gas or electric) lower the temperature setting 25°F/10°C when cooking at all heat levels.

BAKING PAN SIZES

Imperial / U.S.	Metric
9×1$\frac{1}{2}$-inch round cake pan	22- or 23×4-cm (1.5 L)
9×1$\frac{1}{2}$-inch pie plate	22- or 23×4-cm (1 L)
8×8×2-inch square cake pan	20×5-cm (2 L)
9×9×2-inch square cake pan	22- or 23×4.5-cm (2.5 L)
11×7×1$\frac{1}{2}$-inch baking pan	28×17×4-cm (2 L)
2-quart rectangular baking pan	30×19×4.5-cm (3 L)
13×9×2-inch baking pan	34×22×4.5-cm (3.5 L)
15×10×1-inch jelly roll pan	40×25×2-cm
9×5×3-inch loaf pan	23×13×8-cm (2 L)
2-quart casserole	2 L

U.S. / STANDARD METRIC EQUIVALENTS

$\frac{1}{8}$ teaspoon = 0.5 ml	$\frac{1}{3}$ cup = 3 fluid ounces = 75 ml
$\frac{1}{4}$ teaspoon = 1 ml	$\frac{1}{2}$ cup = 4 fluid ounces = 125 ml
$\frac{1}{2}$ teaspoon = 2 ml	$\frac{1}{3}$ cup = 5 fluid ounces = 150 ml
1 teaspoon = 5 ml	$\frac{3}{4}$ cup = 6 fluid ounces = 175 ml
1 tablespoon = 15 ml	1 cup = 8 fluid ounces = 250 ml
2 tablespoons = 25 ml	2 cups = 1 pint = 500 ml
$\frac{1}{4}$ cup = 2 fluid ounces = 50 ml	1 quart = 1 litre